NE능률 영어교과서

대한민국 고등학생 **10**명 중 **4.7**명이 보는 교과서

영어 고등 교과서 점유율 1위

(7차, 2007 개정, 2009 개정, 2015 개정)

능률보카

그동안 판매된
능률VOCA 1,100만 부

대한민국 박스오피스
**천만명을 넘은 영화
단 28개**

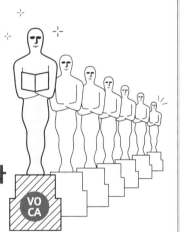

그동안 판매된
리딩튜터 1,900만 부
차곡차곡 쌓으면 19만 미터

**에베레스트
21배 높이**

190,000m

에베레스트 8,848m

그래머존

그동안 판매된 450만 부의 그래머존을 바닥에 쭉 ~ 깔면
1000km 서울-부산 왕복가능

서울

부산

교재 검토에 도움을 주신 선생님들

강건창 광주 살레시오중학교
강수정 인천 석정중학교
구영애 파주 금촌중학교
김민정 순천 엘린 영어교습소
김민정 파주 삼광중학교
김선미 천안 천안서여자중학교
김수연 서울 잉글리시아이 고덕캠퍼스
김수영 광주 숭일중학교
김연숙 서울 휘문중학교
김영현 광주 수피아여자중학교
김유빈(Annie) 동탄 애니원잉글리쉬
김현정 천안 광풍중학교
김혜원 인천 갈산중학교
나은진 서울 화곡중학교
노수정 서울 빌드업 영어교습소
문혜옥 시흥 은행중학교
민세원 광명 소하중학교
박인화 서울 일성여자중고등학교

박창현 광주 고려중학교
박혜숙 서울 경원중학교
반지혜 서울 대원국제중학교
방선영 광명 소하중학교
배영주 부산 이사벨중학교
배정현 서울 대명중학교
변재선 부천 부천중학교
서은조 서울 방배중학교
성수정 부산 주례여자중학교
신주희 서울 광성중학교
신희수 서울 이수중학교
안인숙 울산 현대중학교
양윤정 시흥 능곡고등학교
오영숙 서울 양강중학교
오하연 부산 인지중학교
오형기 서울 배문중학교
윤선경 서울 영국이엠학원
이수경 춘천 강원중학교

이임주 인천 만수북중학교
이정순 서울 일성여자중고등학교
이정재 파주 광탄중학교
이정희 천안 봉서중학교
이진영 울산 신정중학교
이효정 서울 신사중학교
장영진 광주 서강중학교
정찬희 광명 소하중학교
조혜진 성남 동광중학교
최문희 인천 삼산중학교
최수근(Claire) 광교 RISE 어학원
최은주 서울 등명중학교
최지예 대전 삼천중학교
최현우 창원 용원중학교
홍준기 광주 동신중학교
황나리 대전 덕명중학교

1316
LISTENING LEVEL 1

지은이	NE능률 영어교육연구소
영문교열	Curtis Thompson, Keeran Murphy, Angela Lan
디자인	닷츠
내지 일러스트	박응식, 윤병철
맥편집	김재민

NE능률이
미래를
창조합니다.

건강한 배움의 고객가치를 제공하겠다는 꿈을 실현하기 위해
40년이 넘는 시간 동안 열심히 달려왔습니다.

앞으로도 끊임없는 연구와 노력을 통해
당연한 것을 멈추지 않고

고객, 기업, 직원 모두가 함께 성장하는 NE능률이 되겠습니다.

기초부터 실전까지 중학 듣기 완성

1316

1316 LISTENING

LEVEL
1

STRUCTURE & FEATURES

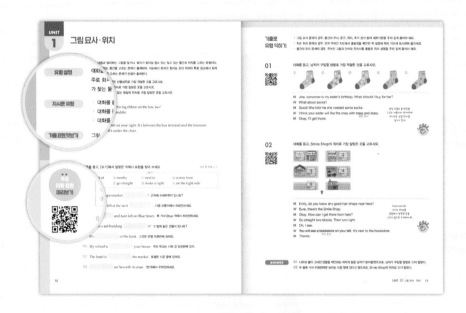

기출로 유형 익히기

기출 문제를 들어보면서 최신 출제 경향을 알 수 있습니다. 내용 파악에 도움이 되는 듣기 전략, 정답의 결정적인 근거가 되는 '정답 단서'와 오답을 유도하는 '오답 함정'을 통해 해당 유형에 대한 적응력을 키울 수 있습니다.

유형 설명 & 지시문 유형 & 기출 표현 맛보기

해당 기출 문제 유형의 전반적인 특징과 대표 지시문을 확인할 수 있습니다.
유형별 실제 기출 문장을 제시하여 해당 문제의 정답과 직결된 표현을 익힐 수 있습니다.

주요 어휘·표현 미리보기

본격적인 문제 풀이에 앞서 해당 단원에 등장할 중요한 어휘와 표현을 미리 학습할 수 있습니다.

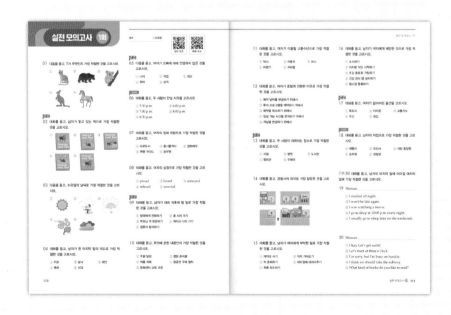

실전 모의고사

실제 중학 영어듣기 능력평가 유형을 충실히 반영한 실전 모의고사 6회분으로 문제 풀이 능력을 향상할 수 있습니다.

LISTENING PRACTICE

다양한 소재와 상황으로 구성된 대화 및 담화를 통해 해당 유형을 집중적으로 훈련할 수 있습니다. 단원마다 고난도 문제와 영국식 발음으로 녹음한 문제가 포함되어 있어 실전에 대한 자신감을 키울 수 있습니다.

DICTATION

주요 표현을 받아쓰면서 시험에 자주 나오는 구문을 익힐 수 있습니다. 또한, '정답 단서'와 '오답 함정'을 참고하여 학습한 내용을 확실히 점검할 수 있습니다.

어휘·표현 다지기

듣기에 등장한 어휘와 표현을 정리하고 복습할 수 있습니다.

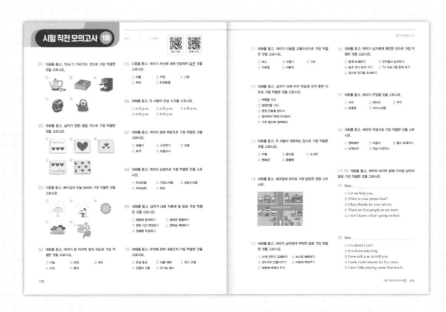

시험 직전 모의고사

실제 시험 형식으로 구성된 2회분의 모의고사로, 중학 영어듣기 능력평가 직전에 활용할 수 있습니다.
듣기 MP3 파일, Dictation, 어휘·표현 테스트지는 www. nebooks.co.kr에서 내려받을 수 있습니다.

CONTENTS

SECTION

2

**실전 모의고사 &
시험 직전 모의고사**

1316 LISTENING

LEVEL 1

중1 기출 문제 유형 분석

	유형	형태	단어 수 (words)	페어 수 (pairs)	2020 2회	2021 1회	2021 2회	2022 1회	2022 2회	2023 1회	계
1	지칭	담화	30~38		1	1	1	1	1	1	6
2	그림 묘사	대화	46~62	2.5~4	1	1	1	1	1	1	6
3	특정 정보	담화	37~44		1	1	1	1	1	1	6
		대화	52~61	3~4	2	1	1	1	1	1	7
4	의도	대화	41~60	2.5~3	1	1	1	1	1	1	6
5	언급	담화	39~51		1	1	1	1	1	1	6
6	시각	대화	51~62	3~3.5	1	1	1	1	1	1	6
7	장래 희망	대화	45~60	3~3.5	1	1	1	1	1	1	6
8	심정	대화	49~58	3	1	1	1	1	1	1	6
9	할 일 · 한 일	대화	48~62	2.5~4	1	2	2	2	2	2	11
10	주제/화제	대화	46~63	3~4	1	1	1	1	1	1	6
11	이유	대화	49~58	3~3.5	1	1	1	1	1	1	6
12	대화 장소	대화	50~61	3.5~4	1	1	1	1	1	1	6
13	위치	대화	47~61	3~3.5	1	1	1	1	1	1	6
14	부탁한 일	대화	47~57	3~3.5	1	1	1	1	1	1	6
15	제안한 일	대화	46~60	3~4	1	1	1	1	1	1	6
16	직업	대화	55~59	2.5~4	1	1	1	1	1	1	6
17	마지막 말에 대한 응답	대화	48~63	3~4	2	2	2	2	2	2	12
	계				20	20	20	20	20	20	

Section

1

유형 설명
UNIT 1-12

그림 묘사·위치

대화를 듣고 내용과 일치하는 그림을 찾거나, 화자가 찾아갈 장소 또는 찾고 있는 물건의 위치를 고르는 유형이다. 주로 화자가 설명하는 물건을 고르는 문제가 출제되며, 지도에서 화자가 찾아갈 곳의 위치와 특정 장소에서 화자가 찾는 물건의 위치를 고르는 문제가 번갈아 출제된다.

- 대화를 듣고, 여자가 꾸민 선물상자로 가장 적절한 것을 고르시오.
- 대화를 듣고, 우체국의 위치로 가장 알맞은 곳을 고르시오.
- 대화를 듣고, 남자가 찾고 있는 명찰의 위치로 가장 알맞은 곳을 고르시오.

그림 묘사
- How about putting this big ribbon on the box, too?
- I like the star in the middle.

위치
- You'll find the hotel on your right. It's between the bus terminal and the museum.
- Oh, I found it. It's under the chair.

다음을 듣고, [보기]에서 알맞은 어휘나 표현을 찾아 쓰세요.   정답 및 해설 p. 2

| 보기 |

| ⓐ in front of | ⓑ nearby | ⓒ next to | ⓓ across from |
| ⓔ corner | ⓕ go straight | ⓖ make a right | ⓗ on the right side |

01   Is there a supermarket _____? 근처에 슈퍼마켓이 있나요?

02   Please turn left at the next _____. 다음 모퉁이에서 좌회전하세요.

03   _____ and turn left on Blue Street. 쭉 가서 Blue 가에서 좌회전하세요.

04   Is there a tall building _____ it? 그 앞에 높은 건물이 있나요?

05   It's _____ of the bank. 그것은 은행 오른편에 있어요.

06   My school is _____ your house. 우리 학교는 너희 집 맞은편에 있어.

07   The hotel is _____ the market. 호텔은 시장 옆에 있어요.

08   _____ on Seventh Avenue. 7번가에서 우회전하세요.

기출로 유형 익히기

- 그림 묘사 문제의 경우, 물건의 무늬, 문구, 위치, 추가 장식 등의 세부사항을 주의 깊게 들어야 해요.
- 지도 위치 문제의 경우, 먼저 주어진 지도에서 출발점을 확인한 뒤 설명에 따라 지도에 표시하며 들으세요.
- 물건의 위치 문제의 경우, 주어진 그림의 단어와 전치사를 활용한 위치 설명을 주의 깊게 들어야 해요.

01

대화를 듣고, 남자가 구입할 양말로 가장 적절한 것을 고르시오.

M Jina, tomorrow is my sister's birthday. What should I buy for her?
W What about socks?
M Good! She told me she needed some socks.
W I think your sister will like the ones with trees and stars.
        정답 단서
M Okay, I'll get those.

생일 선물로 줄 양말을
고르는 내용이야. 한꺼번에
제시되는 정답 단서를
놓치지 말자!

02

대화를 듣고, Smile Shop의 위치로 가장 알맞은 곳을 고르시오.

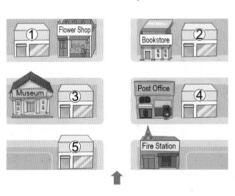

M Emily, do you know any good hair shops near here?
W Sure, there's the Smile Shop.
M Okay. How can I get there from here?
W Go straight two blocks. Then turn right.
M Oh, I see.
W You will see a bookstore on your left. It's next to the bookstore.
        오답 함정
M Thanks.

Bookstore와
Smile Shop을
혼동해서 잘못된 답을
고르지 않도록 주의해야 해.

ANSWER

01 나무와 별이 그려진 양말을 제안하는 여자의 말을 남자가 받아들였으므로, 남자가 구입할 양말로 ③이 알맞다.

02 두 블록 가서 우회전하면 보이는 서점 옆에 있다고 했으므로, Smile Shop의 위치로 ②가 알맞다.

LISTENING PRACTICE

점수   / 12문항

일반 속도   빠른 속도

01
대화를 듣고, 남자가 주문한 케이크로 가장 적절한 것을 고르시오.

①    ②   ③   ④   ⑤

02
대화를 듣고, 여자가 키우는 강아지로 가장 적절한 것을 고르시오.

①   ②   ③   ④   ⑤

03
대화를 듣고, 서점의 위치로 가장 알맞은 곳을 고르시오.

04
대화를 듣고, 여자가 찾고 있는 도서관 카드의 위치로 가장 알맞은 곳을 고르시오.

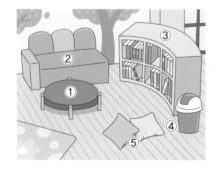

05 대화를 듣고, 여자의 손톱 무늬로 가장 적절한 것을 고르시오.

①   ②   ③   ④   ⑤

06 대화를 듣고, 두 사람이 보고 있는 책 표지로 가장 적절한 것을 고르시오.

①   ②   ③   ④   ⑤

07 대화를 듣고, 세탁소의 위치로 가장 알맞은 곳을 고르시오.

08 대화를 듣고, 남자가 찾고 있는 시계의 위치로 가장 알맞은 곳을 고르시오.

고난도

09 대화를 듣고, 남자가 사는 집으로 가장 적절한 것을 고르시오.

①  ②  ③  ④  ⑤

10 대화를 듣고, 두 사람이 보고 있는 재킷으로 가장 적절한 것을 고르시오.

① ② ③ ④ ⑤

고난도

11 대화를 듣고, 슈퍼마켓의 위치로 가장 알맞은 곳을 고르시오.

12 대화를 듣고, 여자가 찾고 있는 이어폰의 위치로 가장 알맞은 곳을 고르시오.

DICTATION

일반 속도

빠른 속도

01

대화를 듣고, 남자가 주문한 케이크로
가장 적절한 것을 고르시오.

M I ordered a birthday cake from the bakery. It's _____ _____ _____.

W Does it have _____ _____ _____ _____?

M Just one big one.

W Does it say "Happy Birthday" on it?

M No. It doesn't have any words on it.

W Well, it _____ _____ anyway.

02

대화를 듣고, 여자가 키우는 강아지로
가장 적절한 것을 고르시오.

W My puppy is in the dog park. He's _____ _____ the other dogs!

M Which one is he? Does he have pointy ears?

W No. His ears are long, and _____ _____ _____.

M I think I see him. He _____ _____ _____ _____, doesn't he?

W Yes! And he has short legs too.

03

대화를 듣고, 서점의 위치로 가장 알
맞은 곳을 고르시오.

M Excuse me. Is there a bookstore nearby?

W Yes. Just _____ _____ Smith Street and make a right on First Avenue.

M Okay. Is it _____ _____ _____?

W Yes. It's _____ _____ _____ _____ of the street and across from a park.

M Great. Thanks for your help.

04

대화를 듣고, 여자가 찾고 있는 도서관 카드의 위치로 가장 알맞은 곳을 고르시오.

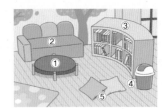

W Uh-oh. I can't find my library card.

M Didn't you just _____ _____ _____ _____ _____?

W No, I didn't. I thought I put it on the bookshelf. But it's not there.

M Hmm… Did you _____ _____ _____ _____?

W Yes, I checked the sofa. But my card's not there.

M How about _____ _____ _____ _____?

W Let me see. Nope! It's not there either.

M Oh, there's something under this cushion!

W That's my library card! Thank you.

05

대화를 듣고, 여자의 손톱 무늬로 가장 적절한 것을 고르시오.

① ②

③   ④

⑤

M _____ _____ _____!

W Thanks. I painted them myself.

M Really? I thought you went to a nail shop.

W No. I _____ _____ _____ _____ on them.

M I like the butterfly on the flower _____ _____ _____.

W Thanks. At first, painting my nails was difficult, but now I enjoy it.

06

대화를 듣고, 두 사람이 보고 있는 책 표지로 가장 적절한 것을 고르시오.

M Is this your new novel, *Moonlight*?

W Yes. What do you think of the _____ _____ on the cover?

M I like it. And there are _____ _____ _____ _____.

W That's right. And the book's title is _____ _____ _____.

M It looks terrific. I can't wait to read it.

16

07

대화를 듣고, 세탁소의 위치로 가장
알맞은 곳을 고르시오.

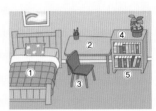

W Excuse me. Is there a dry cleaner's around here?

M Well, you have to _____ _____ and make a left on Green Street.

W I see.

M Then _____ _____ _____ on James Road. The dry cleaner's is _____ _____ _____.

W Great! Thanks for your help!

08

대화를 듣고, 남자가 찾고 있는 시계의
위치로 가장 알맞은 곳을 고르시오.

W What are you doing, Nick?

M _____ _____ _____ my watch. But I can't find it.

W Did you _____ _____ _____ _____?

M Yes, but it's not there. I checked on my desk and under the chair too. But I _____ _____ _____ _____.

W Oh, look! Isn't that your watch on the bookshelf?

M It is! Thanks.

고난도
09

대화를 듣고, 남자가 사는 집으로 가
장 적절한 것을 고르시오.

① ②
③ ④
⑤

[Cell phone rings.]

M Hello?

W Hi, it's me. I'm on your street. Which house is yours?

M It has two floors. And there are three windows _____ _____ _____ _____.

W Okay. Are there two trees _____ _____ _____ it?

M No, there's only one tree. And there's a driveway on the right.

W Is there a car parked _____ _____ _____?

M Yes, there is!

W Aha! I see it!

10

대화를 듣고, 두 사람이 보고 있는 재킷으로 가장 적절한 것을 고르시오.

 ① ②
 ③ ④
⑤

W What do you think of this jacket?

M It's nice. I like the three big buttons.

W Me too. And _____ _____ _____ _____ _____ .

M But it's very long. Do you think _____ _____ _____

_____ ?

W Yes. And it will _____ _____ _____ .

고난도

11

대화를 듣고, 슈퍼마켓의 위치로 가장 알맞은 곳을 고르시오.

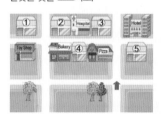

M Excuse me. Is this Third Street?

W No. _____ _____ _____ you see a pizza place on the

corner. That's Third Street.

M I see. Someone said there's a supermarket on Third Street.

W That's right. _____ _____ _____ at the pizza place and

you'll see it.

M Is it next to the pizza place?

W No, it's not. It's _____ _____ _____ _____ .

M Thanks for your help.

W You're welcome.

12

대화를 듣고, 여자가 찾고 있는 이어폰의 위치로 가장 알맞은 곳을 고르시오.

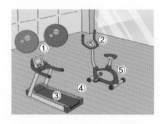

W Hey, Jack. Would you help me find my earphone, please?

M Oh, you _____ _____ _____ _____ ?

W Yes. But I can't find it.

M Did you look around the exercise balls?

W Yes. It's not there. I also _____ _____ _____ in front of the

mirror. But I still can't find it.

M All right. Then why don't we check around the treadmill?

W Okay. *[pause]* Oh, I found it! It's _____ _____ _____

between the exercise bike and the treadmill.

A 다음 영어 어휘나 표현의 뜻을 우리말로 쓰세요.

01 order

02 nail

03 exercise

04 warm

05 street

06 comfortable

07 beside

08 tail

09 driveway

10 in the middle

11 dry cleaner's

12 look for

13 drop

14 between

15 button

16 bakery

B 우리말에 맞는 영어 어휘나 표현을 [보기]에서 찾아 쓰세요.

보기	floor	find	hang down	word	sound
	area	park	walk down	pointy	trash can

01 걸어 내려가다

02 늘어지다

03 찾다

04 구역, 부분

05 끝이 뾰족한

06 쓰레기통

07 주차하다

08 ~처럼 들리다

09 단어, 말

10 층, 바닥

의도·이유

유형 설명
대화를 듣고 화자의 마지막 말의 의도나 특정 행동에 대한 이유를 파악하는 유형이다.

지시문 유형
· 대화를 듣고, 여자의 마지막 말의 의도로 가장 적절한 것을 고르시오.

· 대화를 듣고, 남자가 밤에 잠을 늦게 잔 이유로 가장 적절한 것을 고르시오.

기출 표현 맛보기
의도

· **W**   It's too small for me now. Please buy me a bigger one.

  M   Okay, I'll buy it for you this weekend. (승낙)

· **M**   Do you want to get some? You like ice cream.

  W   I'd love to, but I can't. I have to go to a swimming lesson now. (거절)

이유

· **W**   Sangmin, you look tired. What did you do last night?

  M   I watched a soccer match on TV until 2 a.m. (늦게 잔 이유)

· **W**   Really? It's Saturday. Did you have classes today?

  M   No, I played basketball with my friends. (학교에 간 이유)

주요
어휘·표현
미리보기

다음을 듣고, [보기]에서 알맞은 어휘나 표현을 찾아 쓰세요.   정답 및 해설 p. 5

┌─────────────────────────── | 보기 | ───────────────────────────┐

ⓐ feel bad   ⓑ see a movie   ⓒ until midnight   ⓓ has trouble

ⓔ why don't you   ⓕ interested in   ⓖ ready for   ⓗ something wrong

└──┘

01 I _____ about my mistake. 나는 내 실수 때문에 속상해.

02 Are you _____ the test? 시험 볼 준비가 됐나요?

03 She _____ waking up early. 그녀는 일찍 일어나는 것을 어려워해.

04 Are you _____ music? 너는 음악에 관심이 있니?

05 Would you like to _____ with us? 우리랑 영화 볼래?

06 There's _____ with this phone. 이 전화기에 무언가 문제가 있어.

07 Last night, I watched TV _____. 어젯밤에, 나는 자정까지 TV를 봤어.

08 _____ ask her? She will help you. 그녀에게 물어보는 게 어때? 그녀가 널 도와줄 거야.

• 마지막 말의 의도를 묻는 문제의 경우, 대화 후반부를 특히 주의 깊게 들으세요!
• 이유를 묻는 문제의 경우, 먼저 지시문을 읽고 두 사람 중 누구에 대해 묻는지 확인하세요. 대화 상대가 또 다른 이유를 언급하며 오답을 유도하기도 하므로 주의해야 해요.

01

대화를 듣고, 남자의 마지막 말의 의도로 가장 적절한 것을 고르시오.

① 충고   ② 위로   ③ 축하   ④ 거절   ⑤ 승낙

W   Liam, look. I made this soap with my mom at home.
M   What a cute dolphin!
W   Yes. It's my favorite animal.
M   It smells good. I want to make one. Is it difficult to make?
W   No. It's easy. We're making more soaps this Saturday. Would you like to come?
M   Sure! See you on Saturday, then.

여자가 한 제안에
대해 남자가 뭐라고
대답했을까?

02

대화를 듣고, 남자가 미술관에 가지 <u>못하는</u> 이유로 가장 적절한 것을 고르시오.

① 다리를 다쳐서   ② 강아지가 아파서
③ 날씨가 좋지 않아서   ④ 가족 모임이 있어서
⑤ 숙제를 끝내지 못해서

W   Ben, are you going to the art museum this afternoon?
M   I really want to, but I can't.
W   Why not? You were so excited.
M   My puppy is sick. 정답 단서
W   What's wrong with her?
M   I don't know. I have to take her to the animal doctor.
W   I'm sorry. I hope she's going to be okay.

이유를 묻는 말(Why
not?) 뒤에 나오는 남자의
대답에 집중해 봐.

ANSWER

01 토요일에 함께 비누를 만들자는 여자의 제안에 남자가 그때 보자고 했으므로, 남자의 마지막 말의 의도로 ⑤가 알맞다.

02 남자는 강아지가 아파서 동물 병원에 데려가야 한다고 했으므로, 미술관에 가지 못하는 이유로 ②가 알맞다.

LISTENING PRACTICE

점수 _____ / 10문항

 일반 속도   빠른 속도

01 대화를 듣고, 남자가 한 마지막 말의 의도로 가장 적절한 것을 고르시오.

① 칭찬   ② 감사
③ 위로   ④ 제안
⑤ 요청

02 대화를 듣고, 여자가 한 마지막 말의 의도로 가장 적절한 것을 고르시오.

① 격려   ② 요청
③ 사과   ④ 충고
⑤ 승낙

03 대화를 듣고, 남자가 영화를 보러 갈 수 <u>없는</u> 이유로 가장 적절한 것을 고르시오.

① 병문안을 가야 해서   ② 숙제를 해야 해서
③ 친구를 만나기로 해서   ④ 책을 읽어야 해서
⑤ 친척 집에 가야 해서

04 대화를 듣고, 남자의 기분이 좋지 <u>않은</u> 이유로 가장 적절한 것을 고르시오.

① 식당 예약이 잘못되어서   ② 물건을 잃어버려서
③ 음식 맛이 형편없어서   ④ 좋아하던 식당이 문을 닫아서
⑤ 음식에서 이물질이 나와서

고난도
05 대화를 듣고, 여자가 피곤한 이유로 가장 적절한 것을 고르시오.

① 시험공부를 해서   ② 커피를 많이 마셔서
③ 밤늦게까지 숙제를 해서   ④ 연극을 보고 집에 늦게 와서
⑤ 집에 오는 막차를 놓쳐서

06 대화를 듣고, 남자가 한 마지막 말의 의도로 가장 적절한 것을 고르시오.

① 충고　　　　　　　　　② 감사
③ 격려　　　　　　　　　④ 승낙
⑤ 제안

07 대화를 듣고, 여자가 한 마지막 말의 의도로 가장 적절한 것을 고르시오.

① 위로　　　　　　　　　② 거절
③ 사과　　　　　　　　　④ 제안
⑤ 요청

08 대화를 듣고, 여자가 종업원을 부른 이유로 가장 적절한 것을 고르시오.

① 음식을 추가로 주문하기 위해서　　② 계산이 잘못되어서
③ 음식이 늦게 나와서　　　　　　　④ 음식이 잘못 나와서
⑤ 영수증을 요청하기 위해서

09 대화를 듣고, 남자가 파티에 가지 <u>못한</u> 이유로 가장 적절한 것을 고르시오.

① 배탈이 나서　　　　　　　② 수업이 늦게 끝나서
③ 병간호를 해야 해서　　　　④ 늦잠을 자서
⑤ 파티하는 것을 잊어버려서

고난도
10 대화를 듣고, 남자가 오늘 쇼핑몰에 간 이유로 가장 적절한 것을 고르시오.

① 친구와 저녁을 먹기 위해서　　② 아르바이트를 하기 위해서
③ 새 신발을 사기 위해서　　　　④ 물건을 반품하기 위해서
⑤ 친구의 생일 선물을 사기 위해서

DICTATION

정답 단서 오답 함정

일반 속도 빠른 속도

01

대화를 듣고, 남자가 한 마지막 말의
의도로 가장 적절한 것을 고르시오.

① 칭찬   ② 감사
③ 위로   ④ 제안
⑤ 요청

M How was your day at school, Anna?

W It was terrible. I _____ _____ _____ on a test.

M Don't be _____ _____, honey. Everyone makes mistakes.

W I _____ _____ _____ it.

M You will do fine next time.

02

대화를 듣고, 여자가 한 마지막 말의
의도로 가장 적절한 것을 고르시오.

① 격려   ② 요청
③ 사과   ④ 충고
⑤ 승낙

W Oh no! I can't believe it!

M _____ _____?

W I was writing my research paper, and the computer suddenly _____ _____. I can't turn it back on.

M Uh-oh. You have to finish your paper by tomorrow, don't you?

W That's right. Hey, you know a lot about computers, right? Can you _____ _____ _____ _____?

03

대화를 듣고, 남자가 영화를 보러 갈
수 없는 이유로 가장 적절한 것을 고
르시오.

① 병문안을 가야 해서
② 숙제를 해야 해서
③ 친구를 만나기로 해서
④ 책을 읽어야 해서
⑤ 친척 집에 가야 해서

W What are you doing?

M I'm _____ _____ _____ for homework.

W Oh. Well, I got two free movie tickets. Would you like to _____ _____ _____ tonight?

M Sorry, I can't. I have to _____ _____ _____.

W Maybe next time, then.

M Sure. Enjoy the movie!

04

대화를 듣고, 남자의 기분이 좋지 않은 이유로 가장 적절한 것을 고르시오.

① 식당 예약이 잘못되어서
② 물건을 잃어버려서
③ 음식 맛이 형편없어서
④ 좋아하던 식당이 문을 닫아서
⑤ 음식에서 이물질이 나와서

W _____ _____ _____? You don't look well.

M I just _____ _____ _____ a restaurant.

W Oh. Was the food bad?

M No. But I think I _____ _____ _____ _____.

W You should call the restaurant!

M I did. They said they don't have it.

고난도

05

대화를 듣고, 여자가 피곤한 이유로 가장 적절한 것을 고르시오.

① 시험공부를 해서
② 커피를 많이 마셔서
③ 밤늦게까지 숙제를 해서
④ 연극을 보고 집에 늦게 와서
⑤ 집에 오는 막차를 놓쳐서

M Are you _____ _____ _____ for the test together?

W Well… Do you mind if I get some coffee first?

M No. You look tired.

W Yes, I went to see a play yesterday. I didn't get home _____ _____.

M I understand. But don't drink too much coffee.

W Why not?

M You'll _____ _____ _____ tonight.

W Good point. I'll only have one cup.

06

대화를 듣고, 남자가 한 마지막 말의 의도로 가장 적절한 것을 고르시오.

① 충고   ② 감사
③ 격려   ④ 승낙
⑤ 제안

W Do you _____ _____ _____ this weekend?

M I'm going to see a jazz concert with Cathy.

W Really? Is there a good jazz band in our town?

M Yes. They're new, but I heard _____ _____ _____.

W Really? I want to hear them play.

M _____ _____ _____ come with us?

07

대화를 듣고, 여자가 한 마지막 말의 의도로 가장 적절한 것을 고르시오.

① 위로   ② 거절
③ 사과   ④ 제안
⑤ 요청

W I'm here! What are you doing?

M Hi. I'm just watching the baseball game.

W But you invited me over to _____ _____ _____ _____.

M Yes, but I forgot about the baseball game. Let's watch it together.

W _____ _____ _____ _____ baseball. I'll _____ _____ another time.

08

대화를 듣고, 여자가 종업원을 부른
이유로 가장 적절한 것을 고르시오.

① 음식을 추가로 주문하기 위해서
② 계산이 잘못되어서
③ 음식이 늦게 나와서
④ 음식이 잘못 나와서
⑤ 영수증을 요청하기 위해서

W Excuse me.

M Yes, ma'am? _____ _____ _____ _____?

W There's _____ _____. I didn't order this.

M Oh, I'm sorry. What did you order?

W I wanted the shrimp. But this is beef!

M I'm sorry. I'll _____ _____ _____ with your order.

09

대화를 듣고, 남자가 파티에 가지 못한
이유로 가장 적절한 것을 고르시오.

① 배탈이 나서
② 수업이 늦게 끝나서
③ 병간호를 해야 해서
④ 늦잠을 자서
⑤ 파티하는 것을 잊어버려서

W Hi, Tony! Why didn't you come to the party yesterday? Did you _____ _____ it?

M No. I really wanted to go, but I had to _____ _____ _____.

W Why?

M I ate too much ice cream. So I had a stomachache.

W Oh, that's too bad. Are you okay now?

M Yes, but _____ _____ _____.

고난도
10

대화를 듣고, 남자가 오늘 쇼핑몰에
간 이유로 가장 적절한 것을 고르시오.

① 친구와 저녁을 먹기 위해서
② 아르바이트를 하기 위해서
③ 새 신발을 사기 위해서
④ 물건을 반품하기 위해서
⑤ 친구의 생일 선물을 사기 위해서

W Where have you been?

M I was _____ _____ _____. I just got back.

W The mall? Didn't you buy new shoes there yesterday?

M Yes. But they were _____ _____ _____!

W You're kidding!

M No. I was pretty annoyed. I took them back.

W That's too bad. Anyway, are you _____ _____ _____?

M Sure. Let's go to my favorite Chinese restaurant.

W Okay.

A

다음 영어 어휘나 표현의 뜻을 우리말로 쓰세요.

01 wrong

02 next time

03 anyway

04 terrible

05 maybe

06 upset

07 forget

08 plan

09 finish

10 a lot

11 suddenly

12 annoyed

13 make a mistake

14 visit

15 tired

16 stomachache

B

우리말에 맞는 영어 어휘나 표현을 [보기]에서 찾아 쓰세요.

	보기				
stay in bed	pretty	hurt	take ~ back		Do you mind if ~?
another time	homework		matter	turn off	give a hand

01 도움을 주다

02 상당히, 꽤

03 아프다

04 ~해도 될까요?

05 ~을 돌려주다[반품하다]

06 문제

07 (전원이) 꺼지다

08 침대에 머무르다

09 언제 다시 한번

10 숙제

언급하지 않은 내용

주요
어휘·표현
미리보기

다음을 듣고, [보기]에서 알맞은 어휘나 표현을 찾아 쓰세요.

정답 및 해설 p. 7

| 보기 |

ⓐ terrific   ⓑ on sale   ⓒ available   ⓓ weighs
ⓔ was born   ⓕ misses   ⓖ good at   ⓗ rent a car

01 Those books are _____ this week. 저 책들은 이번 주에 할인 판매 중이야.

02 Their baby _____ 10 kg now. 그들의 아기는 현재 10kg이야.

03 She _____ you very much. 그녀는 너를 몹시 그리워해.

04 The coat is _____ in blue or brown. 그 코트는 파란색이나 갈색으로 구입할 수 있어요.

05 I need to _____ at the airport. 나는 공항에서 차를 빌려야 해.

06 His uncle is a _____ baseball player. 그의 삼촌은 훌륭한 야구 선수야.

07 You are very _____ drawing. 너는 그림을 참 잘 그리는구나.

08 I _____ in Naju in 2000. 나는 2000년에 나주에서 태어났어.

- 먼저 지시문과 선택지를 읽고, 주의해서 들어야 할 내용이 무엇인지 파악하세요.
- 보통 선택지 순서대로 내용이 언급되므로, 들려주는 내용과 선택지를 비교하며 정답을 찾으세요.

01

다음을 듣고, 남자가 엄마에 대해 언급하지 <u>않은</u> 것을 고르시오.

① 직업   ② 귀가 시간   ③ 외모   ④ 고향   ⑤ 취미

M I'd like to introduce my mom to you. She teaches music at Daehan Middle School. Mom goes to work early in the morning and comes back home at 6 p.m. She has short black hair and wears glasses. Her hobby is playing board games.

1번 선택지부터 언급
되는 정보를 하나씩
체크해가며 풀어봐!

02

다음을 듣고, 여자가 Jump Shoes에 대해 언급하지 <u>않은</u> 것을 고르시오.

① 무게   ② 색상   ③ 치수   ④ 할인율   ⑤ 가격

W Hi, everyone. This is Amy from Happy Shopping. Today, I'm introducing Jump Shoes! They're only 400 g. Very good for jogging! The shoes come in blue and pink. Buy now and get 20% off. So, they're only $24. To order, call us at 123-4949!

연락처를 언급했지만
관련 선택지가 없어.
이런 경우도 있다는 걸
기억해야 해.

ANSWER

01 선택지 순서대로 직업, 귀가 시간, 외모, 취미는 언급했지만, 고향은 언급하지 않았으므로 정답은 ④이다.

02 선택지 순서대로 무게, 색상, 할인율, 가격은 언급했지만, 치수는 언급하지 않았으므로 정답은 ③이다.

01 다음을 듣고, 남자가 Eastern Hotel에 대해 언급하지 않은 것을 고르시오.

① 설립 시기   ② 위치   ③ 객실 수
④ 부대시설   ⑤ 숙박 요금

02 다음을 듣고, 남자가 노트북에 대해 언급하지 않은 것을 고르시오.

① 할인율   ② 색상   ③ 가격
④ 너비   ⑤ 무게

03 다음을 듣고, 여자가 Mike에 대해 언급하지 않은 것을 고르시오.

① 고향   ② 현 거주지   ③ 전공
④ 나이   ⑤ 취미

04 다음을 듣고, 남자가 언급하지 않은 것을 고르시오.

① 거주지   ② 재학 중인 학교   ③ 학년
④ 좋아하는 과목   ⑤ 장래 희망

05 다음을 듣고, 여자가 캠핑에 대해 언급하지 않은 것을 고르시오.

① 기간   ② 경비   ③ 이동 수단
④ 활동   ⑤ 신청 방법

06 다음을 듣고, 남자가 미아에 대해 언급하지 <u>않은</u> 것을 고르시오.

① 이름   ② 나이   ③ 인상착의
④ 실종 장소   ⑤ 국적

07 다음을 듣고, 남자가 특별 손님에 대해 언급하지 <u>않은</u> 것을 고르시오.

① 직업   ② 국적   ③ 좋아하는 음악 장르
④ 연주 악기   ⑤ 대표 곡명

08 다음을 듣고, 남자가 자신의 과제에 대해 언급하지 <u>않은</u> 것을 고르시오.

① 해당 과목   ② 분량   ③ 작성 소요 시간
④ 주제   ⑤ 주제 선정 이유

고난도
09 다음을 듣고, 여자가 고모에 대해 언급하지 <u>않은</u> 것을 고르시오.

① 이름   ② 자녀   ③ 나이
④ 직업   ⑤ 거주지

고난도
10 다음을 듣고, 남자가 렌터카에 대해 언급하지 <u>않은</u> 것을 고르시오.

① 색상   ② 대여 비용   ③ 승차 정원
④ 최고 속도   ⑤ 이용 시 주의사항

DICTATION

일반 속도   빠른 속도

01

다음을 듣고, 남자가 Eastern Hotel 에 대해 언급하지 않은 것을 고르시오.

① 설립 시기   ② 위치
③ 객실 수   ④ 부대시설
⑤ 숙박 요금

M Welcome to Eastern Hotel! This beautiful hotel is _____ _____ _____ _____. It has 120 rooms, two terrific restaurants, and three nice swimming pools. You can _____ _____ _____ _____ for just $70 a night.

02

다음을 듣고, 남자가 노트북에 대해 언급하지 않은 것을 고르시오.

① 할인율   ② 색상
③ 가격   ④ 너비
⑤ 무게

M The X87 laptop computer is _____ _____! You can get 25% off _____ _____ _____. It is available in black or silver. It is 33 centimeters wide and weighs _____ _____ one kilogram. Get one today!

03

다음을 듣고, 여자가 Mike에 대해 언급하지 않은 것을 고르시오.

① 고향   ② 현 거주지
③ 전공   ④ 나이
⑤ 취미

W Mike was born in Sydney, but he lives in Tokyo now. He is _____ _____ Japanese history there. His hobby is watching movies, so he often _____ _____ _____ _____ with his friends. Mike is _____ _____ his life in Tokyo, but he misses his parents in Sydney.

04

다음을 듣고, 남자가 언급하지 않은 것을 고르시오.

① 거주지   ② 재학 중인 학교
③ 학년   ④ 좋아하는 과목
⑤ 장래 희망

M Hello! _____ _____ _____ _____. My name is Kim Minjun. I live in Daegu. I am a student at Daegu Middle School. _____ _____ _____ is science. And I want to be a scientist. Thank you for listening.

32

다음을 듣고, 여자가 캠핑에 대해 언급하지 <u>않은</u> 것을 고르시오.
① 기간   ② 경비
③ 이동 수단   ④ 활동
⑤ 신청 방법

W Our class will go to Sokcho for a camping trip. We will _____ _____ September 9 and return on the 11. The cost will be $100. We will _____ _____ _____. At the campsite, we will play games and sing around the campfire. Please _____ _____ _____!

06

다음을 듣고, 남자가 미아에 대해 언급하지 <u>않은</u> 것을 고르시오.
① 이름   ② 나이
③ 인상착의   ④ 실종 장소
⑤ 국적

M Attention, please. We're _____ _____ a missing child. Her name is Kim Jimin, and she is four years old. She _____ _____ _____ and is wearing a yellow T-shirt. She is from Korea, but she speaks English. If you find her, please _____ _____ _____ the information center.

07

다음을 듣고, 남자가 특별 손님에 대해 언급하지 <u>않은</u> 것을 고르시오.
① 직업
② 국적
③ 좋아하는 음악 장르
④ 연주 악기
⑤ 대표 곡명

M Good evening. Today's special guest is Emily Henderson. She is a singer-songwriter from Canada. Her favorite musical genre is jazz. She _____ _____ _____ _____ playing the guitar. She _____ _____ the guitar when she was eleven. Tonight, she will _____ _____ _____ _____ for us.

다음을 듣고, 남자가 자신의 과제에 대해 언급하지 <u>않은</u> 것을 고르시오.

① 해당 과목   ② 분량
③ 작성 소요 시간   ④ 주제
⑤ 주제 선정 이유

M Today I am going to _____ _____ _____ for you. I wrote it for my English homework. It _____ _____ _____ _____ to write it. The topic is polar bears. I chose this topic because I _____ _____ _____ and the environment.

고난도
09

다음을 듣고, 여자가 고모에 대해 언급하지 <u>않은</u> 것을 고르시오.

① 이름   ② 자녀
③ 나이   ④ 직업
⑤ 거주지

W I'd like to _____ _____ _____ my aunt. She is my role model. Her name is Lucy, and she is my father's younger sister. She is 35 years old, and she is a doctor. She _____ _____ a big hospital. I don't see her often because she lives in London. I want to be just like her _____ _____ _____ _____.

고난도
10

다음을 듣고, 남자가 렌터카에 대해 언급하지 <u>않은</u> 것을 고르시오.

① 색상   ② 대여 비용
③ 승차 정원   ④ 최고 속도
⑤ 이용 시 주의사항

M Do you need to _____ _____ _____? Then take a look at this red one. It is only $40 per day, and it _____ _____ _____ up to five people. This attractive red car is _____ _____ _____ _____. It can go 160 kilometers per hour! Why don't you take it on a test drive?

A 다음 영어 어휘나 표현의 뜻을 우리말로 쓰세요.

01 missing child

02 choose

03 grow up

04 major in

05 take a look at

06 attractive

07 swimming pool

08 topic

09 laptop computer

10 wide

11 polar bear

12 scientist

13 introduce

14 history

15 role model

16 bring

B 우리말에 맞는 영어 어휘나 표현을 [보기]에서 찾아 쓰세요.

	보기	per	essay	travel	care about	regular price
		cost	subject	perform	campsite	information center

01 ~당

02 야영지

03 비용

04 과목

05 안내소

06 연주하다

07 정가

08 이동하다

09 과제물

10 ~에 관심을 가지다

시각·대화 장소

정답 및 해설 p. 9

유형 설명
대화를 듣고, 시간 정보나 대화와 관련된 장소를 파악하는 유형이다. 주로 두 사람이 만날 시각을 고르는 문제와 대화가 이루어지는 장소를 묻는 문제가 출제된다.

지시문 유형
· 대화를 듣고, 두 사람이 만날 시각을 고르시오.
· 대화를 듣고, 두 사람이 대화하는 장소로 가장 적절한 곳을 고르시오.

기출 표현 맛보기

시각

· **W** Let's go there at 1 in the afternoon.
  M There are too many people at that time. How about meeting at 12:30?

· **M** The game starts at 7 p.m. So, let's meet in front of the stadium at 6:30.
  W How about 6:00? Let's have burgers for dinner together.

대화 장소

· **M** How may I help you?
  W Can you dry-clean this jacket for me? (세탁소)

· **M** Do you sell puzzles in this bookstore?
  W I'm sorry. We don't. But you can buy them at a toy store nearby. (서점)

주요 어휘·표현 미리보기

다음을 듣고, [보기]에서 알맞은 어휘나 표현을 찾아 쓰세요.

| 보기 |
ⓐ join ⓑ stop by ⓒ destination ⓓ opened an account
ⓔ had better hurry ⓕ pack ⓖ immediately ⓗ would you like

01 Will you _____ us for lunch? 우리랑 점심 함께 할래?

02 I _____ at the bank. 나는 그 은행에서 계좌를 개설했어.

03 He was waiting for me at my _____. 그는 나의 목적지에서 나를 기다리고 있었어.

04 _____ to come to the party? 파티에 올래?

05 You need to go to the hospital _____. 넌 즉시 병원에 가야 해.

06 Do you have time to _____ before leaving? 떠나기 전에 짐을 챙길 시간이 있니?

07 I'll _____ your house tomorrow. 내일 너희 집에 잠시 들를게.

08 You _____ to catch the last train. 마지막 열차를 타려면 서두르는 게 좋을 거야.

- 시간 정보를 묻는 문제의 경우, 현재 시각과 제시된 시간 정보를 메모하며 들으세요. 대화의 끝부분에 내용이 변경될 수 있으므로 끝까지 주의 깊게 듣는 것도 중요해요.
- 대화 장소를 묻는 문제의 경우, 장소 파악에 중요한 단서가 될 수 있는 대화의 주제나 화제를 잘 파악하며 들어야 해요.

01

대화를 듣고, 두 사람이 만날 시각을 고르시오.

① 2:30 p.m.　　② 3:00 p.m.　　③ 3:30 p.m.　　④ 4:00 p.m.　　⑤ 4:30 p.m.

[Cell phone rings.]
M　Hello, Jessica!
W　Hey, Sam! Where are you?
M　I'm on my way to the concert hall now.
W　I'm going there, too. But I will be a little late.
M　No worries. It's 4 o'clock now.　오답 함정
W　Then, let's meet at 4:30 in front of the ticket box.　정답 단서
M　Okay.

각자 공연장으로 향하고 있는 두 사람의 대화 내용이야. 현재 시각과 만날 시각을 잘 들었지?

02

대화를 듣고, 두 사람이 대화하는 장소로 가장 적절한 곳을 고르시오.

① 식당　　② 영화관　　③ 가구점　　④ 음악실　　⑤ 도서관

M　Welcome to Brown Wood. Can I help you?
W　Hi. I'm looking for a dinner table for four people.
M　These are all four-person dinner tables.
W　Which one is the most popular?
M　This one is. People really like the design, and it's not expensive.
W　Good. I really like the color, too.

부분적인 단어만 듣고 푼다면 함정에 빠질 수 있어. 전체적인 주제나 화제에 초점을 두고 들어야 해.

ANSWER
01　현재 시각은 4시이나, 여자가 만나자고 한 시각은 4시 30분이므로 정답은 ⑤이다.
02　여자가 4인용 식탁을 구경하고 있으므로 두 사람이 대화하는 장소로 ③이 알맞다.

LISTENING PRACTICE

점수   / 10문항

일반 속도   빠른 속도

01 대화를 듣고, 두 사람이 만날 시각을 고르시오.

① 4:45 p.m.   ② 5:00 p.m.   ③ 5:30 p.m.
④ 5:45 p.m.   ⑤ 6:00 p.m.

02 대화를 듣고, 두 사람이 만날 시각을 고르시오.

① 9:00 a.m.   ② 10:00 a.m.   ③ 11:00 a.m.
④ 11:30 a.m.   ⑤ 12:00 p.m.

03 대화를 듣고, 두 사람이 만날 시각을 고르시오.

① 2:00 p.m.   ② 2:30 p.m.   ③ 2:40 p.m.
④ 3:00 p.m.   ⑤ 3:10 p.m.

04 대화를 듣고, 두 사람이 대화하는 장소로 가장 적절한 곳을 고르시오.

① 지하철역   ② 비행기 안   ③ 공항
④ 버스 정류장   ⑤ 기차역

05 대화를 듣고, 두 사람이 대화하는 장소로 가장 적절한 곳을 고르시오.

① 동물원   ② 야구 경기장   ③ 콘서트장
④ 기념품점   ⑤ 영화관

고난도

06 대화를 듣고, 두 사람이 만날 시각을 고르시오.

① 3:30 p.m. ② 4:30 p.m. ③ 5:30 p.m.
④ 6:00 p.m. ⑤ 7:00 p.m.

07 대화를 듣고, 두 사람이 만날 시각을 고르시오.

① 5:00 p.m. ② 5:30 p.m. ③ 6:00 p.m.
④ 6:30 p.m. ⑤ 7:00 p.m.

08 대화를 듣고, 두 사람이 대화하는 장소로 가장 적절한 곳을 고르시오.

① 지하철 안 ② 가방 수선 가게 ③ 백화점
④ 분실물 보관소 ⑤ 전자제품 판매점

09 대화를 듣고, 두 사람이 대화하는 장소로 가장 적절한 곳을 고르시오.

① 경찰서 ② 은행 ③ 도서관
④ 매표소 ⑤ 컴퓨터실

고난도

10 대화를 듣고, 두 사람이 대화하는 장소로 가장 적절한 곳을 고르시오.

① 주차장 ② 편의점 ③ 커피 전문점
④ 식료품점 ⑤ 주유소

DICTATION

정답 단서 오답 함정

 일반 속도
 빠른 속도

01

대화를 듣고, 두 사람이 만날 시각을 고르시오.

① 4:45 p.m.　② 5:00 p.m.
③ 5:30 p.m.　④ 5:45 p.m.
⑤ 6:00 p.m.

W Are you going to ＿＿＿＿ ＿＿＿＿ ＿＿＿＿ after volleyball practice, Dad?

M Yes. Let's meet ＿＿＿＿ ＿＿＿＿ ＿＿＿＿ your school at five o'clock.

W Practice doesn't end until 5:30, Dad. And I need time to ＿＿＿＿ ＿＿＿＿ ＿＿＿＿.

M So how about 5:45?

W That's ＿＿＿＿ ＿＿＿＿. I'll see you then.

M Enjoy your practice!

02

대화를 듣고, 두 사람이 만날 시각을 고르시오.

① 9:00 a.m.　② 10:00 a.m.
③ 11:00 a.m.　④ 11:30 a.m.
⑤ 12:00 p.m.

M I'm going to the new cartoon museum tomorrow. ＿＿＿＿ ＿＿＿＿ ＿＿＿＿ ＿＿＿＿ ＿＿＿＿?

W Sure. Where is it?

M It's about thirty minutes away. It opens at 9:00 a.m.

W ＿＿＿＿ ＿＿＿＿ ＿＿＿＿ meet at ten?

M We'll probably be there ＿＿＿＿ ＿＿＿＿ ＿＿＿＿. We should have lunch before we go.

W How about noon, then?

M Sounds good.

03

대화를 듣고, 두 사람이 만날 시각을 고르시오.

① 2:00 p.m.　② 2:30 p.m.
③ 2:40 p.m.　④ 3:00 p.m.
⑤ 3:10 p.m.

W I'm going to go swimming this afternoon. Would you like to join me?

M Sure, that ＿＿＿＿ ＿＿＿＿.

W What time shall we meet?

M ＿＿＿＿ ＿＿＿＿ 2:30 at the gym?

W No, it's already two o'clock. I need ＿＿＿＿ ＿＿＿＿ ＿＿＿＿ ＿＿＿＿.

M Then how about meeting in forty minutes?

W Sounds good.

04

대화를 듣고, 두 사람이 대화하는 장소로 가장 적절한 곳을 고르시오.

① 지하철역　　② 비행기 안
③ 공항　　　　④ 버스 정류장
⑤ 기차역

M Excuse me. I can't find my boarding gate.

W _____ _____ _____?

M I'm flying to Tokyo.

W I see. You need to go to Gate 5 immediately.

M _____ _____ does boarding start?

W It starts at one o'clock.

M It's only 12:30 now. I still have thirty minutes.

W Actually, you must be at the gate _____ _____ twenty minutes before boarding.

M Oh! I _____ _____ _____.

05

대화를 듣고, 두 사람이 대화하는 장소로 가장 적절한 곳을 고르시오.

① 동물원　　　② 야구 경기장
③ 콘서트장　　④ 기념품점
⑤ 영화관

M May I help you?

W Yes. When is _Beauty and the Beast_ showing?

M There's a show starting at five. But you'd have to sit _____ _____ _____ _____.

W When is the next show?

M It starts at 5:45. It's the 3D version, but there are _____ _____ _____.

W Okay. I'll take two tickets.

06

고난도

대화를 듣고, 두 사람이 만날 시각을 고르시오.

① 3:30 p.m.　　② 4:30 p.m.
③ 5:30 p.m.　　④ 6:00 p.m.
⑤ 7:00 p.m.

M Are you going to Minsu's birthday party tomorrow?

W Yes. How about you?

M I _____ _____ _____, too. But I haven't bought a gift yet.

W I haven't either. Let's _____ _____ the mall before going to the party.

M Good idea! It starts at seven.

W _____ _____ _____ at the mall at 4:30?

M That's too early. How about an hour later?

W Sounds good. See you then.

07

대화를 듣고, 두 사람이 만날 시각을 고르시오.

① 5:00 p.m. ② 5:30 p.m.
③ 6:00 p.m. ④ 6:30 p.m.
⑤ 7:00 p.m.

M _____ _____ _____ _____ _____ to Wednesday's soccer game with me?

W I'd love to. What time does it start?

M At six. Let's meet at 5:30 at World Cup Stadium Station.

W _____ _____ thirty minutes earlier?

M Thirty minutes? Why?

W It will _____ _____ _____ to walk to the stadium.

M Okay. See you then.

08

대화를 듣고, 두 사람이 대화하는 장소로 가장 적절한 곳을 고르시오.

① 지하철 안   ② 가방 수선 가게
③ 백화점   ④ 분실물 보관소
⑤ 전자제품 판매점

W I left my bag _____ _____ _____. Do you have it?

M What does it look like?

W It's small and black. And there's a laptop in it.

M Let's see... What's your name? There's a bag _____ _____ _____ _____ on it.

W It's Emily.

M You're lucky. Here's your bag. _____ _____ _____ forget it again.

09

대화를 듣고, 두 사람이 대화하는 장소로 가장 적절한 곳을 고르시오.

① 경찰서   ② 은행
③ 도서관   ④ 매표소
⑤ 컴퓨터실

M How may I help you?

W I'd like to _____ _____ _____.

M Please _____ _____ this form.

W Okay. Do I have to put some money in the account now?

M No, you don't. I just need that form and your ID card.

W _____ _____ _____.

고난도

10

대화를 듣고, 두 사람이 대화하는 장소로 가장 적절한 곳을 고르시오.

① 주차장   ② 편의점
③ 커피 전문점 ④ 식료품점
⑤ 주유소

M Hello. Can you _____ _____ a bit?

W Okay.

M Perfect. How much gas would you like?

W Can you _____ _____ _____, please?

M Okay. [pause] Your tank is full. It's 50,000 won. How would you like to pay?

W _____ _____ _____.

M All right. Please sign here.

A 다음 영어 어휘나 표현의 뜻을 우리말로 쓰세요.

01	stadium	02	ID card
03	forward	04	cartoon
05	station	06	gym
07	volleyball	08	name tag
09	in front of	10	boarding gate
11	at least	12	sign
13	credit card	14	pay
15	noon	16	in the front row

B 우리말에 맞는 영어 어휘나 표현을 [보기]에서 찾아 쓰세요.

보기	hurry end	fill out fill up	change leave	subway practice	probably take a while

01	(옷을) 갈아입다	02	지하철
03	두고 오다	04	아마
05	서두르다	06	연습
07	끝나다	08	시간이 꽤 걸리다
09	~을 작성하다	10	~을 가득 채우다

장래 희망·직업

유형 설명

대화를 듣고 화자의 장래 희망이나 직업을 고르는 유형이다. 주로 대화 중에 장래 희망이 직접적으로 언급되며, 대화 상황과 말을 통해 직업을 유추하는 문제가 출제된다.

지시문 유형

· 대화를 듣고, 남자의 장래 희망으로 가장 적절한 것을 고르시오.

· 대화를 듣고, 여자의 직업으로 가장 적절한 것을 고르시오.

기출표현맛보기

장래 희망

· **M** I like your playing very much.

  W Thank you. I really want to be a guitarist. (기타 연주자)

직업

· **M** Flying Bakery. How can I help you?

  W Hello. I'd like to order a strawberry cake for my daughter's birthday. (제빵사)

주요 어휘·표현 미리보기

다음을 듣고, [보기]에서 알맞은 어휘나 표현을 찾아 쓰세요.

정답 및 해설 p. 12

보기

ⓐ in your free time ⓑ in the future ⓒ get your hair cut ⓓ pick up
ⓔ take care of ⓕ work out ⓖ may I see ⓗ inspired

01 She loves to _____ cats. 그녀는 고양이를 돌보는 걸 매우 좋아해.

02 What do you want to do _____? 장래에 뭘 하고 싶니?

03 You really need to _____ today. 너 오늘 꼭 머리 잘라야 해.

04 I need to _____ my sister at the airport. 나는 공항에 여동생을 마중 나가야 해.

05 What do you usually do _____? 너는 시간이 날 때 보통 무엇을 하니?

06 _____ your ID card? 신분증을 볼 수 있을까요?

07 You should _____ to stay healthy. 여러분은 건강을 유지하기 위해 운동해야 합니다.

08 He _____ us to protect the earth. 그는 우리가 지구를 보호하도록 고무시켰어.

기출로 유형 익히기

- 장래 희망을 고르는 문제의 경우, 과거의 장래 희망이나 취미, 상대의 장래 희망과 혼동하지 않도록 유의하세요.
- 직업을 고르는 문제의 경우, 특정 직업과 관련된 어휘나 표현이 나오므로 잘 들어야 해요.

01

대화를 듣고, 남자의 장래 희망으로 가장 적절한 것을 고르시오.

① 수의사   ② 건축가   ③ 피아니스트
④ 광고 제작자   ⑤ 컴퓨터 프로그래머

W   Mark, are you playing computer games again?
M   Mom, I'm not playing. I'm making a program.
W   Oh, is it part of your school homework?
M   Yes. And it's really fun. I want to be a computer programmer someday. 정답 단서
W   Yes, I believe you can be.
M   Thanks, Mom. I'll do my best.

남자가 무엇이 되고
싶다고 했는지 잘 들어봐.

02

대화를 듣고, 남자의 직업으로 가장 적절한 것을 고르시오.

① 버스 기사   ② 호텔 직원   ③ 동물 조련사
④ 열차 매표원   ⑤ 영화관 직원

M   Hi. May I help you?
W   Yes, I want to buy a train ticket to New York. When is the next train?
M   Let me check. *[pause]* The next train for New York leaves in 20 minutes.
W   Okay. I will take that one. One ticket, please.
M   That will be 30 dollars.
W   Here you are.
M   Thanks.

'티켓'이 어떤
상황에서 등장했을까?

ANSWER

01 남자가 자신은 컴퓨터 프로그래머가 되고 싶다고 했으므로, 남자의 장래 희망으로 ⑤가 알맞다.
02 여자가 남자로부터 뉴욕행 열차표를 구입하는 상황이므로, 남자의 직업으로 ④가 알맞다.

LISTENING PRACTICE

점수 ___ / 10문항

일반 속도

빠른 속도

01 대화를 듣고, 여자의 장래 희망으로 가장 적절한 것을 고르시오.

① 프로게이머　　　② 조종사　　　③ 여행 가이드
④ 승무원　　　⑤ 컴퓨터 프로그래머

02 대화를 듣고, 남자의 장래 희망으로 가장 적절한 것을 고르시오.

① 교수　　　② 작가　　　③ 여행가
④ 건축가　　　⑤ 외교관

03 대화를 듣고, 여자의 장래 희망으로 가장 적절한 것을 고르시오.

① 운동선수　　　② 영화감독　　　③ 배우
④ 코미디언　　　⑤ 방송작가

04 대화를 듣고, 남자의 직업으로 가장 적절한 것을 고르시오.

① 승무원　　　② 기자　　　③ 박물관장
④ 여행 가이드　　　⑤ 조종사

05 대화를 듣고, 여자의 직업으로 가장 적절한 것을 고르시오.

① 주차 관리원　　　② 주유소 직원　　　③ 교통경찰
④ 매표원　　　⑤ 카레이서

[고난도]

06 대화를 듣고, 남자의 장래 희망으로 가장 적절한 것을 고르시오.

① 요리사　　　　　② 제빵사　　　　　③ 영양사
④ 파티 플래너　　　⑤ 음식 평론가

07 대화를 듣고, 여자의 장래 희망으로 가장 적절한 것을 고르시오.

① 수의사　　　　　② 교사　　　　　③ 동물원 사육사
④ 사회 복지사　　　⑤ 애견미용사

[고난도]

08 대화를 듣고, 남자의 직업으로 가장 적절한 것을 고르시오.

① 모델　　　　　　② 배우　　　　　③ 경찰관
④ 미용사　　　　　⑤ 아나운서

09 대화를 듣고, 여자의 직업으로 가장 적절한 것을 고르시오.

① 엔지니어　　　　② 렌터카 회사 직원　　　③ 자동차 판매원
④ 의상 디자이너　　⑤ 자동차 디자이너

10 대화를 듣고, 남자의 직업으로 가장 적절한 것을 고르시오.

① 음식 평론가　　　② 바리스타　　　③ 음식점 종업원
④ 잡지 기자　　　　⑤ 주차관리원

DICTATION

정답 단서 오답 함정

일반 속도

빠른 속도

01

대화를 듣고, 여자의 장래 희망으로
가장 적절한 것을 고르시오.

① 프로게이머   ② 조종사
③ 여행 가이드   ④ 승무원
⑤ 컴퓨터 프로그래머

M What do you do _____ _____ _____ _____?

W I like playing computer games.

M Do you want to be a pro gamer _____ _____ _____?

W No. It's just a hobby. I want to be a pilot.

M Wow! You could _____ _____ _____ _____!

W That's right.

02

대화를 듣고, 남자의 장래 희망으로
가장 적절한 것을 고르시오.

① 교수   ② 작가
③ 여행가   ④ 건축가
⑤ 외교관

W What are you doing, David?

M I'm _____ _____ _____ about Antoni Gaudí.

W Who is he?

M He was _____ _____ _____ _____ _____ in the world.

W Are you _____ _____ _____?

M Yes. I want to be like him in the future.

03

대화를 듣고, 여자의 장래 희망으로
가장 적절한 것을 고르시오.

① 운동선수   ② 영화감독
③ 배우   ④ 코미디언
⑤ 방송작가

M Oh! It's two o'clock. I'm going to the gym.

W Again? You _____ _____ a lot.

M I do. Why don't you come with me?

W No, thanks. I'm going to the movie theater.

M You seem to _____ _____ _____.

W Yes. Actually, I hope to make my own movies someday. I _____ _____ _____ _____.

M You want to be a director?

W That's right! And watching comedies inspires me.

04

대화를 듣고, 남자의 직업으로 가장 적절한 것을 고르시오.

① 승무원　　② 기자
③ 박물관장　④ 여행 가이드
⑤ 조종사

W Tim, are you going to the airport again?

M Yes. I need to _____ _____ a group of people from Thailand.

W Will you _____ _____ _____ the city?

M Yes. I'll take them to some museums and palaces.

W You have _____ _____ _____ _____.

M I like it. I get to tell people all about Korean culture.

05

대화를 듣고, 여자의 직업으로 가장 적절한 것을 고르시오.

① 주차 관리원　② 주유소 직원
③ 교통경찰　　④ 매표원
⑤ 카레이서

W Excuse me. _____ _____ _____ your driver's license?

M Okay. Here you are. But what did I do wrong?

W You were driving _____ _____ _____ _____. The speed limit here is sixty-five kilometers per hour, but you were doing almost eighty.

M Oh, I am sorry. I didn't know.

W I'll have to _____ _____ _____ _____ for speeding.

고난도

06

대화를 듣고, 남자의 장래 희망으로 가장 적절한 것을 고르시오.

① 요리사　　② 제빵사
③ 영양사　　④ 파티 플래너
⑤ 음식 평론가

W What's your favorite food?

M Well, I can't just pick one. I really _____ _____ _____ _____.

W Me too. That's why I want to be a chef.

M That sounds awesome.

W Do you want to _____ _____ _____, too?

M I don't think I'm _____ _____ _____. I want to be a food critic.

07

대화를 듣고, 여자의 장래 희망으로 가장 적절한 것을 고르시오.

① 수의사　　② 교사
③ 동물원 사육사　④ 사회 복지사
⑤ 애견미용사

W I'm going to the animal hospital _____ _____ _____.

M Why are you going there?

W I'm a volunteer. I _____ _____ _____ and clean their cages.

M You must really love _____ _____ _____ animals.

W I do. I want to be a zookeeper when I grow up.

M That sounds really interesting!

08

대화를 듣고, 남자의 직업으로 가장
적절한 것을 고르시오.

① 모델　　　② 배우
③ 경찰관　　④ 미용사
⑤ 아나운서

W Did you _____ _____ _____ _____, Ken?

M Yes. What do you think?

W The style is great! You look like a model.

M Thanks! I have to _____ _____ _____ tomorrow.

W What is it for?

M A new TV show. It's called *Beach Police*.

W Would you _____ _____ _____ _____?

M No. A big star will play him. I'd play his best friend.

W Well, I hope you are successful.

09

대화를 듣고, 여자의 직업으로 가장
적절한 것을 고르시오.

① 엔지니어
② 렌터카 회사 직원
③ 자동차 판매원
④ 의상 디자이너
⑤ 자동차 디자이너

W Hello! How may I help you?

M I'm thinking about _____ _____ _____ _____. What do you recommend?

W This is our best-selling model. It can _____ _____ _____.

M It looks great! _____ _____ _____ _____ blue?

W I'm afraid not. It only comes in black and grey.

M I see. Can I look at them now?

W Sure. This way, please.

10

대화를 듣고, 남자의 직업으로 가장
적절한 것을 고르시오.

① 음식 평론가　② 바리스타
③ 음식점 종업원　④ 잡지 기자
⑤ 주차관리원

M Hello. What would you like to order?

W I would like the tomato pasta and a seafood salad.

M Okay. Do you want _____ _____ _____?

W Can I use these coupons _____ _____ _____?

M Yes, you can.

W Great! _____ _____ _____ lemonade, please.

M All right. Here are some breadsticks.

W Thanks.

A 다음 영어 어휘나 표현의 뜻을 우리말로 쓰세요.

01 cage

02 entertain

03 director

04 speed limit

05 volunteer

06 hobby

07 museum

08 main character

09 driver's license

10 culture

11 movie theater

12 recommend

13 chef

14 palace

15 best-selling

16 pilot

B 우리말에 맞는 영어 어휘나 표현을 [보기]에서 찾아 쓰세요.

| 보기 | pick | play | speeding | zookeeper | architecture |
| | fit | ticket | awesome | successful | critic |

01 속도위반

02 굉장한

03 합격한

04 (벌금) 딱지

05 고르다

06 건축

07 동물원 사육사

08 평론가, 비평가

09 맞다, 적합하다

10 (영화 등에서) 연기하다

심정

대화를 듣고, 남자 또는 여자의 심정을 파악하는 유형이다. 대화 상황을 고려하여 화자가 느낄 전반적인 심정을 고르는 문제가 출제된다.

· 대화를 듣고, 남자의 심정으로 가장 적절한 것을 고르시오.
· 대화를 듣고, 여자의 심정으로 가장 적절한 것을 고르시오.

· You don't look well. Are you all right? (worried)
· Wow, I really wanted to ride the roller coaster there! (excited)
· Please, Tom. You're wearing it now. I'm worried about you. (걱정스러움)
· Well, I practiced a lot, but I didn't win a prize. (실망스러움)

주요
어휘·표현
미리보기

다음을 듣고, [보기]에서 알맞은 어휘나 표현을 찾아 쓰세요.

정답 및 해설 p. 15

───	보기	───	
ⓐ make friends	ⓑ gets well	ⓒ a birthday present	ⓓ waiting for
ⓔ can't believe	ⓕ on time	ⓖ have you been	ⓗ had fun

01 I'm _____ you at the station. 나는 역에서 너를 기다리고 있어.

02 The train left from Seoul _____. 그 기차는 정시에 서울에서 출발했어.

03 It's already 11:00 p.m.? I _____ it! 벌써 밤 11시야? 믿을 수 없어!

04 It's too hard to _____ here. 여기에서는 친구를 사귀기가 너무 어려워.

05 We _____ at Lisa's party. 우리는 Lisa의 파티에서 재미있게 놀았어.

06 Oh, it was _____ from her. 아, 그건 그녀에게 받은 생일 선물이었어.

07 _____ to London before? 전에 런던에 가본 적 있니?

08 I hope your father _____ soon. 너희 아버지께서 건강을 곧 회복하시길 바랄게.

기출로 유형 익히기

- 먼저 지시문을 읽고 누구의 심정을 골라야 하는지 파악하세요.
- 선택지가 영어로 출제되기도 하므로 관련 어휘를 미리 익혀두는 것이 좋아요.
- 기쁨, 자랑스러움, 지루함, 걱정스러움 등 감정을 나타내는 어구나 감탄사, 화자의 어조에 유의하며 들어보세요.

01

대화를 듣고, 남자의 심정으로 가장 적절한 것을 고르시오.

① 기쁨   ② 지루함   ③ 부러움
④ 걱정스러움   ⑤ 자랑스러움

W What's wrong, Mike?
M My mom told me to walk the dog yesterday.
W Then, what happened?
M When I talked with my friend, my dog ran away.
W Oh, no! Did you find your dog?
M No, I couldn't find it anywhere. What shall I do? 정답 단서

여자는 산책을 하다 개를 잃어버린 남자와 대화를 나누고 있어.

02

대화를 듣고, 여자의 심정으로 가장 적절한 것을 고르시오.

① shy   ② bored   ③ relaxed
④ worried   ⑤ excited

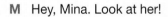

M Hey, Mina. Look at her!
W Oh! What a cute dog! Where did you get her?
M Tom's dog had four puppies. He let us have one.
W She's so lovely, Dad. I love dogs so much.
M I know. Please take good care of her.
W Of course. I can't believe I have a dog now.

남자가 데려온 강아지에 대하여 여자가 어떻게 표현했지?

ANSWER

01 남자가 개를 잃어버렸다고 말하는 내용이므로 남자의 심정으로 ④가 알맞다.

02 여자가 강아지를 키우게 되어 기뻐하는 내용이므로 여자의 심정으로 ⑤가 알맞다.

LISTENING PRACTICE

일반 속도

빠른 속도

01 대화를 듣고, 남자의 심정으로 가장 적절한 것을 고르시오.

① 자랑스러움   ② 부러움   ③ 외로움
④ 지루함   ⑤ 당황스러움

02 대화를 듣고, 여자의 심정으로 가장 적절한 것을 고르시오.

① 부끄러움   ② 자랑스러움   ③ 부러움
④ 기쁨   ⑤ 실망스러움

03 대화를 듣고, 남자의 심정으로 가장 적절한 것을 고르시오.

① 후회스러움   ② 만족스러움   ③ 놀라움
④ 부끄러움   ⑤ 걱정스러움

04 대화를 듣고, 여자의 심정으로 가장 적절한 것을 고르시오.

① bored   ② excited   ③ shy
④ angry   ⑤ relaxed

고난도
05 대화를 듣고, 남자의 심정으로 가장 적절한 것을 고르시오.

① surprised   ② sad   ③ interested
④ peaceful   ⑤ nervous

06 대화를 듣고, 여자의 심정으로 가장 적절한 것을 고르시오.

① relaxed   ② excited   ③ disappointed

④ proud   ⑤ jealous

고난도

07 대화를 듣고, 남자의 심정으로 가장 적절한 것을 고르시오.

① worried   ② bored   ③ proud

④ satisfied   ⑤ surprised

08 대화를 듣고, 여자의 심정으로 가장 적절한 것을 고르시오.

① 슬픔   ② 걱정스러움   ③ 부끄러움

④ 무관심함   ⑤ 자랑스러움

09 대화를 듣고, 남자의 심정으로 가장 적절한 것을 고르시오.

① 지루함   ② 화남   ③ 부러움

④ 즐거움   ⑤ 당황스러움

10 대화를 듣고, 여자의 심정으로 가장 적절한 것을 고르시오.

① 신남   ② 두려움   ③ 초조함

④ 아쉬움   ⑤ 걱정스러움

DICTATION

정답 단서 오답 함정

일반 속도

빠른 속도

01

대화를 듣고, 남자의 심정으로 가장
적절한 것을 고르시오.
① 자랑스러움 　② 부러움
③ 외로움　　　④ 지루함
⑤ 당황스러움

W Hi, Jimmy. _____ _____ _____ _____ your new school?

M Well, my classes are interesting, and my teachers are nice.

W That's great.

M I guess. But I don't have any friends here.

W Oh, I see. You'll _____ _____ soon.

M I hope so. I _____ _____ _____ _____.

02

대화를 듣고, 여자의 심정으로 가장
적절한 것을 고르시오.
① 부끄러움　② 자랑스러움
③ 부러움　　④ 기쁨
⑤ 실망스러움

M I have _____ _____ _____ for you.

W Thanks, Dad. What is it?

M Open the envelope and _____ _____.

W Wow, it's _____ _____ _____ *Dream Girls*! I really wanted to see this musical. Thank you.

M I'm glad you like it.

03

대화를 듣고, 남자의 심정으로 가장
적절한 것을 고르시오.
① 후회스러움　② 만족스러움
③ 놀라움　　　④ 부끄러움
⑤ 걱정스러움

W Hey, Eddie, _____ _____? You haven't smiled all day.

M My grandma is very sick. She is _____ _____ _____ now.

W Oh, really? That's too bad.

M I was at the hospital all day yesterday.

W I hope she _____ _____ _____.

M Thanks. I really hope so, too.

04

대화를 듣고, 여자의 심정으로 가장
적절한 것을 고르시오.
① bored　　② excited
③ shy　　　④ angry
⑤ relaxed

M Hey, Minsun. What are you doing here?

W I'm waiting for the bus. But I've already waited for thirty minutes.

M Thirty minutes? I _____ _____ _____!

W I'm going to be late for my appointment.

M How about _____ _____ _____ instead? It usually _____ _____ _____.

W I think I should. I hate the bus!

05

대화를 듣고, 남자의 심정으로 가장
적절한 것을 고르시오.

① surprised　② sad
③ interested　④ peaceful
⑤ nervous

M What are you reading, Mina?

W It's a sad book about a famous woman.

M Really? _____ _____ _____ her?

W She was a great scientist, but she _____ _____. It's a great book. I'm so happy that I found it.

M I'd like to learn more about her. Can I read it _____ _____ _____?

W Yes, you can.

06

대화를 듣고, 여자의 심정으로 가장
적절한 것을 고르시오.

① relaxed　② excited
③ disappointed　④ proud
⑤ jealous

M Haru, I heard you're going on a school trip to Jeju.

W Yes, we're going next week. I can't wait!

M _____ _____ _____ there before?

W No, but my parents said that it is a beautiful island.

M Well, I hope _____ _____ _____.

W I will. I'm really _____ _____ _____ the trip!

07

대화를 듣고, 남자의 심정으로 가장
적절한 것을 고르시오.

① worried　② bored
③ proud　④ satisfied
⑤ surprised

W I'm glad that test _____ _____ _____. Let's go have lunch!

M I don't _____ _____ _____.

W Is something wrong?

M I think I might have done poorly on the test.

W Don't be silly. You always _____ _____ _____.

M Maybe not this time. That test was hard.

W I'm confident that you _____ _____.

M I hope you're right.

08

대화를 듣고, 여자의 심정으로 가장
적절한 것을 고르시오.
① 슬픔　　　② 걱정스러움
③ 부끄러움　　④ 무관심함
⑤ 자랑스러움

W That painting of _____ _____ _____ is mine.

M You painted that? It's very good.

W Thanks. It's my _____ _____.

M What will you do with it?

W I will hang it _____ _____ _____ so everyone can see it.

09

대화를 듣고, 남자의 심정으로 가장
적절한 것을 고르시오.
① 지루함　　　② 화남
③ 부러움　　　④ 즐거움
⑤ 당황스러움

W Aren't you going to Mark's house tonight?

M No. He's not my friend anymore.

W _____ _____? You said he's funny and interesting.

M He is. But he _____ _____ _____.

W Oh. Well, maybe he'll apologize.

M _____ _____ _____. I'm not talking to him.

10

대화를 듣고, 여자의 심정으로 가장
적절한 것을 고르시오.
① 신남　　　② 두려움
③ 초조함　　　④ 아쉬움
⑤ 걱정스러움

M You went to the amusement park yesterday, _____ _____?

W Yes. How did you know?

M Your sister said you were _____ _____ _____ the roller coaster.

W I was. But the roller coaster _____ _____ _____ _____.

M Really? Well, were the other rides fun?

W They were okay. But I really wanted to ride the roller coaster.

UNIT 6 어휘·표현 다지기

A

다음 영어 어휘나 표현의 뜻을 우리말로 쓰세요.

01 classmate

02 silly

03 anymore

04 clown

05 confident

06 wall

07 appointment

08 interesting

09 painting

10 excited

11 school trip

12 envelope

13 famous

14 ride

15 island

16 happen

B

우리말에 맞는 영어 어휘나 표현을 [보기]에서 찾아 쓰세요.

보기	lie	hang	closed	feel like v-ing	look forward to
	care	score	poorly	find out	be in the hospital

01 알아내다

02 ~을 고대하다

03 입원 중이다

04 상관하다

05 걸다

06 문을 닫은

07 형편없이

08 ~하고 싶다

09 거짓말하다

10 점수

할 일·한 일

유형 설명
대화를 듣고 앞으로 할 일이나 과거에 한 일을 고르는 유형이다. 주로 대화가 끝난 직후에 화자가 할 일이나, 과거의 특정한 날에 화자가 한 일을 묻는 문제가 출제된다.

지시문 유형
· 대화를 듣고, 남자가 대화 직후에 할 일로 가장 적절한 것을 고르시오.
· 대화를 듣고, 두 사람이 주말에 할 일로 가장 적절한 것을 고르시오.
· 대화를 듣고, 여자가 지난 토요일에 한 일로 가장 적절한 것을 고르시오.

기출 표현 맛보기
할 일

W   Why don't you find it on the Internet?
M   Okay, I will do that right now.

한 일

W   Did you watch the baseball game last Saturday?
M   No, I missed it. How was it?
W   It was so exciting. I watched it at the stadium with my dad.

주요
어휘·표현
미리보기

다음을 듣고, [보기]에서 알맞은 어휘나 표현을 찾아 쓰세요.　　　　정답 및 해설 p. 17

보기
ⓐ get moving　　ⓑ cousins　　ⓒ take this photo　　ⓓ spend the day
ⓔ was canceled　　ⓕ go shopping　　ⓖ late for　　ⓗ on my way to

01   We're going to _____ at the park. 우리는 공원에서 하루를 보낼 거야.

02   I'm _____ school now. 나는 지금 학교에 가는 길이야.

03   _____ now or you'll miss the bus. 지금 빨리 움직이지 않으면 버스를 놓칠 거야.

04   That student is often _____ school. 저 학생은 학교에 자주 지각해.

05   Did he _____ yesterday? 그가 어제 이 사진을 찍었니?

06   The game _____ because of rain. 비 때문에 경기가 취소되었어.

07   Did you have fun with your _____? 네 사촌들과 즐거운 시간 보냈니?

08   Let's _____ tomorrow. 내일 쇼핑하러 가자.

- 대화를 듣기 전에 지시문을 읽고, 누가 언제 할 일 또는 한 일을 묻는지 확인하세요.
- 상대방의 할 일이나 한 일이 함정으로 등장하는 경우가 많으니 주의하세요.

01

대화를 듣고, 여자가 대화 직후에 할 일로 가장 적절한 것을 고르시오.

① 양초 만들기   ② 종이접기 배우기   ③ 티셔츠 만들기
④ 페이스 페인팅하기   ⑤ 물풍선 터뜨리기

M Wow, this school festival is really fun.

W Yes, it is.

M What do you want to do next?

W Let's make a candle in the gym. 오답 함정

M But it will take too much time. Why don't we do face painting? 정답 단서

W Sounds good! Let's go right now.

대화 직후에 할 일은 주로 대화 후반부에 나와.

02

대화를 듣고, 남자가 휴일에 한 일로 가장 적절한 것을 고르시오.

① 꽃 심기   ② 창문 닦기   ③ 그림 그리기
④ 뮤지컬 보기   ⑤ 친구 만나기

W Good morning, Dongjoon. How was your holiday?

M It was great! I planted flowers in my garden.

W That's interesting! What kind of flowers did you plant?

M They were roses and sunflowers. I hope they grow well.

W Wow, you had a wonderful holiday.

휴일을 어떻게 보냈냐는 여자의 질문에 남자가 뭐라고 대답했는지 잘 들어봐.

ANSWER

01 페이스 페인팅을 하자는 남자의 말에 여자가 동의했으므로, 여자가 대화 직후에 할 일은 ④이다.

02 남자가 자신의 정원에 꽃들을 심었다고 했으므로, 정답은 ①이다.

LISTENING PRACTICE

점수 _____ / 10문항

일반 속도

빠른 속도

01 대화를 듣고, 여자가 대화 직후에 할 일로 가장 적절한 것을 고르시오.

① 거실 청소하기 ② 쓰레기 분리수거하기 ③ 설거지하기
④ 욕실 청소하기 ⑤ 빨래하기

고난도
02 대화를 듣고, 남자가 대화 직후에 할 일로 가장 적절한 것을 고르시오.

① 공항에 마중 나가기 ② 결혼식 참석하기 ③ 기차 시간표 확인하기
④ 정비소 가기 ⑤ 항공편 변경하기

03 대화를 듣고, 여자가 어제 한 일로 가장 적절한 것을 고르시오.

① 쇼핑하기 ② 게임하기 ③ 산책하기
④ 친구와 점심 먹기 ⑤ 이삿짐 싸는 것 돕기

04 대화를 듣고, 남자가 어제 한 일로 가장 적절한 것을 고르시오.

① TV 보기 ② 친구 만나기 ③ 병원 진료받기
④ 놀이공원 가기 ⑤ 집 청소하기

05 대화를 듣고, 여자가 지난 토요일에 한 일로 가장 적절한 것을 고르시오.

① 외식하기 ② 동물원 가기 ③ 사진관 가기
④ 앵무새 먹이 주기 ⑤ 카페에서 친구 만나기

06

대화를 듣고, 여자가 일요일에 할 일로 가장 적절한 것을 고르시오.

① 숙제하기　　　　② 해변 가기　　　　③ 바이올린 수업 가기
④ 시험공부 하기　　⑤ 연주회 가기

07

대화를 듣고, 남자가 대화 직후에 할 일로 가장 적절한 것을 고르시오.

① 휴대전화 구입하기　　② 선생님과 면담하기　　③ 버스 타러 가기
④ 앱 내려받기　　　　　⑤ 웹사이트 접속하기

고난도
08

대화를 듣고, 여자가 대화 직후에 할 일로 가장 적절한 것을 고르시오.

① 스키장 가기　　　② 책 반납하러 가기　　③ 쇼핑하러 가기
④ 스웨터 반품하기　⑤ 겨울옷 세탁하기

09

대화를 듣고, 여자가 지난 토요일에 한 일로 가장 적절한 것을 고르시오.

① 영화 보기　　　　② 음악 듣기　　　　③ 수족관 가기
④ 체험학습 다녀오기　⑤ 뮤지컬 관람하기

10

대화를 듣고, 남자가 지난 주말에 한 일로 가장 적절한 것을 고르시오.

① 캠핑하기　　　② 수영하기　　　③ 시험공부 하기
④ 모래성 만들기　⑤ 사촌 집 방문하기

DICTATION

설명 및 해설 pp. 17-20

정답 단서 오답 함정

일반 속도

빠른 속도

01

대화를 듣고, 여자가 대화 직후에 할 일로 가장 적절한 것을 고르시오.

① 거실 청소하기
② 쓰레기 분리수거하기
③ 설거지하기
④ 욕실 청소하기
⑤ 빨래하기

W Are you busy now?

M No, I just finished my homework.

W Good. Let's _____ _____ _____ and finish before Dad gets home.

M Okay, Mom. I'll do the dishes and wash the clothes.

W Okay. I'll _____ _____ _____ _____.

M Dad will be very surprised.

W Yes, he will. _____ _____ _____!

02

고난도

대화를 듣고, 남자가 대화 직후에 할 일로 가장 적절한 것을 고르시오.

① 공항에 마중 나가기
② 결혼식 참석하기
③ 기차 시간표 확인하기
④ 정비소 가기
⑤ 항공편 변경하기

[Cell phone rings.]

W Hello?

M It's Jake. I'm sorry, but I can't come to your wedding tomorrow.

W Why not? I really want to see you.

M Unfortunately, _____ _____ _____ _____ because of the bad weather.

W Oh no! What about driving?

M My car is in the repair shop.

W Why don't you take the train?

M Will it _____ _____ _____ _____?

W I'm not sure. I don't know the schedule.

M I'll check online and then _____ _____ _____.

03

대화를 듣고, 여자가 어제 한 일로 가장 적절한 것을 고르시오.

① 쇼핑하기
② 게임하기
③ 산책하기
④ 친구와 점심 먹기
⑤ 이삿짐 싸는 것 돕기

M Hi, Amanda. I saw you walking down Main Street yesterday.

W Oh, you did? I was _____ _____ _____ _____ Hannah's place.

M Oh, I haven't seen her in a while. Did you two have lunch together?

W No. I mostly _____ _____ _____ _____ _____. She's moving to Atlanta tomorrow.

M Oh, I didn't know that. _____ _____ _____.

W Me too.

64

대화를 듣고, 남자가 어제 한 일로 가장 적절한 것을 고르시오.
① TV 보기   ② 친구 만나기
③ 병원 진료받기 ④ 놀이공원 가기
⑤ 집 청소하기

W Hey, _____ _____ _____ _____ at the amusement park yesterday?

M Actually, I didn't go.

W Oh, didn't you say you were going to go with Jack?

M I did. But Jack got sick yesterday. So he _____ _____ _____ _____ _____.

W I'm sorry to hear that.

M Yeah. So I just _____ _____ and watched TV.

05

대화를 듣고, 여자가 지난 토요일에 한 일로 가장 적절한 것을 고르시오.
① 외식하기
② 동물원 가기
③ 사진관 가기
④ 앵무새 먹이 주기
⑤ 카페에서 친구 만나기

W Hey, look at this. I _____ _____ _____ last Saturday.

M Wow, this parrot in the photo is cute! Did you go to the zoo?

W No, I visited a special café. There were several parrots, and I _____ _____ _____ _____!

M That sounds amazing. I'd like to _____ _____ _____ sometime too.

W Then let's go together next time.

06

대화를 듣고, 여자가 일요일에 할 일로 가장 적절한 것을 고르시오.
① 숙제하기
② 해변 가기
③ 바이올린 수업 가기
④ 시험공부 하기
⑤ 연주회 가기

W I'm going to _____ _____ _____ at the beach on Saturday!

M Sounds great. But I thought you _____ _____ _____ _____ on Saturday.

W No, that's on Sunday.

M Oh, I see.

W What will you do this weekend?

M Unfortunately, I have to _____ _____ _____ _____ _____.

대화를 듣고, 남자가 대화 직후에 할 일로 가장 적절한 것을 고르시오.
① 휴대전화 구입하기
② 선생님과 면담하기
③ 버스 타러 가기
④ 앱 내려받기
⑤ 웹사이트 접속하기

W This is a great app!

M What does it do?

W It _____ _____ _____ _____ the bus will arrive.

M I need that app. I often _____ _____ _____ and get to school late.

W You can download it _____ _____.

M I'll do that now. And I'll never be late for school again.

08

대화를 듣고, 여자가 대화 직후에 할
일로 가장 적절한 것을 고르시오.

① 스키장 가기
② 책 반납하러 가기
③ 쇼핑하러 가기
④ 스웨터 반품하기
⑤ 겨울옷 세탁하기

M Honey, how about _____ _____ together?

W Okay. Are there any sales at the department store?

M Yes. _____ _____ _____, so winter clothes are 40% off.

W Wow! I can buy a sweater for my ski trip.

M That's a good idea.

W But can we go later? I need to return some library books first.

M Sure. _____ _____ _____ _____.

W Great. I'll be back in about an hour.

M No problem.

09

대화를 듣고, 여자가 지난 토요일에
한 일로 가장 적절한 것을 고르시오.

① 영화 보기
② 음악 듣기
③ 수족관 가기
④ 체험학습 다녀오기
⑤ 뮤지컬 관람하기

M Hi, Irene. _____ _____ _____ _____ last Saturday?

W I saw *Matilda*. It was really good.

M *Matilda*? Do you mean the movie?

W No, the musical. _____ _____ _____, Mike? What did you do?

M I _____ _____ _____ _____ with my parents.

W Sounds fun!

10

대화를 듣고, 남자가 지난 주말에 한
일로 가장 적절한 것을 고르시오.

① 캠핑하기   ② 수영하기
③ 시험공부 하기 ④ 모래성 만들기
⑤ 사촌 집 방문하기

M Did you have a nice weekend?

W Yes, I did. I _____ _____ _____ _____ with my cousins.

M You must have had fun!

W Yeah. We swam in the sea and made a big sandcastle. Did you _____ _____ _____ too?

M Yes, I _____ _____ with my family.

W Oh, that sounds lovely!

A 다음 영어 어휘나 표현의 뜻을 우리말로 쓰세요.

01 surprised

02 stay

03 arrive

04 beach

05 in time

06 lesson

07 mostly

08 parrot

09 housework

10 living room

11 exactly

12 busy

13 repair shop

14 aquarium

15 do the dishes

16 sandcastle

B 우리말에 맞는 영어 어휘나 표현을 [보기]에서 찾아 쓰세요.

	보기	off	flight	somewhere	see a doctor	department store
		miss	move	download	unfortunately	amusement park

01 놀이공원

02 백화점

03 이사하다

04 할인되어

05 항공편

06 의사의 진찰을 받다

07 놓치다

08 어딘가에

09 (데이터를) 내려받다

10 유감스럽게도, 불행하게도

지칭·주제/화제

담화나 대화를 듣고, 들려주는 내용이 무엇에 관한 것인지 파악하는 유형이다. 담화에서 지칭하는 'this'나 'I'가 무엇인지 추론하는 문제가 출제된다. 대화의 전반적인 주제나 화제를 묻는 문제도 출제된다.

지시문 유형
- 다음을 듣고, 'this'가 가리키는 것으로 가장 적절한 것을 고르시오.
- 다음을 듣고, 'I'가 무엇인지 가장 적절한 것을 고르시오.
- 대화를 듣고, 무엇에 관한 내용인지 가장 적절한 것을 고르시오.

기출표현맛보기

지칭
- I have black lines on my body. I am a member of the cat family. (호랑이)
- You can put this on the stove and make pancakes or fried eggs with this. (프라이팬)

주제/화제
- Nahee, we need to clean the music room now. (음악실 청소하기)
- Hey, Jihye. What do you do for volunteer work? (봉사 활동)

주요 어휘·표현 미리보기

다음을 듣고, [보기]에서 알맞은 어휘나 표현을 찾아 쓰세요.   정답 및 해설 p. 20

보기
ⓐ a kind of ⓑ weather ⓒ wash ⓓ feed
ⓔ useful ⓕ how to ⓖ good for ⓗ made of

01 This chair is _____ wood. 이 의자는 나무로 만들어졌어.

02 How is the _____ today? 오늘 날씨가 어때?

03 I want to learn _____ drive a car. 나는 차를 운전하는 법을 배우고 싶어.

04 Chickens are _____ bird. 닭은 조류의 일종이야.

05 I have to _____ my cat every morning. 나는 매일 아침 고양이에게 먹이를 줘야 해.

06 Running is _____ your health. 달리기는 네 건강에 좋아.

07 Let me help you _____ your dog. 내가 네 개 씻기는 걸 도와줄게.

08 This book is very _____ for learning English. 이 책은 영어를 배우는 데 아주 유용해.

기출로 유형 익히기

- 지칭 문제의 경우, 사물이나 동물의 특징을 설명하는 형용사나 표현을 주의 깊게 듣고 종합하여 정답을 유추해 보세요.
- 주제/화제 문제의 경우, 대화나 담화의 일부가 아닌 전체 내용과 관련된 선택지를 고르세요.

01

다음을 듣고, 'this'가 가리키는 것으로 가장 적절한 것을 고르시오.

①  ② ③  ④ ⑤

M When you want to wash your hands, you turn this on. Then, water will come out from this. You can also use this to wash the dishes or clothes. But don't forget to turn this off when you are not using this. What is this?

오답 함정 / 정답 단서

일부 단어에 집중하지 말고 여러 단서들을 조합해서 정답을 추론해야 해.

02

대화를 듣고, 무엇에 관한 내용인지 가장 적절한 것을 고르시오.

① 체육 대회　　　　② 합창 대회　　　　③ 봉사 활동
④ 영어 캠프　　　　⑤ 박물관 방문

W James, you look excited. What's new?
M Today my class will visit the Bike museum.
W Cool. What are you going to do there?
M We'll learn about the history of bikes.
W Will you do anything else?
M We'll also ride special bikes. It will be fun.

주제나 화제를 암시하는 키워드는 대화 초반에 언급되는 경우가 많아.

ANSWER
01 손을 씻을 때 트는 것으로, 설거지하거나 빨래하는 데도 사용한다고 했으므로 정답은 ②이다.
02 남자가 자전거 박물관에서 할 일에 대해 말하고 있으므로 정답은 ⑤이다.

LISTENING PRACTICE

일반 속도   빠른 속도

01 다음을 듣고, 'this'가 가리키는 것으로 가장 적절한 것을 고르시오.

① 　② 　③ 　④ 　⑤

02 다음을 듣고, 'I'가 무엇인지 가장 적절한 것을 고르시오.

① 　② 　③ 　④ 　⑤

03 대화를 듣고, 무엇에 관한 내용인지 가장 적절한 것을 고르시오.

① 유기견 입양하기　　② 산책로 탐방하기　　③ 봉사활동 하기
④ 반려동물 돌보기　　⑤ 건강한 식습관 기르기

고난도
04 대화를 듣고, 무엇에 관한 내용인지 가장 적절한 것을 고르시오.

① 최근 지진 피해 현황　　② 전자제품 구입 요령
③ 지진 발생 시 안전수칙　　④ 엘리베이터 이용 시 주의사항
⑤ 전력 공급 중단 시 대처방안

고난도
05 대화를 듣고, 무엇에 관한 내용인지 가장 적절한 것을 고르시오.

① 물놀이 안전 수칙　　② 여름 휴가지 추천　　③ 수영장 재개장 안내
④ 응급 처치의 중요성　　⑤ 수영 강습의 필요성

06

다음을 듣고, 'this'가 가리키는 것으로 가장 적절한 것을 고르시오.

①   ②   ③   ④    ⑤

07

다음을 듣고, 'this'가 가리키는 것으로 가장 적절한 것을 고르시오.

①   ②   ③    ④   ⑤

08

다음을 듣고, 'this'가 가리키는 것으로 가장 적절한 것을 고르시오.

①    ②   ③   ④   ⑤

09

대화를 듣고, 무엇에 관한 내용인지 가장 적절한 것을 고르시오.

① 주말 활동   ② 일정 관리 요령   ③ 스트레스 해소법
④ 가족사항   ⑤ 하루 일과

10

대화를 듣고, 무엇에 관한 내용인지 가장 적절한 것을 고르시오.

① 대기오염   ② 운전 연수   ③ 전기 자동차
④ 졸음 운전   ⑤ 교통 소음

DICTATION

정답 단서 오답 함정

일반 속도 빠른 속도

01

다음을 듣고, 'this'가 가리키는 것으로 가장 적절한 것을 고르시오.

①   ②

③   ④

⑤

M You can see this in homes, offices and schools. This is _____ _____ _____ furniture. People _____ _____ _____ when they are doing work or studying. This sometimes has drawers. There are often books or a computer _____ _____ _____ this. What is this?

02

다음을 듣고, 'I'가 무엇인지 가장 적절한 것을 고르시오.

①   ②

③   ④

⑤

W I live in China. My ears and feet are black, and I have black circles _____ _____ _____. The rest of my body is white. I like to eat bamboo, and I _____ _____ _____ _____. What am I?

03

대화를 듣고, 무엇에 관한 내용인지 가장 적절한 것을 고르시오.

① 유기견 입양하기
② 산책로 탐방하기
③ 봉사활동 하기
④ 반려동물 돌보기
⑤ 건강한 식습관 기르기

W You _____ _____, David.

M Yes, I have to walk my dog every morning.

W I don't have to walk my cat. But I _____ _____ _____ _____.

M I feed my dog three times a day. And I wash him too.

W Now I understand _____ _____ _____.

72

04

대화를 듣고, 무엇에 관한 내용인지
가장 적절한 것을 고르시오.

① 최근 지진 피해 현황
② 전자제품 구입 요령
③ 지진 발생 시 안전수칙
④ 엘리베이터 이용 시 주의사항
⑤ 전력 공급 중단 시 대처방안

M I saw an earthquake _____ _____ _____. It looked scary.

W What should we do if one occurs?

M We should hide under some furniture. And we shouldn't use anything electrical.

W _____ _____ _____. What else?

M We shouldn't use elevators. We should _____ _____ _____ instead.

05

대화를 듣고, 무엇에 관한 내용인지
가장 적절한 것을 고르시오.

① 물놀이 안전 수칙
② 여름 휴가지 추천
③ 수영장 재개장 안내
④ 응급 처치의 중요성
⑤ 수영 강습의 필요성

W Did you _____ _____ _____ _____ at the swimming pool?

M Actually, a young girl fell in. She couldn't swim.

W That's terrible! Is she okay?

M Yes. A man pulled her from the pool and _____ _____ _____ _____. He saved her life.

W That's great. First aid is very useful.

M Yes. We really need to learn _____ _____ _____ it.

W I agree.

06

다음을 듣고, 'this'가 가리키는 것으
로 가장 적절한 것을 고르시오.

① ②
③ ④
⑤

W You can carry this. When you close this, it is _____ _____ _____. But this _____ _____ when you open it. This is useful if you don't want to _____ _____ when the weather is bad. What is this?

07

다음을 듣고, 'this'가 가리키는 것으
로 가장 적절한 것을 고르시오.

① ②
③ ④
⑤

W You can find this _____ _____ _____. This is small, and it is usually _____ _____ metal or wood. One end is shaped like a small bowl. You can hold this in your hand and use it to _____ _____ _____. What is this?

08

다음을 듣고, 'this'가 가리키는 것으로 가장 적절한 것을 고르시오.

① ②

③ ④

⑤

W People use this when _____ _____ _____. You must use this in cars and on airplanes. You find this on some buses too. This has _____ _____ _____. They can be connected by a metal or plastic part in the middle. This _____ _____ _____ if there is an accident. What is this?

09

대화를 듣고, 무엇에 관한 내용인지 가장 적절한 것을 고르시오.

① 주말 활동
② 일정 관리 요령
③ 스트레스 해소법
④ 가족사항
⑤ 하루 일과

W Hi, Matthew! What are you doing on Saturday?

M I'm not sure yet. I usually _____ _____ _____ my friends.

W What do you and your friends usually do together on weekends?

M We like to _____ _____ _____ and watch movies. How about you?

W I _____ _____ _____ with my husband every Saturday. I also take piano lessons on Sundays.

10

대화를 듣고, 무엇에 관한 내용인지 가장 적절한 것을 고르시오.

① 대기오염　② 운전 연수
③ 전기 자동차　④ 졸음 운전
⑤ 교통 소음

W Those cars are so quiet! I didn't even hear them.

M That's because they _____ _____ electricity, not gasoline.

W I see. That must be very _____ _____ _____ _____.

M It is. But some people don't like them because they are slow.

W _____ _____ _____. I want to buy one someday.

A

다음 영어 어휘나 표현의 뜻을 우리말로 쓰세요.

01 furniture

02 learn

03 earthquake

04 drawer

05 first aid

06 connect

07 on top of

08 metal

09 electricity

10 scary

11 office

12 thin

13 accident

14 environment

15 understand

16 bamboo

B

우리말에 맞는 영어 어휘나 표현을 [보기]에서 찾아 쓰세요.

보기	hold	occur	carry	matter	pick up
	pull	walk	save	stairs	make sense

01 가지고 다니다

02 쥐다

03 끌어당기다, 잡아당기다

04 계단

05 ~을 집어 들다

06 말이 되다, 이해가 되다

07 중요하다

08 (생명 등을) 구하다

09 (동물을) 산책시키다

10 일어나다, 발생하다

UNIT 9 특정 정보

담화나 대화를 듣고 문제에서 요구하는 특정 정보를 찾아내는 유형이다. 주로 날씨나 교통수단을 묻는 문제가 출제된다. 구입할 물건이나 잃어버린 물건을 고르는 문제가 출제되기도 한다.

지시문 유형

· 다음을 듣고, 금요일의 날씨로 가장 적절한 것을 고르시오.
· 대화를 듣고, 여자가 오늘 집에 갈 방법으로 가장 적절한 것을 고르시오.
· 대화를 듣고, 남자가 잃어버린 물건을 고르시오.

기출 표현 맛보기

날씨
· On Friday, the temperature will go down and it will snow a lot.
· We had rain yesterday. But today, there will be no rain, just a lot of clouds.

교통수단
· How about going with me in my mom's car?
· I usually take a bus, but I think I have to take a taxi today.

주요 어휘·표현 미리보기

다음을 듣고, [보기]에서 알맞은 어휘나 표현을 찾아 쓰세요.   정답 및 해설 p. 22

| 보기 |
| ⓐ get to | ⓑ takes too long | ⓒ woke up | ⓓ take |
| ⓔ look good on | ⓕ continue | ⓖ drove | ⓗ idea |

01 It _____ to get there by bus. 버스로 그곳을 가려면 너무 오래 걸려.

02 My mom _____ me to school. 엄마가 나를 학교에 태워다주셨어.

03 These pants _____ you. 이 바지는 네게 잘 어울려.

04 The heavy rain will _____ all day. 폭우가 종일 계속되겠습니다.

05 How can we _____ the airport? 우리 공항에 어떻게 가지?

06 He _____ late and missed the school bus. 그는 늦게 일어나서 통학 버스를 놓쳤어.

07 It's a better _____ to walk there. 걸어서 거기에 가는 게 나은 생각이야.

08 I usually _____ the subway when I go to school. 나는 학교 갈 때 보통 지하철을 타.

기출로 유형 익히기

- 날씨를 묻는 문제의 경우, 전체적인 내용보다는 문제에서 요구하는 특정 정보에 집중하여 들어보세요.
- 교통수단이나 구입할 물건을 묻는 문제의 경우, 대화 끝부분에서 내용이 바뀔 때가 많으므로 끝까지 잘 들어야 해요.

01

다음을 듣고, 내일의 날씨로 가장 적절한 것을 고르시오.

① ② ③ ④ ⑤

W Good morning. Here's the weather report. It's raining a lot now, but it's going to stop tonight. After today's rain, it will be sunny tomorrow. The sky will not be cloudy anymore. You can enjoy outdoor activities.

정답 단서   오답 함정

오늘의 날씨도 함께
언급하고 있으니 주의하자!

02

대화를 듣고, 남자가 이용할 교통수단으로 가장 적절한 것을 고르시오.

① 도보   ② 기차   ③ 자동차   ④ 자전거   ⑤ 지하철

M How will you go to Jake's birthday party, Stella?
W I will walk there after my piano lesson. How about you?
M My mom said she would take me there by car.
W Okay, see you at the party.
M See you there.

친구의 생일 파티에
어떻게 갈지 대화하는 내용이야.
두 사람이 이용할
교통수단이 다르네!

ANSWER

01 오늘 비가 내린 뒤, 내일은 화창할 것이라고 했으므로, 내일의 날씨로 ①이 알맞다.

02 남자의 엄마가 파티 장소에 차로 데려다 준다고 했으므로, 남자가 이용할 교통수단으로 ③이 알맞다.

LISTENING PRACTICE

점수 _____ / 10문항

01 다음을 듣고, 내일 오전의 날씨로 가장 적절한 것을 고르시오.

① 　② 　③ 　④ 　⑤

02 다음을 듣고, 서울의 내일 오후 날씨로 가장 적절한 것을 고르시오.

① 　② 　③ 　④ 　⑤

03 대화를 듣고, 여자가 이용할 교통수단으로 가장 적절한 것을 고르시오.

① 자동차　　　② 자전거　　　③ 지하철
④ 버스　　　⑤ 도보

04 대화를 듣고, 남자가 어제 학교에 간 방법으로 가장 적절한 것을 고르시오.

① 도보　　　② 택시　　　③ 통학 버스
④ 자동차　　　⑤ 자전거

05 대화를 듣고, 여자가 구입할 물건을 고르시오.

① 구두　　　② 스카프　　　③ 셔츠
④ 바지　　　⑤ 모자

06 다음을 듣고, 내일 오후의 날씨로 가장 적절한 것을 고르시오.

①   ②   ③   ④   ⑤

고난도

07 다음을 듣고, 오늘 대구의 날씨로 가장 적절한 것을 고르시오.

①   ②   ③   ④   ⑤

08 대화를 듣고, 여자가 이동할 방법으로 가장 적절한 것을 고르시오.

① 자동차   ② 도보   ③ 지하철
④ 버스   ⑤ 자전거

고난도

09 대화를 듣고, 두 사람이 토론토에 갈 방법으로 가장 적절한 것을 고르시오.

① 자동차   ② 버스   ③ 기차
④ 비행기   ⑤ 택시

10 대화를 듣고, 남자가 구입할 물건을 고르시오.

① 케이크   ② 설탕   ③ 밀가루
④ 우유   ⑤ 달걀

DICTATION

정답 단서 오답 함정

일반 속도

빠른 속도

01

다음을 듣고, 내일 오전의 날씨로 가장 적절한 것을 고르시오.

① 　②

③ 　④

⑤

M Good morning! This is your daily weather report. It's snowing right now, but the snow will _____ _____ _____ this evening. Tomorrow it will be _____ _____ _____ _____ but cold and sunny in the afternoon.

02

다음을 듣고, 서울의 내일 오후 날씨로 가장 적절한 것을 고르시오.

① ② ③ ④ ⑤

M Hello, everyone! I'm Alan Johnson, and here is tomorrow's weather forecast for Seoul. It _____ _____ _____ in the morning, but it will become cloudy in the afternoon. _____ _____ _____ late in the evening and continue all night. So _____ _____ your umbrella!

03

대화를 듣고, 여자가 이용할 교통수단으로 가장 적절한 것을 고르시오.

① 자동차　② 자전거
③ 지하철　④ 버스
⑤ 도보

M _____ _____ _____ _____, Kimberly?

W I'm going to the mall. I need some new shoes.

M Are you going to _____ _____ _____?

W Yes. I usually take the bus, but _____ _____ _____.

M Can I go with you?

W Sure! That would be great!

04

대화를 듣고, 남자가 어제 학교에 간
방법으로 가장 적절한 것을 고르시오.

① 도보　　　　② 택시
③ 통학 버스　　④ 자동차
⑤ 자전거

W Hi, Matt. I didn't see you on the school bus yesterday.

M That's because I _____ _____ _____ and missed it.

W Oh, no. Did your father _____ _____ _____ _____?

M No, he was too busy. I had to _____ _____ _____.

W That's too bad.

05

대화를 듣고, 여자가 구입할 물건을
고르시오.

① 구두　　　　② 스카프
③ 셔츠　　　　④ 바지
⑤ 모자

W _____ _____ _____, Derek. What do you think of this scarf?

M I like it a lot. It's _____ _____ _____ _____ my shirt.

W Yes, but it's too expensive. I'll just get this hat instead.

M It _____ _____ _____ _____!

W Thanks! You should get one too.

06

다음을 듣고, 내일 오후의 날씨로 가
장 적절한 것을 고르시오.

①　　　②
③
④
⑤

W Good morning. I'm Tina Wilson. Here is the ABC weather forecast. Today we'll have heavy rain with strong winds all day. Please _____ _____ _____ an umbrella with you. Tomorrow, _____ _____ _____ _____ in the morning. But by the afternoon, it will be nice and sunny. The sunny weather will continue _____ _____ _____ as well.

고난도
07

다음을 듣고, 오늘 대구의 날씨로 가
장 적절한 것을 고르시오.

①　　　②
③
④
⑤

W I'm Diana Lee, and here is the national weather report. There are sunny skies over Seoul and Incheon today, but the weather _____ _____ _____ in Daegu. Heavy rain started this morning and _____ _____ _____ _____ all day. It will be cloudy in Busan, but it won't rain. And Jeju will _____ _____ _____ because of a storm.

W Have a good day today, Joey.

M You too, Laura. _____ _____ your subway card. I'll put it on your desk.

W Thanks, but I _____ _____ _____ today.

M Why not? Will one of your coworkers pick you up instead?

W No, I'm going to _____ _____ _____. I need some exercise.

M Oh, okay.

고난도
09

대화를 듣고, 두 사람이 토론토에 갈
방법으로 가장 적절한 것을 고르시오.
① 자동차   ② 버스
③ 기차   ④ 비행기
⑤ 택시

M Let's go to the festival in Toronto next week!

W All right. We can take my car.

M No, it would _____ _____ _____ to drive there.

W Then _____ _____ _____ take the train? It's faster than driving.

M That's true. But flying is the fastest way to get to Toronto.

W Yes, but it's also _____ _____ _____ _____. My idea is better.

M I guess you're right.

M I want to _____ _____ _____. Let's go to the market.

W Okay. You'll need sugar and flour.

M I'll get some sugar, but I already have _____ _____ _____.

W You'll need eggs too.

M Don't worry. I have plenty of eggs.

W I _____ _____ _____ your cake!

A   다음 영어 어휘나 표현의 뜻을 우리말로 쓰세요.

01 mall

02 storm

03 different

04 festival

05 market

06 windy

07 way

08 remember

09 as well

10 instead

11 change

12 usually

13 strong

14 weather report

15 bake

16 flour

B   우리말에 맞는 영어 어휘나 표현을 [보기]에서 찾아 쓰세요.

보기	same	national	high wind	coworker	expensive
	foggy	plenty of	heavy rain	experience	be expected to-v

01 많은

02 경험하다

03 안개가 낀

04 강풍

05 비싼

06 직장 동료

07 폭우

08 전국적인

09 같은

10 ~하기로 예상되다

부탁·제안한 일

유형 설명 대화를 듣고, 남자나 여자가 상대에게 부탁한 일이나 제안한 것을 고르는 유형이다. 주로 대화가 일어나는 상황을 통해 한 사람이 다른 사람에게 부탁이나 제안한 일을 파악하는 문제가 출제된다.

지시문 유형
- 대화를 듣고, 남자가 여자에게 부탁한 일로 가장 적절한 것을 고르시오.
- 대화를 듣고, 여자가 남자에게 제안한 것으로 가장 적절한 것을 고르시오.

기출 표현 맛보기 부탁한 일

- **M** Can you look up the weather on the Internet now?
  W Sure!

- **W** Then, can I borrow your book?
  M Sure, I'll bring it tomorrow.

제안한 일

- **M** Why don't you drink some warm water?
  W Good idea. Warm water will help me.

- **M** Will you join me? They need more volunteers.
  W Okay, I'll join you.

주요 어휘·표현 미리보기

다음을 듣고, [보기]에서 알맞은 어휘나 표현을 찾아 쓰세요.   정답 및 해설 p. 25

| 보기 |
| ⓐ shut | ⓑ graduated from | ⓒ add | ⓓ a piece of |
| ⓔ go out | ⓕ give it a try | ⓖ take a walk | ⓗ look down |

01 I usually ⎯⎯⎯⎯⎯ on Sundays. 나는 보통 일요일에 산책을 해.

02 Can you give me ⎯⎯⎯⎯⎯ paper? 종이 한 장만 줄 수 있니?

03 He ⎯⎯⎯⎯⎯ high school last year. 그는 작년에 고등학교를 졸업했어.

04 We're going to ⎯⎯⎯⎯⎯ tonight. 우리는 오늘 밤에 외출할 예정이야.

05 Are you okay? You ⎯⎯⎯⎯⎯ today. 너 괜찮니? 오늘 우울해 보여.

06 Can you ⎯⎯⎯⎯⎯ more salt to this soup? 이 수프에 소금 좀 더 넣어줄 수 있니?

07 The door is open. Could you ⎯⎯⎯⎯⎯ it? 문이 열려 있네. 닫아줄 수 있니?

08 I want to ⎯⎯⎯⎯⎯. 한번 시도해 보고 싶어.

기출로 유형 익히기

- 'Can I / Can you / Could you / Will you / Would you / Please ~'로 시작하는 표현에 집중하세요.
- 대화 상대가 제안하는 내용이 오답 함정일 수 있으니 주의하세요.

01

대화를 듣고, 남자가 여자에게 부탁한 일로 가장 적절한 것을 고르시오.

① 책 사주기   ② 책 빌려주기   ③ 퍼즐 맞추기
④ 게임 CD 빌려주기   ⑤ 삼촌에게 전화하기

W   Jeff, how was your Christmas?
M   It was great.
W   What presents did you get?
M   My parents gave me a jigsaw puzzle. What about you?   오답 함정
W   I got Korean history books from my uncle.
M   Really? I need those for my homework. Can you lend them to me?
W   Sure.   정답 단서

크리스마스 선물로
각자 무엇을 받았는지
이야기를 나누고 있어.

02

대화를 듣고, 남자가 여자에게 제안한 것으로 가장 적절한 것을 고르시오.

① 패션 프로그램 시청하기   ② 패션디자이너 만나기   ③ 의상 디자인하기
④ 방송국 방문하기   ⑤ 패션 잡지 읽기

M   Are you watching a fashion show, Mina? I didn't know you were interested in fashion.
W   Yes, I really want to design clothes, Dad.
M   Oh, my friend, Andrew, is a fashion designer. Why don't we visit him soon?
W   Really? That's so exciting!

남자는 패션디자이너가
되고 싶다는 여자에게
어떤 제안을 할까?

ANSWER

01 남자가 여자에게 한국사에 대한 책을 빌려달라고 했으므로 정답은 ②이다.
02 남자가 여자에게 패션디자이너인 자신의 친구를 만나보지 않겠냐고 제안했으므로 정답은 ②이다.

LISTENING PRACTICE

일반 속도   빠른 속도

01 대화를 듣고, 여자가 남자에게 부탁한 일로 가장 적절한 것을 고르시오.

① 스웨터 빌려주기   ② 조명 끄기   ③ 창문 닫기
④ 에어컨 끄기   ⑤ 난방기 켜기

고난도

02 대화를 듣고, 여자가 남자에게 부탁한 일로 가장 적절한 것을 고르시오.

① 게임 중단하기   ② 동생 데리러 가기   ③ 책 빌려주기
④ 생일선물 준비하기   ⑤ 택배 받기

03 대화를 듣고, 남자가 여자에게 부탁한 일로 가장 적절한 것을 고르시오.

① 샌드위치 포장하기   ② 재료 건네주기   ③ 치즈 추가하기
④ 설거지하기   ⑤ 채소 씻기

04 대화를 듣고, 여자가 남자에게 제안한 것으로 가장 적절한 것을 고르시오.

① 동아리 가입하기   ② 친구에게 먼저 연락하기   ③ 방과 후 활동 신청하기
④ 선생님께 말씀드리기   ⑤ 조별 모임 장소 알아보기

05 대화를 듣고, 남자가 여자에게 제안한 것으로 가장 적절한 것을 고르시오.

① 학생복 사기   ② 졸업식 참석하기   ③ 축하파티 준비하기
④ 지갑 사기   ⑤ 학용품 선물하기

06 대화를 듣고, 남자가 여자에게 부탁한 일로 가장 적절한 것을 고르시오.

① 시계 수리받기　② 공항에 데려다주기　③ 고양이 돌봐주기
④ 공항에 마중 나오기　⑤ 조카와 놀아주기

07 대화를 듣고, 여자가 남자에게 부탁한 일로 가장 적절한 것을 고르시오.

① 강의실 데려다주기　② 책 주문하기　③ 수업 준비하기
④ 책 꺼내주기　⑤ 책장 정리하기

고난도
08 대화를 듣고, 여자가 남자에게 제안한 것으로 가장 적절한 것을 고르시오.

① 양파 구입하기　② 배달음식 주문하기　③ 요리하기
④ 식료품 배달시키기　⑤ 외식하기

09 대화를 듣고, 남자가 여자에게 제안한 것으로 가장 적절한 것을 고르시오.

① 산책하기　② 함께 과제하기　③ 과제 미리 제출하기
④ 세탁기 구입하기　⑤ 빨래하기

10 대화를 듣고, 남자가 여자에게 제안한 것으로 가장 적절한 것을 고르시오.

① 수리점 찾아보기　② 새 카메라 구입하기　③ 사진 정리하기
④ 친구에게 사과하기　⑤ 카메라 빌리기

DICTATION

정답 단서 오답 함정

일반 속도

빠른 속도

01

대화를 듣고, 여자가 남자에게 부탁한
일로 가장 적절한 것을 고르시오.

① 스웨터 빌려주기
② 조명 끄기
③ 창문 닫기
④ 에어컨 끄기
⑤ 난방기 켜기

M Is something wrong, Lisa?

W Yes. It's _____ _____ _____ _____. I'm freezing.

M Yes, it is a little cold. Would you like to _____ _____ _____?

W No. But the window is open. _____ _____ _____ _____?

M Sure. Sorry about that.

고난도

02

대화를 듣고, 여자가 남자에게 부탁한
일로 가장 적절한 것을 고르시오.

① 게임 중단하기
② 동생 데리러 가기
③ 책 빌려주기
④ 생일선물 준비하기
⑤ 택배 받기

W Jake, are you playing phone games?

M No! I'm reading an e-book.

W Oh, okay. _____ _____ _____ _____ after you finish?

M I don't have any plans. Why?

W I have to _____ _____ _____ _____, but a delivery man is coming soon.

M Did you order something for Dad's birthday?

W Yes. Can you get the package when it arrives?

M Sure, Mom. And I'll hide it _____ _____ _____.

W Thanks, honey!

03

대화를 듣고, 남자가 여자에게 부탁한
일로 가장 적절한 것을 고르시오.

① 샌드위치 포장하기
② 재료 건네주기
③ 치즈 추가하기
④ 설거지하기
⑤ 채소 씻기

M What are you doing with that bread?

W I'm _____ _____ _____. Can you give me a piece of ham?

M Sure. Here you are.

W Thanks. Now, I'll just cut two slices of cheese. And _____ _____! Here! You can have half!

M Thanks. But _____ _____ _____ more cheese for me?

W Sure!

04

대화를 듣고, 여자가 남자에게 제안한
것으로 가장 적절한 것을 고르시오.

① 동아리 가입하기
② 친구에게 먼저 연락하기
③ 방과 후 활동 신청하기
④ 선생님께 말씀드리기
⑤ 조별 모임 장소 알아보기

W What's wrong, Mark? You look down.

M Some students _____ _____ _____ these days.

W Oh. Would you like me to talk to them?

M No! That would just _____ _____ _____.

W How about talking to your teacher? She might be able to help.

M Okay. I'll _____ _____ _____ _____, Mom.

05

대화를 듣고, 남자가 여자에게 제안한
것으로 가장 적절한 것을 고르시오.

① 학생복 사기
② 졸업식 참석하기
③ 축하파티 준비하기
④ 지갑 사기
⑤ 학용품 선물하기

W Alex is _____ _____ _____ _____ tomorrow. What will you get him?

M I already bought his present. It's a new wallet. What about you?

W I haven't _____ _____ _____. I don't have any good ideas.

M _____ _____ _____ buy him some new school clothes?

W That's a good idea. Thanks!

06

대화를 듣고, 남자가 여자에게 부탁한
일로 가장 적절한 것을 고르시오.

① 시계 수리받기
② 공항에 데려다주기
③ 고양이 돌봐주기
④ 공항에 마중 나오기
⑤ 조카와 놀아주기

M I'm going on vacation tomorrow.

W That's great! Do you _____ _____ _____ to the airport?

M No, but I need _____ _____ _____ Fluffy.

W Fluffy? Is that your cat?

M Yes, can you _____ _____ and play with her?

W Sure! I'd be glad to.

07

대화를 듣고, 여자가 남자에게 부탁한
일로 가장 적절한 것을 고르시오.

① 강의실 데려다주기
② 책 주문하기
③ 수업 준비하기
④ 책 꺼내주기
⑤ 책장 정리하기

W Edward, can you _____ _____ _____ _____?

M Well, I don't have much time. My class starts in five minutes.

W It _____ _____ _____. I just need a book from the top shelf.

M Oh! You can't reach it?

W No, I can't. Could you _____ _____ _____ _____?

M No problem.

08

대화를 듣고, 여자가 남자에게 제안한
것으로 가장 적절한 것을 고르시오.

① 양파 구입하기
② 배달음식 주문하기
③ 요리하기
④ 식료품 배달시키기
⑤ 외식하기

M Do we have any onions?

W No. We used the last ones yesterday.

M I was going to _____, but I need onions.

W Would you like me to go to the store and get some?

M No, it's _____ _____ _____ .

W Why don't you just _____ _____ _____ from the restaurant around the corner?

M Good idea. I can cook tomorrow night.

09

대화를 듣고, 남자가 여자에게 제안한
것으로 가장 적절한 것을 고르시오.

① 산책하기
② 함께 과제하기
③ 과제 미리 제출하기
④ 세탁기 구입하기
⑤ 인터넷 검색하기

M How's your essay going?

W Terrible. I _____ _____ _____ any new ideas.

M Why don't you _____ _____ _____? It will refresh your brain.

W Really? Okay. Do you want to come with me?

M No, thanks. I have to _____ _____ _____ .

W All right. Thanks for the suggestion.

10

대화를 듣고, 남자가 여자에게 제안한
것으로 가장 적절한 것을 고르시오.

① 수리점 찾아보기
② 새 카메라 구입하기
③ 사진 정리하기
④ 친구에게 사과하기
⑤ 카메라 빌리기

W I borrowed Holly's camera and accidentally broke it.

M She _____ _____ _____ .

W She is. I would buy her a new one, but I can't afford it. I don't know _____ _____ _____ .

M Why don't you just tell her that you're sorry?

W You're right. I should.

M It was an accident, so she'll probably _____ _____ .

A

다음 영어 어휘나 표현의 뜻을 우리말로 쓰세요.

01 suggestion

02 do laundry

03 wallet

04 shelf

05 half

06 hide

07 closet

08 package

09 borrow

10 deliver

11 take long

12 hard

13 forgive

14 bully

15 afford

16 make dinner

B

우리말에 맞는 영어 어휘나 표현을 [보기]에서 찾아 쓰세요.

보기	slice	freezing	refresh	accidentally	make worse
	watch	reach	pick up	do ~ a favor	go on vacation

01 꽁꽁 얼게 추운

02 (음식을 얇게 썬) 조각

03 ~을 태우러 가다

04 (손이) 닿다

05 상쾌하게 하다

06 휴가를 가다

07 (잠깐 동안) 봐주다

08 뜻하지 않게 잘못하여

09 ~의 부탁을 들어주다

10 악화시키다

마지막 말에 대한 응답

유형 설명 　대화를 듣고, 마지막 말에 대한 응답을 고르는 유형이다. 내용의 전체적인 흐름을 파악하여 대화의 마지막 말에 이어질 응답으로 적절한 것을 고르는 문제가 출제된다.

지시문 유형
- 대화를 듣고, 남자의 마지막 말에 이어질 여자의 말로 가장 적절한 것을 고르시오.
- 대화를 듣고, 여자의 마지막 말에 이어질 남자의 말로 가장 적절한 것을 고르시오.

기출표현맛보기
- W　He broke his leg when he was playing basketball this morning.
  M　Oh, I'm sorry to hear that.
- M　I'm going to buy a baseball cap this afternoon. Do you want to come with me?
  W　Sure. Why not?

주요 어휘·표현 미리보기

다음을 듣고, [보기]에서 알맞은 어휘나 표현을 찾아 쓰세요.　　　　정답 및 해설 p. 27

| 보기 |
| ⓐ looks sad | ⓑ apologize | ⓒ sold out | ⓓ cost |
| ⓔ fixed | ⓕ urgent | ⓖ far away | ⓗ smells good |

01 My office is ＿＿＿＿＿＿ from my home.　내 사무실은 우리 집에서 멀어.

02 I want to ＿＿＿＿＿＿ for my mistake.　내 실수에 대해 사과하고 싶어.

03 It ＿＿＿＿＿＿. What is it?　냄새가 좋네. 뭐야?

04 The train tickets are all ＿＿＿＿＿＿.　기차표가 모두 매진되었어.

05 That boy ＿＿＿＿＿＿.　저 소년은 슬퍼 보여.

06 I got my bicycle ＿＿＿＿＿＿ yesterday.　나는 어제 내 자전거를 수리 맡겼어.

07 How much does it ＿＿＿＿＿＿ to buy the book?　그 책을 사는 데 비용이 얼마나 드니?

08 Please hurry. This is ＿＿＿＿＿＿!　서둘러줘. 정말 급해!

• 대화의 전반적인 내용을 파악하는 동시에 마지막 말을 주의 깊게 들으세요. 특히 대화의 마지막 말이 질문이라면 의문사를 놓치지 마세요.
• 대화 중에 언급된 어휘를 이용한 오답 선택지에 유의하세요.

01

대화를 듣고, 남자의 마지막 말에 이어질 여자의 말로 가장 적절한 것을 고르시오.

Woman: _____

① Don't worry about it.　　② Sorry to hear that.
③ Three times a week.　　④ I play it at the gym.
⑤ Of course. Here you are.

W　Hi, Minsu. What will you do after school?
M　I will play badminton with my friends.
W　I like badminton, too.
M　Do you play any other sports?
W　I also play table tennis.
M　How often do you play table tennis?
W　_____

방과 후에 하는 활동에 대한 대화야.

02

대화를 듣고, 여자의 마지막 말에 이어질 남자의 말로 가장 적절한 것을 고르시오.

Man: _____

① That's a good idea.　　② She is good at tennis, too.
③ Well, I couldn't find anything good.　　④ The badminton game was exciting.
⑤ Yes. I saw him in the supermarket.

M　Nina. Did you get anything at the school flea market today?
W　Yes. I bought this badminton racket. 오답 함정
M　Wow! It's almost new. How much was it?
W　It was very cheap, only 1,000 won.
M　That's great!
W　I know! What did you buy?
M　_____

교내 벼룩시장에서 구입한 물건에 대한 대화야.

ANSWER

01 탁구를 얼마나 자주 치냐는 남자의 마지막 말에 이어질 여자의 말로 ③이 알맞다.
02 벼룩시장에서 무엇을 샀냐고 묻는 여자의 마지막 말에 이어질 남자의 말로 ③이 알맞다.

LISTENING PRACTICE

점수 _____ / 10문항

일반 속도

빠른 속도

[01-02] 대화를 듣고, 남자의 마지막 말에 이어질 여자의 말로 가장 적절한 것을 고르시오.

01   Woman: _____

① It was yesterday.   ② What a surprise!

③ When is your birthday?   ④ You don't have to apologize.

⑤ Why don't you buy them?

02   Woman: _____

① I came here at 5:00 p.m.   ② I'm too busy to go back.

③ No, I'm going there next week. ④ Yes, I did. But I missed you a lot.

⑤ I went there with my family.

[03-05] 대화를 듣고, 여자의 마지막 말에 이어질 남자의 말로 가장 적절한 것을 고르시오.

03   Man: _____

① Yes, it is very far.   ② It takes fifty minutes.

③ School begins at nine o'clock. ④ No, I don't take a bus.

⑤ Only when I am late.

04   Man: _____

① I'm afraid the tickets are sold out. ② That show was amazing.

③ Okay, I'll see you then.   ④ How much do they cost?

⑤ Sorry, I'm not interested.

고난도
05   Man: _____

① Okay, but this is the last time. ② No, I don't have one anymore.

③ Sure, you can come with me.   ④ Sorry, but I don't know how.

⑤ Yes, I will fix it tomorrow.

정답 및 해설 p. 27

[06-07] 대화를 듣고, 여자의 마지막 말에 이어질 남자의 말로 가장 적절한 것을 고르시오.

06

Man: ______________________________

① I ate some cookies already.
② No, I don't have anything.
③ Soda is not a healthy drink.
④ Just a glass of water, please.
⑤ Yes, I ordered a salad and a steak.

고난도

07

Man: ______________________________

① They sent me an email.
② Let me check the schedule.
③ I will call you when I get there.
④ You're a very careful driver.
⑤ My flight arrives at 9:30 p.m.

[08-10] 대화를 듣고, 남자의 마지막 말에 이어질 여자의 말로 가장 적절한 것을 고르시오.

08

Woman: ______________________________

① Thanks, but I'm full.
② Yes, but I'm still hungry.
③ I will have chicken for lunch.
④ Yes, this new restaurant is excellent.
⑤ No, we're going to be late for the party.

09

Woman: ______________________________

① It's my pleasure.
② Okay, I'll ask someone else.
③ Sorry, but I have to go now.
④ That would be great. Thanks.
⑤ Walk two blocks and turn left.

10

Woman: ______________________________

① We'll go there by plane.
② Let's meet at five o'clock.
③ You can go there, too.
④ I've never been there before.
⑤ We'll leave next Wednesday.

DICTATION

정답 단서 오답 함정

일반 속도

빠른 속도

01

대화를 듣고, 남자의 마지막 말에 이어질 여자의 말로 가장 적절한 것을 고르시오.

Woman: _____

① It was yesterday.
② What a surprise!
③ When is your birthday?
④ You don't have to apologize.
⑤ Why don't you buy them?

M What's wrong, Marie? _____ _____ _____.

W Today is a special day, but you forgot.

M _____ _____ _____ _____?

W It's my birthday!

M I didn't really forget. Here are some flowers.

W _____

02

대화를 듣고, 남자의 마지막 말에 이어질 여자의 말로 가장 적절한 것을 고르시오.

Woman: _____

① I came here at 5:00 p.m.
② I'm too busy to go back.
③ No, I'm going there next week.
④ Yes, I did. But I missed you a lot.
⑤ I went there with my family.

M Sumi! You're home!

W It's _____ _____ _____ _____, Junwoo. I'm finally back in Seoul.

M Why did you come back early?

W Because my work schedule changed.

M I see. Did you _____ _____ _____ _____ there?

W _____

03

대화를 듣고, 여자의 마지막 말에 이어질 남자의 말로 가장 적절한 것을 고르시오.

Man: _____

① Yes, it is very far.
② It takes fifty minutes.
③ School begins at nine o'clock.
④ No, I don't take a bus.
⑤ Only when I am late.

M Do you take the bus to school?

W No, I walk to school. My home isn't very _____ _____.

M How lucky you are!

W How do you _____ _____ _____?

M By bus, and it _____ _____ _____ _____.

W How long does it take?

M _____

04

대화를 듣고, 여자의 마지막 말에 이어질 남자의 말로 가장 적절한 것을 고르시오.

Man: _____

① I'm afraid the tickets are sold out.
② Wow! That show was amazing.
③ Okay, I'll see you then.
④ How much do they cost?
⑤ Sorry, I'm not interested.

W Do you like the opera, Harry?

M No, I don't. Actually, I hate it. I think _____ _____.

W Oh. I have two _____ _____ _____ _____ for tonight.

M Really? Who are you going with?

W Well, I was going to ask you _____ _____ _____ _____.

M _____

05

대화를 듣고, 여자의 마지막 말에 이어질 남자의 말로 가장 적절한 것을 고르시오.

Man: _____

① Okay, but this is the last time.
② No, I don't have one anymore.
③ Sure, you can come with me.
④ Sorry, but I don't know how.
⑤ Yes, I will fix it tomorrow.

W What are you doing, Steven?

M I'm _____ _____ _____ go out.

W Oh! Where are you going?

M My friend's house. Did you need something?

W Yes. Can I borrow your computer again?

M Again? Didn't you _____ _____ _____?

W Not yet. I've been too busy.

M Well, you can't keep using mine.

W But it's _____ _____. Please?

M _____

06

대화를 듣고, 여자의 마지막 말에 이어질 남자의 말로 가장 적절한 것을 고르시오.

Man: _____

① I ate some cookies already.
② No, I don't have anything.
③ Soda is not a healthy drink.
④ Just a glass of water, please.
⑤ Yes, I ordered a salad and a steak.

W May I _____ _____ _____?

M Yes, I'll have the corn salad and the steak.

W _____ _____ _____ _____ your steak?

M Well-done, please.

W And _____ _____ _____?

M _____

07

대화를 듣고, 여자의 마지막 말에 이어질 남자의 말로 가장 적절한 것을 고르시오.

Man: _____

① They sent me an email.
② Let me check the schedule.
③ I will call you when I get there.
④ You're a very careful driver.
⑤ My flight arrives at 9:30 p.m.

W I guess I should be going.

M Yes. We'll be boarding soon.

W _____ _____ _____. And be careful, honey.

M Don't worry, Mom. I'll be fine.

W How will you get to your dormitory in Vancouver?

M Someone from the school will _____ _____ _____ at the airport.

W _____ _____ _____ _____ that you arrived safely?

M _____

08

대화를 듣고, 남자의 마지막 말에 이어질 여자의 말로 가장 적절한 것을 고르시오.

Woman: _____

① Thanks, but I'm full.
② Yes, but I'm still hungry.
③ I will have chicken for lunch.
④ Yes, this new restaurant is excellent.
⑤ No, we're going to be late for the party.

W What's that smell?

M I think it's chicken.

W Is Mom cooking for the party?

M Yes, she is.

W It _____ _____ _____. Maybe she'll let us have some.

M Didn't you just _____ _____ _____ _____?

W _____

09

대화를 듣고, 남자의 마지막 말에 이어질 여자의 말로 가장 적절한 것을 고르시오.

Woman: _____

① It's my pleasure.
② Okay, I'll ask someone else.
③ Sorry, but I have to go now.
④ That would be great. Thanks.
⑤ Walk two blocks and turn left.

W Hey, Jason. Could you _____ _____ _____ this box?

M Sure. Where are you going?

W I'm going to the bus stop.

M Oh, _____ _____ _____ _____ now?

W Yes, I am.

M Then I'll _____ _____ _____ _____ home. I'm going in the same direction.

W _____

10

대화를 듣고, 남자의 마지막 말에 이어질 여자의 말로 가장 적절한 것을 고르시오.

Woman: _____

① We'll go there by plane.
② Let's meet at five o'clock.
③ You can go there, too.
④ I've never been there before.
⑤ We'll leave next Wednesday.

W Summer _____ _____ _____.

M Yes, it is. Do you _____ _____ _____?

W My family is going to visit my uncle's house in Sydney.

M Wow, _____ _____ _____ _____.

W Yes, I am very excited.

M When will you go there?

W _____

A

다음 영어 어휘나 표현의 뜻을 우리말로 쓰세요.

01 careful

02 direction

03 amazing

04 a glass of

05 early

06 lucky

07 begin

08 interested

09 special

10 schedule

11 go back

12 dormitory

13 help

14 boring

15 finally

16 get ready to-v

B

우리말에 맞는 영어 어휘나 표현을 [보기]에서 찾아 쓰세요.

보기	board	healthy	well-done	give a ride	have a big lunch
	get to	surprise	excellent	I'm afraid (that)	have a good time

01 놀라운 일[소식]

02 유감이지만 ~이다

03 훌륭한

04 건강에 좋은

05 ~에 가다[도착하다]

06 즐거운 시간을 보내다

07 점심을 푸짐하게 먹다

08 ~을 태워주다

09 탑승하다

10 (고기가) 잘 익은

내용 불일치

유형 설명 대화를 듣고, 대화의 내용과 일치하지 않는 것을 고르는 문제 유형이다.

지시문 유형
- 대화를 듣고, 남자의 고양이에 대한 내용으로 일치하지 <u>않는</u> 것을 고르시오.
- 대화를 듣고, 남자가 다녀온 여행에 대한 내용으로 일치하지 <u>않는</u> 것을 고르시오.

기출 표현 맛보기
- **W** What's his name?
  M His name is Prince.

- **W** What else did you do there?
  M I visited many museums.

주요 어휘·표현 미리보기

다음을 듣고, [보기]에서 알맞은 어휘나 표현을 찾아 쓰세요.   정답 및 해설 p. 31

| 보기 |
| ⓐ lost | ⓑ younger than | ⓒ decided to | ⓓ share |
| ⓔ free | ⓕ have to return | ⓖ can't wait to | ⓗ in third grade |

01 I used to _____ the room with my sister. 나는 언니와 방을 함께 썼었어.

02 My brother is _____. 내 남동생은 3학년이야.

03 I _____ watch the movie! 나는 빨리 그 영화를 보고 싶어!

04 Are you _____ this weekend? 너 이번 주말에 시간 있니?

05 I've _____ my cell phone. 나는 내 휴대전화를 잃어버렸어.

06 You _____ these books today. 너는 오늘 이 책들을 반납해야 해.

07 Is Christine _____ you? Christine이 너보다 더 어리니?

08 He _____ go skiing this winter. 그는 이번 겨울에 스키를 타러 가기로 했어.

기출로 유형 익히기

- 대화를 듣기 전에 선택지를 미리 읽고, 대화의 내용을 예상해 보세요.
- 보통 선택지 순서대로 내용이 나오므로, 들려주는 내용과 선택지를 비교하며 정답을 찾으세요.

01

대화를 듣고, 남자의 고양이에 대한 내용으로 일치하지 <u>않는</u> 것을 고르시오.

① 삼촌이 주셨다.　　　　② 흰색 털을 가지고 있다.
③ 작년에 태어났다.　　　　④ 이름이 Prince이다.
⑤ 눈이 갈색이다.

W　Tom, is this your cat?
M　Yes, my uncle gave him to me.
W　Oh, his white hair is so soft. How old is he?
M　Um... He was born last year.
W　What's his name?
M　His name is Prince.
W　I love his blue eyes. 정답 단서

①번 선택지부터 두 사람이
나누는 대화에 나오는 정보를
하나씩 확인하며 풀어봐!

02

대화를 듣고, 남자가 다녀온 여행에 대한 내용으로 일치하지 <u>않는</u> 것을 고르시오.

① 제주도에 다녀왔다.　　　　② 해산물을 먹었다.
③ 박물관을 방문했다.　　　　④ 한라산에 갔다.
⑤ 바다에서 수영했다.

W　Minho, I heard you went to Jeju.
M　Yes, it was wonderful! I ate lots of sea food.
W　That's nice. What else did you do there?
M　I visited many museums.
W　Did you go to Hallasan? 오답 함정
M　No, I didn't.
W　Then, what did you do?
M　I swam in the sea.

대화 중에 언급은
되었지만, 실제로
하지 않은 일은 무엇일까?

ANSWER

01　여자가 고양이의 파란 눈이 마음에 든다고 했으므로 정답으로 ⑤가 알맞다.
02　여자가 남자에게 한라산에 갔냐고 물었는데 남자는 가지 않았다고 대답했으므로 정답으로 ④가 알맞다.

LISTENING PRACTICE

일반 속도

빠른 속도

01 대화를 듣고, 파티에 대한 내용으로 일치하지 <u>않는</u> 것을 고르시오.

① 이번 주 토요일이다.　　　　　② 생일 축하 파티이다.

③ 9명의 친구를 초대했다.　　　　④ 남자의 집에서 열린다.

⑤ 오후에 시작한다.

02 대화를 듣고, 두 사람이 갈 현장 학습에 대한 내용으로 일치하지 <u>않는</u> 것을 고르시오.

① 놀이공원으로 간다.　　　　　② 이번 주 금요일에 간다.

③ 버스를 타고 간다.　　　　　　④ 학교에 8시 반까지 모여야 한다.

⑤ 도시락을 가져가야 한다.

고난도
03 대화를 듣고, 남자의 반려동물에 대한 내용으로 일치하지 <u>않는</u> 것을 고르시오.

① 반려동물 세 마리가 있다.　　　② 반려동물끼리 사이가 좋다.

③ 고양이들은 수줍음이 있다.　　　④ 개가 고양이들보다 나이가 많다.

⑤ 집에 오는 손님들을 좋아한다.

04 대화를 듣고, 사진 속 인물에 대한 내용으로 일치하지 <u>않는</u> 것을 고르시오.

① 남자의 사촌이다.　　　　　　② 남자보다 한 살 더 어리다.

③ 키가 약 180cm이다.　　　　　④ 축구를 좋아한다.

⑤ 작가가 되고 싶어 한다.

05 대화를 듣고, 여자의 새 운동화에 대한 내용으로 일치하지 <u>않는</u> 것을 고르시오.

① 흰색이다.　　　　　　　　　② 온라인으로 구매했다.

③ 반품할 예정이다.　　　　　　④ 10사이즈이다.

⑤ 잘못된 사이즈를 주문했다.

06 대화를 듣고, 여자의 여행 계획에 대한 내용으로 일치하지 <u>않는</u> 것을 고르시오.

① 하와이에 갈 예정이다.
② 다음 주 금요일에 출발할 것이다.
③ 5일간 체류 예정이다.
④ 해변 가까이에 묵을 것이다.
⑤ 서핑을 배울 것이다.

07 대화를 듣고, 남자의 방에 대한 내용으로 일치하지 <u>않는</u> 것을 고르시오.

① 잘 정돈되어 있다.
② 남동생과 함께 쓴다.
③ 책상이 2개 있다.
④ 2층 침대가 있다.
⑤ 책꽂이에 책이 많다.

08 대화를 듣고, 여자의 필통에 대한 내용으로 일치하지 <u>않는</u> 것을 고르시오.

① 빨간색이다.
② 천으로 만들어졌다.
③ 연필과 지우개가 들어 있다.
④ 이름이 써 있다.
⑤ 꽃이 그려져 있다.

09 대화를 듣고, 남자의 가족에 대한 내용으로 일치하지 <u>않는</u> 것을 고르시오.

① 다섯 식구이다.
② 형과 여동생이 있다.
③ 형은 24살이다.
④ 동생은 3학년이다.
⑤ 형은 수학 선생님이다.

고난도
10 대화를 듣고, Taste of Venice에 대한 내용으로 일치하지 <u>않는</u> 것을 고르시오.

① 여자는 가 본 적이 없다.
② 이탈리아 음식점이다.
③ Main 가에 있다.
④ 최근에 문을 열었다.
⑤ 월요일은 운영하지 않는다.

DICTATION

정답 단서 오답 함정

일반 속도   빠른 속도

01

대화를 듣고, 파티에 대한 내용으로 일치하지 <u>않는</u> 것을 고르시오.

① 이번 주 토요일이다.
② 생일 축하 파티이다.
③ 9명의 친구를 초대했다.
④ 남자의 집에서 열린다.
⑤ 오후에 시작한다.

M Hi, Emily. _____ _____ _____ this Saturday?

W Yes, what's up?

M It's my birthday. I want you to come to my party.

W _____ _____ _____ _____. How many people will there be?

M I invited eight friends _____ _____. Please come to my house at 2:00 p.m.

W Okay. See you then.

02

대화를 듣고, 두 사람이 갈 현장 학습에 대한 내용으로 일치하지 <u>않는</u> 것을 고르시오.

① 놀이공원으로 간다.
② 이번 주 금요일에 간다.
③ 버스를 타고 간다.
④ 학교에 8시 반까지 모여야 한다.
⑤ 도시락을 가져가야 한다.

M We are going to the amusement park for a field trip this Friday! I'm so excited!

W Me too. We will go there _____ _____, won't we?

M Yes. We have to be at school by 8:30. Then we will take a bus together.

W Cool. Should we _____ _____ _____ _____?

M If you want to. But you can just buy some food there.

W All right. I _____ _____ _____ _____!

고난도
03

대화를 듣고, 남자의 반려동물에 대한 내용으로 일치하지 <u>않는</u> 것을 고르시오.

① 반려동물 세 마리가 있다.
② 반려동물끼리 사이가 좋다.
③ 고양이들은 수줍음이 있다.
④ 개가 고양이들보다 나이가 많다.
⑤ 집에 오는 손님들을 좋아한다.

W Do you have any pets, Danny?

M Actually, I have three pets, a puppy and two cats.

W That's awesome! Do they _____ _____ _____ each other?

M Yes. My dog, Larry, is very friendly. My cats, Coco and Choco, are _____ _____ _____, but they like Larry.

W How old are they?

M Larry is three years old, and Coco and Choco are four years old.

W Oh, I want to see them.

M _____ _____ _____. They all love visitors.

대화를 듣고, 사진 속 인물에 대한 내용으로 일치하지 <u>않는</u> 것을 고르시오.

① 남자의 사촌이다.
② 남자보다 한 살 더 어리다.
③ 키가 약 180cm이다.
④ 축구를 좋아한다.
⑤ 작가가 되고 싶어 한다.

W Who is the boy in this picture? Is he your classmate?

M No, he is my cousin, Andrew. He is a year _____ _____ _____.

W Really? But he seems very tall.

M Yeah. _____ _____ _____ 180 cm.

W Wow. Does he like to play soccer like you?

M Not really. He likes to _____ _____. He wants to be a writer in the future.

05

대화를 듣고, 여자의 새 운동화에 대한 내용으로 일치하지 <u>않는</u> 것을 고르시오.

① 흰색이다.
② 온라인으로 구매했다.
③ 반품할 예정이다.
④ 10사이즈이다.
⑤ 잘못된 사이즈를 주문했다.

M Why are there white sneakers in this box?

W I ordered them online, but I _____ _____ _____ _____.

M Why?

W They're too big. I usually wear size 8. But those are size 10.

M Then why did you order _____ _____ _____?

W I ordered size 8. But they sent me the wrong ones.

M Oh, in that case, they'll probably _____ _____ _____ _____.

06

대화를 듣고, 여자의 여행 계획에 대한 내용으로 일치하지 <u>않는</u> 것을 고르시오.

① 하와이에 갈 예정이다.
② 다음 주 금요일에 출발할 것이다.
③ 5일간 체류 예정이다.
④ 해변 가까이에 묵을 것이다.
⑤ 서핑을 배울 것이다.

M Where are you going this vacation? Are you going to Seattle again?

W No, I _____ _____ _____ to Hawaii this time.

M Sounds cool. When are you leaving?

W Next Friday. I'll be there _____ _____ _____.

M Do you have any plans?

W I'll stay at a hotel near the beach and _____ _____ _____.

M That sounds really fun.

07

대화를 듣고, 남자의 방에 대한 내용으로 일치하지 <u>않는</u> 것을 고르시오.

① 잘 정돈되어 있다.
② 남동생과 함께 쓴다.
③ 책상이 2개 있다.
④ 2층 침대가 있다.
⑤ 책꽂이에 책이 많다.

W Wow, your room is very tidy. Do you _____ _____ _____ _____ _____?

M Yes. That's why there are two desks here.

W I see. But there's only one bed.

M Right. But it's _____ _____ for both of us.

W And you guys _____ _____ _____. I see a lot of books on the bookshelf.

M Yes. We really do.

08

대화를 듣고, 여자의 필통에 대한 내용으로 일치하지 <u>않는</u> 것을 고르시오.

① 빨간색이다.
② 천으로 만들어졌다.
③ 연필과 지우개가 들어 있다.
④ 이름이 써 있다.
⑤ 꽃이 그려져 있다.

W Uh-oh. I think I lost my pencil case.

M What does it look like? Let me help you find it.

W It's red and _____ _____ _____.

M Okay. Is it big?

W It's _____ _____ _____. And it only has a few pencils in it.

M All right. Did you _____ _____ _____ _____ _____?

W Yes. And I also drew a flower next to my name.

09

대화를 듣고, 남자의 가족에 대한 내용으로 일치하지 <u>않는</u> 것을 고르시오.

① 다섯 식구이다.
② 형과 여동생이 있다.
③ 형은 24살이다.
④ 동생은 3학년이다.
⑤ 형은 수학 선생님이다.

W _____ _____ _____ are there in your family?

M There are five people in my family: Mom, Dad, my brother, my sister, and me.

W How old are your siblings? _____ _____ _____ _____?

M No, my older brother is twenty-four, and my younger sister is nine. She's _____ _____ _____.

W What does your brother do?

M He's a college student. He studies math and wants to be a math teacher.

W Cool.

10

대화를 듣고, Taste of Venice에 대한 내용으로 일치하지 <u>않는</u> 것을 고르시오.

① 여자는 가 본 적이 없다.
② 이탈리아 음식점이다.
③ Main 가에 있다.
④ 최근에 문을 열었다.
⑤ 월요일은 운영하지 않는다.

M Hi, Judy. _____ _____ _____ to Taste of Venice?

W No, I haven't. What is that?

M It's an Italian restaurant on Main Street. It opened last week.

W Oh, I didn't know that. Have you been there yet?

M Yes. I had dinner there yesterday. Everything _____ _____.

W I'll try going there tomorrow, then.

M Unfortunately, it's closed on Sundays.

W Oh, thanks for _____ _____ _____. I'll visit next Monday, then.

A

다음 영어 어휘나 표현의 뜻을 우리말로 쓰세요.

01 bowl

02 draw

03 college

04 tidy

05 cloth

06 near

07 both of

08 anytime

09 excited

10 each other

11 visitor

12 writer

13 exchange

14 invite

15 including

16 in that case

B

우리말에 맞는 영어 어휘나 표현을 [보기]에서 찾아 쓰세요.

보기	sneaker	actually	sibling	for free	come over
	taste	enough	field trip	a few	get along with

01 맛이 ~하다

02 사실은

03 형제자매

04 약간의, 소수의

05 현장 학습

06 (~의 집에) 들르다

07 운동화

08 ~와 잘 지내다

09 무료로

10 (~할 만큼) 충분히

Section

2

실전 모의고사
1-6 회

시험 직전 모의고사
1-2 회

점수   / 20문항

 일반 속도   빠른 속도

01 다음을 듣고, 'I'가 무엇인지 가장 적절한 것을 고르시오.

① ② ③
④ ⑤

02 대화를 듣고, 남자가 읽고 있는 책으로 가장 적절한 것을 고르시오.

①  ② ③
④ ⑤

03 다음을 듣고, 수요일의 날씨로 가장 적절한 것을 고르시오.

① ② ③
④ ⑤

04 대화를 듣고, 남자가 한 마지막 말의 의도로 가장 적절한 것을 고르시오.

① 위로   ② 승낙   ③ 제안
④ 축하   ⑤ 사과

05 다음을 듣고, 여자가 오빠에 대해 언급하지 <u>않은</u> 것을 고르시오.

① 나이   ② 직업   ③ 외모
④ 취미   ⑤ 성격

고난도

06 대화를 듣고, 두 사람이 만날 시각을 고르시오.

① 5:30 p.m.   ② 6:00 p.m.
③ 7:00 p.m.   ④ 8:00 p.m.
⑤ 8:30 p.m.

07 대화를 듣고, 여자의 장래 희망으로 가장 적절한 것을 고르시오.

① 프로듀서   ② 동시통역사   ③ 영화배우
④ 여행 가이드   ⑤ 승무원

08 대화를 듣고, 여자의 심정으로 가장 적절한 것을 고르시오.

① proud   ② bored   ③ annoyed
④ relaxed   ⑤ worried

09 대화를 듣고, 남자가 대화 직후에 할 일로 가장 적절한 것을 고르시오.

① 엄마에게 전화하기   ② 꽃 사러 가기
③ 부모님 댁 방문하기   ④ 케이크 사러 가기
⑤ 결혼식 참석하기

10 대화를 듣고, 무엇에 관한 내용인지 가장 적절한 것을 고르시오.

① 주말 일정   ② 캠핑 준비물
③ 여름 계획   ④ 항공권 구매 절차
⑤ 문화센터 교육 과정

11 대화를 듣고, 여자가 이용할 교통수단으로 가장 적절한 것을 고르시오.

① 택시   ② 자동차   ③ 버스
④ 비행기   ⑤ 지하철

12 대화를 듣고, 여자가 호텔에 전화한 이유로 가장 적절한 것을 고르시오.

① 예약 날짜를 변경하기 위해서
② 투어 프로그램을 예약하기 위해서
③ 예약을 취소하기 위해서
④ 입실 가능 시간을 문의하기 위해서
⑤ 객실을 변경하기 위해서

13 대화를 듣고, 두 사람이 대화하는 장소로 가장 적절한 곳을 고르시오.

① 서점   ② 병원   ③ 도서관
④ 영화관   ⑤ 우체국

14 대화를 듣고, 경찰서의 위치로 가장 알맞은 곳을 고르시오.

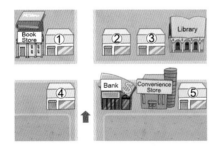

15 대화를 듣고, 남자가 여자에게 부탁한 일로 가장 적절한 것을 고르시오.

① 케이크 사기   ② 의자 가져오기
③ 차 준비하기   ④ 파티장에 데려다주기
⑤ 위층 청소하기

16 대화를 듣고, 남자가 여자에게 제안한 것으로 가장 적절한 것을 고르시오.

① 소식하기
② 저지방 식단 시작하기
③ 조깅 동호회 가입하기
④ 건강 관리 앱 설치하기
⑤ 헬스장 등록하기

17 대화를 듣고, 여자가 잃어버린 물건을 고르시오.

① 목도리   ② 이어폰   ③ 교통카드
④ 우산   ⑤ 장갑

고난도
18 대화를 듣고, 남자의 직업으로 가장 적절한 것을 고르시오.

① 제빵사   ② 요리사   ③ 식당 종업원
④ 승무원   ⑤ 경찰관

[19-20] 대화를 듣고, 남자의 마지막 말에 이어질 여자의 말로 가장 적절한 것을 고르시오.

19 Woman: _____

① I studied all night.
② I won't be late again.
③ I was watching a movie.
④ I go to sleep at 10:00 p.m. every night.
⑤ I usually go to sleep later on the weekends.

20 Woman: _____

① Okay. Let's get sushi!
② Let's meet at three o'clock.
③ I'm sorry, but I'm busy on Sunday.
④ I think we should take the subway.
⑤ What kind of books do you like to read?

DICTATION

01 ◀ 지칭

다음을 듣고, 'I'가 무엇인지 가장 적절한 것을 고르시오.

①   ②
③   ④
⑤

W I have light brown fur _____ _____ _____ _____.
I also have strong back legs and a long tail. My back legs _____
_____ _____ and kick, while I use my tail to keep my balance.
I _____ _____ _____ in a small pouch. I live in Australia.
What am I?

02 ◀ 그림 묘사

대화를 듣고, 남자가 읽고 있는 책으로 가장 적절한 것을 고르시오.

①   ②
③ ④
⑤

W What are you reading, Tom?
M It's a _____ _____ _____. It's called *Insects and You*.
W Oh, okay. I like the picture of the fly _____ _____ _____.
M Actually, that's a bumblebee.
W Really? I guess I don't know much about bugs.
M Then _____ _____ _____ this book!

03 ◀ 날씨

다음을 듣고, 수요일의 날씨로 가장 적절한 것을 고르시오.

① ②
③ ④
⑤

M Hello, this is Ethan Holmes from Channel 4 News with the weather. On
Monday, it will be windy for most of the day. The _____ _____
_____ _____ on Tuesday, but it will rain on Wednesday. The
temperature _____ _____ on Thursday, and it will be cloudy in
the afternoon.

04 ◀ 의도

대화를 듣고, 남자가 한 마지막 말의 의도로 가장 적절한 것을 고르시오.

① 위로 　　　② 승낙
③ 제안 　　　④ 축하
⑤ 사과

W I can't believe this!

M What is it, Maggie? _____ _____ _____?

W Samantha didn't invite me to her pool party.

M _____ _____ _____ _____ that?

W She passed out invitations at school today, but she didn't give me one.

M _____ _____. Maybe she will give you one tomorrow.

05 ◀ 언급하지 않은 내용

다음을 듣고, 여자가 오빠에 대해 언급하지 않은 것을 고르시오.

① 나이 　　　② 직업
③ 외모 　　　④ 취미
⑤ 성격

W This is my older brother, Max. He is twenty-four years old. He is a wedding photographer. _____ _____ _____ _____, Max likes to take kickboxing lessons and spend time with his friends. He and I like to play computer games together. He is very _____ _____ _____.

고난도

06 ◀ 시각

대화를 듣고, 두 사람이 만날 시각을 고르시오.

① 5:30 p.m. 　　② 6:00 p.m.
③ 7:00 p.m. 　　④ 8:00 p.m.
⑤ 8:30 p.m.

[Cell phone rings.]

W Hello?

M Hi, Jasmine. This is Brandon. Do you want to go to a concert tonight in Lake Park?

W Sure! _____ _____ _____ _____?

M It starts at 8:30. But I want to get there early.

W All right. It's 5:30 now. Let's meet _____ _____ _____ _____.

M Okay, I'll _____ _____ _____ at your house.

W All right. See you then.

M What are you watching, Debbie?

W I'm watching a travel show on Spain. I'm going there next month.

M Really? That's great! _____ _____ _____ _____ there?

W I have so many ideas! _____ _____ _____ _____ my travel plans!

M Wow! They look so professional. You should be a tour guide.

W Thanks. I want _____ _____ _____ _____.

08 ◀ 심정

대화를 듣고, 여자의 심정으로 가장 적절한 것을 고르시오.
① proud ② bored
③ annoyed ④ relaxed
⑤ worried

M Kate, don't forget that you _____ _____ _____ _____ tomorrow.

W I don't want to go.

M Why? Last week you said you _____ _____ _____.

W I know. But _____ _____ _____ the dentist.

M Don't worry. It will be okay.

09 ◀ 할 일

대화를 듣고, 남자가 대화 직후에 할 일로 가장 적절한 것을 고르시오.
① 엄마에게 전화하기
② 꽃 사러 가기
③ 부모님 댁 방문하기
④ 케이크 사러 가기
⑤ 결혼식 참석하기

[Cell phone rings.]

W Hey, Derek! _____ _____?

M Hey, Tiffany! I just talked to Mom this morning.

W Oh, really? _____ _____ _____?

M Today is her and Dad's 40th anniversary. I totally forgot!

W So did I. I'll pick up some flowers _____ _____ _____ _____ their house. Could you pick up a cake?

M Sure. I'll get one right now.

10 ◀ 주제

대화를 듣고, 무엇에 관한 내용인지 가장 적절한 것을 고르시오.

① 주말 일정
② 캠핑 준비물
③ 여름 계획
④ 항공권 구매 절차
⑤ 문화센터 교육 과정

W Hi, Bill. What are you doing?

M I'm _____ _____ _____ to Canada.

W Wow! When are you leaving?

M This summer. We're going to _____ _____ for a week. Do you have any plans?

W Yes, I _____ _____ _____ a ballet class. I can't wait!

11 ◀ 특정 정보

대화를 듣고, 여자가 이용할 교통수단으로 가장 적절한 것을 고르시오.

① 택시   ② 자동차
③ 버스   ④ 비행기
⑤ 지하철

[Cell phone rings.]

M Hello?

W It's me. I'm finally in Seoul. It was a long flight.

M I _____ _____ _____ _____ _____. But it's 1:00 a.m. It's too late for the bus.

W Yes, but maybe the subway is still running.

M _____ _____ _____ online. *[pause]* Nope. It stopped at 12:00 a.m.

W Then I'll _____ _____ _____.

12 ◀ 이유

대화를 듣고, 여자가 호텔에 전화한 이유로 가장 적절한 것을 고르시오.

① 예약 날짜를 변경하기 위해서
② 투어 프로그램을 예약하기 위해서
③ 예약을 취소하기 위해서
④ 입실 가능 시간을 문의하기 위해서
⑤ 객실을 변경하기 위해서

[Telephone rings.]

M Hello, this is Sunnyhill Hotel. How may I help you?

W Hi, this is Erica Marshall. I _____ _____ _____ _____ for two nights from June 25 to June 27.

M Yes, I remember.

W My friend can't _____ _____ _____ _____, so I need a single room, instead.

M Okay. I'll _____ _____ _____ to your reservation.

13 ◀ 대화 장소

대화를 듣고, 두 사람이 대화하는 장소로 가장 적절한 곳을 고르시오.

① 서점　　② 병원
③ 도서관　④ 영화관
⑤ 우체국

M How can I help you?

W Do you have _____ _____ _____ Charlotte's Web?

M Yes. Would you like to _____ _____ _____?

W Yes, please. How long can I keep it?

M _____ _____ _____ _____. Can I see your student ID card?

W Here it is.

14 ◀ 위치

대화를 듣고, 경찰서의 위치로 가장 알맞은 곳을 고르시오.

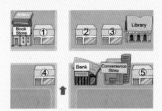

W Excuse me, I'm lost. Could you help me? _____ _____ _____ the police station.

M Sure. _____ _____ for 30 meters and turn right at the bank.

W Okay.

M The police station is _____ _____ _____ _____ of the street, next to the convenience store.

W Thanks for your help!

15 ◀ 부탁한 일

대화를 듣고, 남자가 여자에게 부탁한 일로 가장 적절한 것을 고르시오.

① 케이크 사기
② 의자 가져오기
③ 차 준비하기
④ 파티장에 데려다주기
⑤ 위층 청소하기

W I think _____ _____ _____ the party.

M I still need to buy a cake.

W Oh, I can _____ _____ _____. Don't worry.

M Thanks, but it's okay. I can do it.

W Okay. Is there anything else _____ _____ _____?

M Can you bring some chairs from upstairs? We need three more.

W Sure.

16 ◀ 제안한 일

대화를 듣고, 남자가 여자에게 제안한
것으로 가장 적절한 것을 고르시오.

① 소식하기
② 저지방 식단 시작하기
③ 조깅 동호회 가입하기
④ 건강 관리 앱 설치하기
⑤ 헬스장 등록하기

M Why didn't you have any lunch today?

W I don't want to _____ _____, so I'm trying to eat less.

M That's not healthy. Why don't you _____ _____?

W I don't like exercising. It's boring.

M You should join a jogging club! It will be fun, and you'll _____ _____ _____.

W That's a great idea!

17 ◀ 특정 정보

대화를 듣고, 여자가 잃어버린 물건을
고르시오.

① 목도리   ② 이어폰
③ 교통카드   ④ 우산
⑤ 장갑

M Where are you going, Mia? You just _____ _____.

W I'm going to the bus station.

M Are you _____ _____ _____ there?

W No, Dad. I'm going to look for my glove. I think I _____ _____ _____ _____.

M Oh, no. I hope you find it. Those are your favorite gloves.

고난도

18 ◀ 직업

대화를 듣고, 남자의 직업으로 가장
적절한 것을 고르시오.

① 제빵사   ② 요리사
③ 식당 종업원   ④ 승무원
⑤ 경찰관

W How is your new job so far, David?

M I like it, but it _____ _____ _____ sometimes.

W What are some of your duties?

M I _____ _____ _____ _____, and then I tell them to the cook.

W Does anyone help you serve the dishes to the customers?

M Sometimes. But I usually _____ _____ _____.

19 ◀ 마지막 말에 대한 응답

대화를 듣고, 남자의 마지막 말에 이어질 여자의 말로 가장 적절한 것을 고르시오.

Woman: _____

① I studied all night.
② I won't be late again.
③ I was watching a movie.
④ I go to sleep at 10:00 p.m. every night.
⑤ I usually go to sleep later on the weekends.

W I'm really tired today.

M Why? Are you _____ _____?

W No, I _____ _____ _____ 1:00 a.m. last night.

M Oh. Were you studying for the English test?

W No! I _____ _____ _____ _____!

M Then what were you doing?

W _____

20 ◀ 마지막 말에 대한 응답

대화를 듣고, 남자의 마지막 말에 이어질 여자의 말로 가장 적절한 것을 고르시오.

Woman: _____

① Okay. Let's get sushi!
② Let's meet at three o'clock.
③ I'm sorry, but I'm busy on Sunday.
④ I think we should take the subway.
⑤ What kind of books do you like to read?

M What are you going to do this Sunday?

W _____ _____.

M I'm going to a bookstore downtown. Do you want to _____ _____?

W Sure. I want to buy some comic books.

M Great! Would you like to _____ _____ _____ first?

W _____

어휘 · 표현 다지기

A

다음 영어 어휘나 표현의 뜻을 우리말로 쓰세요.

01 friendly _____   **02** below _____

03 still _____   **04** up to _____

05 downtown _____   **06** fur _____

07 pouch _____   **08** stressful _____

09 totally _____   **10** invitation _____

11 customer _____   **12** keep one's balance _____

13 anniversary _____   **14** reserve _____

15 temperature _____   **16** professional _____

B

우리말에 맞는 영어 어휘나 표현을 [보기]에서 찾아 쓰세요.

	보기	rise	glove	upstairs	check out	sign up for
		serve	half an hour	outgoing	pass out	convenience store

01 위층 _____   **02** 장갑 _____

03 30분 _____   **04** 외향적인 _____

05 (기온 등이) 올라가다 _____   **06** 편의점 _____

07 (책 등을) 대출하다 _____   **08** ~을 나눠주다 _____

09 (음식 등을) 제공하다 _____   **10** ~을 등록하다 _____

01 다음을 듣고, 'this'가 가리키는 것으로 가장 적절한 것을 고르시오.

①   ②   ③

④   ⑤

02 대화를 듣고, 여자의 우산으로 가장 적절한 것을 고르시오.

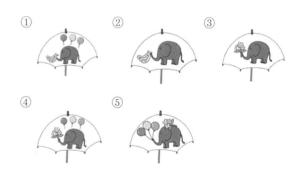

①   ②   ③

④   ⑤

03 다음을 듣고, 내일의 날씨로 가장 적절한 것을 고르시오.

①   ②   ③

④   ⑤

🇬🇧
04 대화를 듣고, 남자가 한 마지막 말의 의도로 가장 적절한 것을 고르시오.

① 승낙   ② 동의   ③ 거절
④ 축하   ⑤ 위로

05 다음을 듣고, 남자가 Lisa's Supermarket에 대해 언급하지 않은 것을 고르시오.

① 매장 위치   ② 재개점 이유   ③ 행사 날짜
④ 행사 시간   ⑤ 행사 품목

고난도
06 대화를 듣고, 두 사람이 만날 시각을 고르시오.

① 2:00 p.m.   ② 5:00 p.m.   ③ 6:30 p.m.
④ 7:00 p.m.   ⑤ 10:30 p.m.

07 대화를 듣고, 여자의 장래 희망으로 가장 적절한 것을 고르시오.

① 변호사   ② 교사   ③ 디자이너
④ 화가   ⑤ 과학자

🇬🇧
08 대화를 듣고, 여자의 심정으로 가장 적절한 것을 고르시오.

① 실망함   ② 기쁨   ③ 자랑스러움
④ 지루함   ⑤ 걱정스러움

09 대화를 듣고, 여자가 대화 직후에 할 일로 가장 적절한 것을 고르시오.

① 청소하기   ② 짐 풀기   ③ 산책하기
④ 창문 열기   ⑤ 에어컨 켜기

10 대화를 듣고, 무엇에 관한 내용인지 가장 적절한 것을 고르시오.

① 정리정돈의 효과   ② 시간 관리 비법
③ 자투리 공간 활용   ④ 집안일 분담
⑤ 스트레스 해소법

11 대화를 듣고, 남자가 이용할 교통수단으로 가장 적절한 것을 고르시오.

① 버스 ② 자전거 ③ 지하철
④ 택시 ⑤ 기차

🇬🇧
12 대화를 듣고, 여자가 방을 바꾸고 싶어 하는 이유로 가장 적절한 것을 고르시오.

① 너무 좁아서
② 너무 어두워서
③ 방음이 잘 안 되어서
④ 다른 방이 마음에 들어서
⑤ 인테리어가 마음에 들지 않아서

13 대화를 듣고, 두 사람이 대화하는 장소로 가장 적절한 곳을 고르시오.

① 병원 ② 약국 ③ 아이스링크
④ 호텔 ⑤ 식당

고난도
14 대화를 듣고, 남자가 찾고 있는 지갑의 위치로 가장 알맞은 곳을 고르시오.

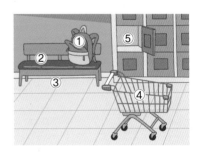

15 대화를 듣고, 여자가 남자에게 부탁한 일로 가장 적절한 것을 고르시오.

① 문단속하기 ② 이동 주차하기
③ 현관문 열어두기 ④ 장 보기
⑤ 짐 옮기기

🇬🇧
16 대화를 듣고, 남자가 여자에게 제안한 것으로 가장 적절한 것을 고르시오.

① 미술학원 등록하기 ② 블로그 개설하기
③ 만화책 만들기 ④ 블로그에 만화 연재하기
⑤ 만화 공모전 응모하기

17 대화를 듣고, 여자가 어제 한 일로 가장 적절한 것을 고르시오.

① 영화 보기 ② 쇼핑하기
③ 박물관 관람하기 ④ 집에서 휴식하기
⑤ 공룡 모형 만들기

18 대화를 듣고, 남자의 직업으로 가장 적절한 것을 고르시오.

① 기자 ② 조종사 ③ 여행 가이드
④ 소설가 ⑤ 연구원

[19-20] 대화를 듣고, 여자의 마지막 말에 이어질 남자의 말로 가장 적절한 것을 고르시오.

19 Man: _____

① For about two years.
② He lives in California.
③ He has been there twice.
④ He is almost 170 cm tall.
⑤ He went there to study English.

🇬🇧
20 Man: _____

① No, I don't want to go there.
② Central Park is very big.
③ I recommend taking the subway.
④ Yes, people enjoy walking in the park.
⑤ You can pick up your bike next week.

DICTATION

01 ◀ 지칭

다음을 듣고, 'this'가 가리키는 것으로 가장 적절한 것을 고르시오.

M This egg-shaped fruit is often grown in New Zealand. _____ _____ _____ _____ is brown and covered with short hairs. We _____ _____ this part before we eat this. Inside, this is usually green, although it is sometimes yellow. There are many small, black seeds _____ _____ _____. What is this?

02 ◀ 그림 묘사

대화를 듣고, 여자의 우산으로 가장 적절한 것을 고르시오.

M Did you buy a new umbrella, Ashley?

W No, it was _____ _____ _____ _____ _____.

M The elephant on the umbrella is so cute. It looks like it is _____ _____.

W It is actually holding flowers! Also, I really like the _____ _____ _____.

M It's a lovely design.

03 ◀ 날씨

다음을 듣고, 내일의 날씨로 가장 적절한 것을 고르시오.

W Good morning! This is Sandra Collins with the weather report. It will be cloudy for most of the day today, and there is a 40% _____ _____ _____ this afternoon. Tomorrow, it is going to _____ _____ _____. You should try to _____ _____.

04 ◀ 의도

대화를 듣고, 남자가 한 마지막 말의 의도로 가장 적절한 것을 고르시오.
① 승낙　② 동의
③ 거절　④ 축하
⑤ 위로

W What are you doing this weekend, Jason?
M I _____ _____ _____ yet. What about you?
W I'm going to a musical. I _____ _____ _____ yesterday!
M Oh, wow! I'm sure you'll have a great time.
W You like musicals too, right? Would you _____ _____ _____ _____ with me?
M I'd love to.

05 ◀ 언급하지 않은 내용

다음을 듣고, 남자가 Lisa's Supermarket에 대해 언급하지 <u>않은</u> 것을 고르시오.
① 매장 위치　② 재개점 이유
③ 행사 날짜　④ 행사 시간
⑤ 행사 품목

M Lisa's Supermarket _____ _____ _____ Main Street this week. The grand reopening event will be on Thursday, March 3 from 10:00 a.m. to 9:00 p.m. There will be free ice cream for kids, and all fresh fruit and vegetables _____ _____ _____ _____. Please come and visit!

고난도
06 ◀ 시각

대화를 듣고, 두 사람이 만날 시각을 고르시오.
① 2:00 p.m.　② 5:00 p.m.
③ 6:30 p.m.　④ 7:00 p.m.
⑤ 10:30 p.m.

M Gina, _____ _____ _____ _____ _____ to the Paradise Zoo with me?
W I'd love to.
M How about this Saturday?
W I _____ _____ _____ _____ at two on Saturdays. It should end at five.
M That's okay. The zoo is only open at night, from seven o'clock to 10:30 p.m.
W That's perfect! Let's meet thirty minutes _____ _____ _____ _____.
M Okay.

대화를 듣고, 여자의 장래 희망으로
가장 적절한 것을 고르시오.
① 변호사   ② 교사
③ 디자이너   ④ 화가
⑤ 과학자

M Beth, would you like to _____ _____ _____ _____

_____ with me this afternoon?

W That sounds fun, but I can't. I have to _____ _____ _____.

M All right, maybe next time. Isn't tutoring stressful, though?

W No, I really enjoy teaching. I want to be a math teacher someday.

M Oh, okay. Then tutoring is a _____ _____ _____!

대화를 듣고, 여자의 현재 심정으로
가장 적절한 것을 고르시오.
① 실망함   ② 기쁨
③ 자랑스러움   ④ 지루함
⑤ 걱정스러움

M Happy birthday, Jenny! This is for you.

W Wow! Thank you!

M It's my pleasure.

W I didn't think anyone remembered my birthday, so _____ _____

_____.

M I wanted to surprise you, so I _____ _____ _____ until

now.

W I was really surprised. I'm going to remember this day _____

_____ _____ _____.

대화를 듣고, 여자가 대화 직후에 할
일로 가장 적절한 것을 고르시오.
① 청소하기   ② 짐 풀기
③ 산책하기   ④ 창문 열기
⑤ 에어컨 켜기

W I'm so exhausted!

M Yeah, it was a long trip. I'm _____ _____ _____ _____!

W Me too. I want to rest, but I should unpack first.

M Before you do that, could you open the windows? It's _____

_____ _____ in here.

W No problem. We _____ _____ _____ _____.

10 ◀ 주제

대화를 듣고, 무엇에 관한 내용인지 가장 적절한 것을 고르시오.

① 정리정돈의 효과
② 시간 관리 비법
③ 자투리 공간 활용
④ 집안일 분담
⑤ 스트레스 해소법

W Jack, why is your room always so messy?

M I don't know. I am usually _____ _____ _____ _____ to clean it.

W _____ _____ _____ _____ is very important. It makes you feel better.

M Really? I didn't know that.

W Try it. You'll _____ _____ _____.

11 ◀ 특정 정보

대화를 듣고, 남자가 이용할 교통수단으로 가장 적절한 것을 고르시오.

① 버스   ② 자전거
③ 지하철   ④ 택시
⑤ 기차

W It's raining now, Sean. _____ _____ _____ _____.

M Thanks, Stacy. I'll remember.

W I hope you don't have to _____ _____ _____ _____ _____ for very long.

M I'm actually not taking the bus home tonight.

W Really? Why not?

M The new subway line opened last week, so I'm going to _____ _____ _____ instead.

12 ◀ 이유

대화를 듣고, 여자가 방을 바꾸고 싶어 하는 이유로 가장 적절한 것을 고르시오.

① 너무 좁아서
② 너무 어두워서
③ 방음이 잘 안 되어서
④ 다른 방이 마음에 들어서
⑤ 인테리어가 마음에 들지 않아서

M Good morning, Ms. Taylor. Do you like your room?

W _____ _____ _____. I would like a different room.

M I'm sorry to hear that. Is it too small?

W No, it's _____ _____ _____.

M What's wrong, then?

W It is very _____ _____ _____ _____. Can I switch to a brighter room?

13 ◀ 대화 장소

대화를 듣고, 두 사람이 대화하는 장소로 가장 적절한 곳을 고르시오.

① 병원　　② 약국
③ 아이스링크　④ 호텔
⑤ 식당

W Do you have an appointment?

M No, I don't.

W Sorry, but you can't see the doctor if you didn't _____ _____

_____.

M I know. But I just slipped on some ice and _____ _____

_____.

W I see. _____ _____ _____ _____?

M It's serious. I can't move it.

W In that case, I'll talk to the doctor. Wait for a moment, please.

고난도

14 ◀ 위치

대화를 듣고, 남자가 찾고 있는 지갑의 위치로 가장 알맞은 곳을 고르시오.

M Have you seen my wallet?

W Your wallet? Didn't you just _____ _____ _____ _____

_____?

M No, I didn't.

W Why don't you _____ _____ _____ _____?

M Well, there's nothing under the bench.

W Hmm… What about in the shopping cart?

M My wallet's not there either. Oh, wait. I think my wallet is _____

_____ _____.

W Oh yes. Here it is.

---

15 ◀ 부탁한 일

대화를 듣고, 여자가 남자에게 부탁한 일로 가장 적절한 것을 고르시오.

① 문단속하기
② 이동 주차하기
③ 현관문 열어두기
④ 장 보기
⑤ 짐 옮기기

[Cell phone rings.]

W Hi, Mark.

M Hi, Shannon! Where are you now?

W I'm in the parking lot. I just _____ _____ _____ the grocery

store.

M Good! I'll _____ _____ _____ _____ _____ for

you.

W Actually, could you come down and help me _____ _____

_____? They're really heavy.

M Sure. I'll be there in a minute.

16 ◀ 제안한 일

대화를 듣고, 남자가 여자에게 제안한 것으로 가장 적절한 것을 고르시오.

① 미술학원 등록하기
② 블로그 개설하기
③ 만화책 만들기
④ 블로그에 만화 연재하기
⑤ 만화 공모전 응모하기

M Becky, I was just _____ _____ _____ _____.

W Oh, really? What do you think?

M It's very well written. But the cartoons are the best part.

W Thanks! I _____ _____ _____ _____.

M I can tell. They're unique.

W I want more people to see them.

M Why don't you _____ _____ _____ _____ _____?

W Maybe I will!

17 ◀ 한 일

대화를 듣고, 여자가 어제 한 일로 가장 적절한 것을 고르시오.

① 영화 보기
② 쇼핑하기
③ 박물관 관람하기
④ 집에서 휴식하기
⑤ 공룡 모형 만들기

W Happy Monday!

M Hi, Julie. What did you do yesterday?

W I went to the dinosaur museum. But it turns out that it _____ _____ _____ _____. So I couldn't enter.

M Oh, that's too bad. So did you _____ _____ _____?

W I started to. But on my way home, I saw a big mall. So I _____ _____ instead.

M That's good.

18 ◀ 직업

대화를 듣고, 남자의 직업으로 가장 적절한 것을 고르시오.

① 기자   ② 조종사
③ 여행 가이드   ④ 소설가
⑤ 연구원

W Frank, I just _____ _____ _____ in the newspaper this morning. It was great!

M Thanks, Megan. I really enjoyed interviewing that Chinese novelist.

W Did you _____ _____ _____ _____ China?

M Yes, I was there for a month because I had to _____ _____ _____.

W Oh, wow! How long did it take to write the article?

M About a week.

19 ◄ 마지막 말에 대한 응답

대화를 듣고, 여자의 마지막 말에 이어질 남자의 말로 가장 적절한 것을 고르시오.

Man: _____

① For about two years.
② He lives in California.
③ He has been there twice.
④ He is almost 170 cm tall.
⑤ He went there to study English.

W What are you doing?
M I'm _____ _____ _____ to my brother.
W Really? Don't you live with him?
M No, he's studying in the US.
W Wow! _____ _____ _____ _____ _____ there?
M _____

20 ◄ 마지막 말에 대한 응답

대화를 듣고, 여자의 마지막 말에 이어질 남자의 말로 가장 적절한 것을 고르시오.

Man: _____

① No, I don't want to go there.
② Central Park is very big.
③ I recommend taking the subway.
④ Yes, people enjoy walking in the park.
⑤ You can pick up your bike next week.

W Excuse me, sir. _____ _____ is Central Park from here?
M It takes about forty minutes to get there _____ _____.
W Oh, wow. That's a long time.
M Do you have a bike? It only takes fifteen minutes by bicycle.
W No, I don't. Is there _____ _____ _____ I can get there?
M _____

128

A 다음 영어 어휘나 표현의 뜻을 우리말로 쓰세요.

01 disappointed

02 slip

03 bright

04 tutor

05 above

06 dark

07 parking lot

08 outside

09 article

10 enter

11 unique

12 do research

13 flea market

14 grocery store

15 reopen

16 novelist

B 우리말에 맞는 영어 어휘나 표현을 [보기]에서 찾아 쓰세요.

보기	heavy	chance	stressed	experience	exhausted
	messy	on foot	switch to	serious	be covered with

01 무거운

02 가능성

03 지저분한

04 ~로 바꾸다

05 경험

06 지친

07 걸어서

08 심각한

09 스트레스를 받는

10 ~로 덮이다

01 다음을 듣고, 'this'가 가리키는 것으로 가장 적절한 것을 고르시오.

 ①
 ②
 ③

 ④
 ⑤

02 대화를 듣고, 여자가 선택한 식탁보로 가장 적절한 것을 고르시오.

 ①
 ②
 ③

 ④
 ⑤

03 다음을 듣고, 오늘의 날씨로 가장 적절한 것을 고르시오.

 ①
 ②
 ③

 ④
 ⑤

04 🇬🇧 대화를 듣고, 남자가 한 마지막 말의 의도로 가장 적절한 것을 고르시오.

① 요청 　　② 감사 　　③ 충고
④ 사과 　　⑤ 불평

05 다음을 듣고, 여자가 반려동물에 대해 언급하지 않은 것을 고르시오.

① 이름 　　② 생김새 　　③ 나이
④ 성격 　　⑤ 좋아하는 음식

06 대화를 듣고, 두 사람이 만날 시각을 고르시오.

① 6:00 p.m. 　② 6:30 p.m. 　③ 7:00 p.m.
④ 7:30 p.m. 　⑤ 8:00 p.m.

07 대화를 듣고, 여자의 장래 희망으로 가장 적절한 것을 고르시오.

① 작곡가 　　② 가수 　　③ 배우
④ 기자 　　⑤ 라디오 진행자

08 🇬🇧 대화를 듣고, 여자의 심정으로 가장 적절한 것을 고르시오.

① 기쁨 　　② 무서움 　　③ 지루함
④ 무관심함 　　⑤ 자랑스러움

고난도

09 대화를 듣고, 남자가 대화 직후에 할 일로 가장 적절한 것을 고르시오.

① 양파 썰기 　　② 상 차리기
③ 카레 요리법 찾기 　　④ 그릇 꺼내기
⑤ 감자 껍질 벗기기

10 대화를 듣고, 무엇에 관한 내용인지 가장 적절한 것을 고르시오.

① 동아리 가입 　② 방학 계획 　③ 독후감 과제
④ 장래 희망 　⑤ 취미 생활

11 대화를 듣고, 남자가 학교에 갈 방법으로 가장 적절한 것을 고르시오.

① 버스　　　② 지하철　　　③ 도보
④ 자전거　　　⑤ 자동차

12 대화를 듣고, 여자가 선생님을 찾아온 이유로 가장 적절한 것을 고르시오.

① 연습 일정을 변경하기 위해서
② 연습 불참 소식을 전하기 위해서
③ 시험 성적을 문의하기 위해서
④ 오디션 참가 신청을 하기 위해서
⑤ 숙제에 대해 도움을 요청하기 위해서

13 대화를 듣고, 두 사람이 대화하는 장소로 가장 적절한 곳을 고르시오.

① 세탁소　　　② 공연장　　　③ 옷 가게
④ 음식점　　　⑤ 분실물 보관소

14 대화를 듣고, 호텔의 위치로 가장 알맞은 곳을 고르시오.

15 대화를 듣고, 여자가 남자에게 부탁한 일로 가장 적절한 것을 고르시오.

① 짐 맡아주기　　　② 버스 시간 알려주기
③ 조기 입실하기　　　④ 택시 부르기
⑤ 근교 식당 추천해주기

16 대화를 듣고, 남자가 여자에게 제안한 것으로 가장 적절한 것을 고르시오.

① 수영 배우기　　　② 선생님께 편지 쓰기
③ 영어 원서 읽기　　　④ 선생님 뵈러 가기
⑤ 수영 수업시간 변경하기

17 대화를 듣고, 여자가 어제 한 일로 가장 적절한 것을 고르시오.

① 게임하기　　　② SNS하기　　　③ 영화 보기
④ 소설 읽기　　　⑤ 숙제하기

18 대화를 듣고, 남자의 직업으로 가장 적절한 것을 고르시오.

① 여행 가이드　　　② 식당 종업원　　　③ 전시 해설가
④ 호텔 직원　　　⑤ 버스 기사

[19-20] 대화를 듣고, 여자의 마지막 말에 이어질 남자의 말로 가장 적절한 것을 고르시오.

19 Man: _____

① I think he needs to wear glasses.
② Luke is very quiet.
③ You should give him more attention.
④ Don't worry. He likes his new school.
⑤ The teachers' office is just around the corner.

고난도
20 Man: _____

① I already picked out your desk.
② It will fit in your room.
③ They will deliver the desk next week.
④ The furniture store is very close to my house.
⑤ Of course! I'll ask the salesman to give me one.

DICTATION

정답 단서 오답 함정

  일반 속도   빠른 속도

01 ◀ 지칭

다음을 듣고, 'this'가 가리키는 것으로 가장 적절한 것을 고르시오.

① ② ③ ④ ⑤

W You can find this in a bathroom. This has a _____ _____ _____ and a brush at the end. You use this about three times a day to _____ _____ _____. You should buy a new one _____ _____ _____. What is this?

02 ◀ 그림 묘사

대화를 듣고, 여자가 선택한 식탁보로 가장 적절한 것을 고르시오.

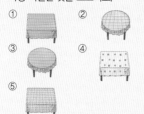

① ② ③ ④ ⑤

W I need to _____ _____ _____ _____ for tonight's dinner. Can you help me?

M Sure. I like the _____ _____.

W I like that one too, but it's too small. How about the _____ _____?

M Okay. Should we get a round tablecloth or a square one?

W A round one.

03 ◀ 날씨

다음을 듣고, 오늘의 날씨로 가장 적절한 것을 고르시오.

① ② ③ ④ ⑤

M Good morning, Philadelphia! This is Jerry Miller with the weather report. It's cloudy today, and there is _____ _____ _____ _____ _____ tomorrow. The skies will be clear on Saturday, but there will be a lot of wind _____ _____ _____. On Sunday, it will be warm and sunny.

04 ◀ 의도

대화를 듣고, 남자가 한 마지막 말의 의도로 가장 적절한 것을 고르시오.

① 요청　　　② 감사
③ 충고　　　④ 사과
⑤ 불평

W　What are you looking for, Eric?

M　My earphones. They were in my pocket. Maybe _____ _____ _____.

W　Did you check your backpack? You usually _____ _____ _____ _____.

M　I did, but they weren't in there. Will you check the living room for me?

W　Sure. [pause] I can't find your earphones here.

M　Then _____ _____ _____ _____ today? I really need them now.

05 ◀ 언급하지 않은 내용

다음을 듣고, 여자가 반려동물에 대해 언급하지 <u>않은</u> 것을 고르시오.

① 이름　　　② 생김새
③ 나이　　　④ 성격
⑤ 좋아하는 음식

W　Hi, everyone. This is my pet rabbit, Samantha. As you can see, her ears and nose are black, and _____ _____ _____ _____ _____ is white. She is very friendly and playful. She likes it when I _____ _____ _____ _____. Her favorite food is carrots.

06 ◀ 시각

대화를 듣고, 두 사람이 만날 시각을 고르시오.

① 6:00 p.m.　　② 6:30 p.m.
③ 7:00 p.m.　　④ 7:30 p.m.
⑤ 8:00 p.m.

M　Caroline, will you _____ _____ _____ _____ with me tonight?

W　Sure!

M　It starts at seven thirty. Is that okay?

W　Yes. But let's have dinner _____ _____ _____.

M　Sounds good. How about meeting an hour before it starts?

W　Six thirty? I don't think _____ _____ _____. How about meeting thirty minutes earlier?

M　All right. See you then.

대화를 듣고, 여자의 장래 희망으로
가장 적절한 것을 고르시오.
① 작곡가　　② 가수
③ 배우　　　④ 기자
⑤ 라디오 진행자

M　Hi, Christine. Do you want to study together after school today?

W　I can't. Our school radio station is _____ _____ _____ _____ at 6:00 p.m.

M　Oh, okay. You're hosting the show, right?

W　I am! I _____ _____ _____ _____ . I really love it.

M　You should be a DJ and have _____ _____ _____ someday!

W　That's my dream job!

대화를 듣고, 여자의 심정으로 가장
적절한 것을 고르시오.
① 기쁨　　　② 무서움
③ 지루함　　④ 무관심함
⑤ 자랑스러움

W　What was that noise?

M　I _____ _____ _____ .

W　There it is again! Don't you hear footsteps? I think _____ _____ _____ _____ .

M　It's probably just the wind. Don't worry.

W　What if it's a dangerous animal? I want to _____ _____ _____ _____ !

M　All right. Let's go.

대화를 듣고, 남자가 대화 직후에 할
일로 가장 적절한 것을 고르시오.
① 양파 썰기
② 상 차리기
③ 카레 요리법 찾기
④ 그릇 꺼내기
⑤ 감자 껍질 벗기기

M　Do you need help with anything, Brittany? I can _____ _____ _____ .

W　Oh, I'll do that after the curry is done.

M　I can chop the onions, then.

W　I've decided not to use onions this time. Could you _____ _____ _____ instead?

M　Sure. How many do you need?

W　Five _____ _____ _____ .

10 ◀ 주제

대화를 듣고, 무엇에 관한 내용인지
가장 적절한 것을 고르시오.

① 동아리 가입   ② 방학 계획
③ 독후감 과제   ④ 장래 희망
⑤ 취미 생활

M What are you looking at, Joan? Are they club posters?

W Yes. I'm thinking about _____ _____ _____ _____.

M Would you like to join the book club with me?

W I _____ _____ _____ _____ to read books.

M What about the French club? I think it would be fun.

W Good idea. _____ _____ _____!

11 ◀ 특정 정보

대화를 듣고, 남자가 학교에 갈 방법
으로 가장 적절한 것을 고르시오.

① 버스   ② 지하철
③ 도보   ④ 자전거
⑤ 자동차

W Are you _____ _____ _____ _____ now, Mike?

M Yeah.

W Please don't ride your bike today. The roads are _____ _____.

M Actually, my bike broke yesterday. I'll just walk.

W Are you sure? I can ask Mrs. Johnson to pick you up.

M No, it's okay. I _____ _____ _____.

12 ◀ 이유

대화를 듣고, 여자가 선생님을 찾아온
이유로 가장 적절한 것을 고르시오.

① 연습 일정을 변경하기 위해서
② 연습 불참 소식을 전하기 위해서
③ 시험 성적을 문의하기 위해서
④ 오디션 참가 신청을 하기 위해서
⑤ 숙제에 대해 도움을 요청하기 위해서

W Mr. Lee, can I talk to you _____ _____ _____?

M Sure. Do you have a question about the homework?

W No, I need to talk to you about the drama club.

M Okay.

W I want to _____ _____ for a while. I need more time to study for my final exams.

M I understand. Studying is more important. I'll see you _____ _____ _____ _____.

M May I help you?

W Yes, please. Is this sweater _____ _____?

M Yes. You can try it on if you'd like.

W Okay. *[pause]* It's great! I really love the picture of _____ _____ _____ _____ on the pocket.

M It's one of our _____ _____ _____. And it's machine washable.

W How much is it?

M It's $10.

W Excuse me. Where is the New World Hotel?

M Turn right at the hospital over there. Then _____ _____ one block and turn left.

W Turn left?

M Yes. It will be on your right. It's _____ _____ _____ _____.

W Okay. Thanks for your help.

15 ◀ 부탁한 일

대화를 듣고, 여자가 남자에게 부탁한 일로 가장 적절한 것을 고르시오.

① 짐 맡아주기
② 버스 시간 알려주기
③ 조기 입실하기
④ 택시 부르기
⑤ 근처 식당 추천해주기

W I'd like to _____ _____, please.

M Okay. Did you enjoy your trip?

W I did! By the way, how can I _____ _____ _____ _____?

M You could take a bus, but you have a lot of luggage. A taxi would be better.

W Good idea. Could you _____ _____ _____ _____?

M Sure.

16 ◀ 제안한 일

대화를 듣고, 남자가 여자에게 제안한 것으로 가장 적절한 것을 고르시오.

① 수영 배우기
② 선생님께 편지 쓰기
③ 영어 원서 읽기
④ 선생님 뵈러 가기
⑤ 수영 수업시간 변경하기

M What are you doing tomorrow afternoon?

W I _____ _____ _____ _____ at 2:00 p.m.

M I think you should skip it. Why don't you _____ _____ _____ to visit Ms. Smith?

W Our old English teacher? Why?

M Tomorrow is Teachers' Day. Did you forget?

W I did! Thanks for _____ _____.

17 ◀ 한 일

대화를 듣고, 여자가 어제 한 일로 가장 적절한 것을 고르시오.

① 게임하기   ② SNS하기
③ 영화 보기   ④ 소설 읽기
⑤ 숙제하기

M Are you okay? You look very tired.

W I am. I _____ _____ _____ last night.

M Why? Were you playing games on your phone?

W No, I was _____ _____ _____ _____.

M So did you finish it?

W Yes. It was so interesting that I _____ _____ _____ _____.

18 ◀ 직업

대화를 듣고, 남자의 직업으로 가장 적절한 것을 고르시오.

① 여행 가이드   ② 식당 종업원
③ 전시 해설가   ④ 호텔 직원
⑤ 버스 기사

W Good afternoon. I would like to _____ _____. My name is Hyejin Kim.

M Let me see… [typing sound] Here is your room key. Breakfast is served on the 10th floor from 6:00 a.m. to 10:00 a.m.

W Oh, great! I'm thinking of _____ _____ _____ tomorrow. Do you have any suggestions?

M The Prado Museum is a must-see. I can _____ _____ _____ _____ for you.

W Thank you!

대화를 듣고, 여자의 마지막 말에 이어질 남자의 말로 가장 적절한 것을 고르시오.

Man: _____

① I think he needs to wear glasses.
② Luke is very quiet.
③ You should give him more attention.
④ Don't worry. He likes his new school.
⑤ The teachers' office is just around the corner.

[Cell phone rings.]

W Hello?

M Hi, this is Bill Taylor. I'm Luke's teacher. Do you _____ _____ _____?

W Sure. Did something happen at school?

M No, I'm just _____ _____ Luke. He seems very quiet recently.

W Luke just _____ _____ _____ _____ a few months ago. He thinks everyone likes his new brother more than him.

M _____

대화를 듣고, 여자의 마지막 말에 이어질 남자의 말로 가장 적절한 것을 고르시오.

Man: _____

① I already picked out your desk.
② It will fit in your room.
③ They will deliver the desk next week.
④ The furniture store is very close to my house.
⑤ Of course! I'll ask the salesman to give me one.

[Cell phone rings.]

M Hi, Jin. I'm at the furniture store now.

W Hey, Dad. Did you _____ _____ _____ _____ for me?

M Not yet. What do you think of a wooden desk?

W Hmm… _____ _____ _____ drawers?

M It does. But I think it's a little small.

W Can you _____ _____ _____ _____? Then we can look at it together.

M _____

A

다음 영어 어휘나 표현의 뜻을 우리말로 쓰세요.

01 checkered

02 square

03 clear

04 footstep

05 follow

06 wooden

07 recently

08 chop

09 striped

10 set the table

11 luggage

12 what if ~?

13 dangerous

14 remind

15 mystery novel

16 slippery

B

우리말에 맞는 영어 어휘나 표현을 [보기]에서 찾아 쓰세요.

	보기				
	peel	host	pick out	stay up late	throughout the day
	skip	handle	arrange	attention	be concerned about

01 손잡이

02 종일

03 마련하다

04 관심, 주의

05 ~을 걱정하다

06 늦게까지 깨어 있다

07 진행하다

08 껍질을 벗기다

09 ~을 선택하다[고르다]

10 (일을) 거르다, 빠지다

점수 _____ / 20문항

 일반 속도
 빠른 속도

01 다음을 듣고, 'I'가 무엇인지 가장 적절한 것을 고르시오.

02 대화를 듣고, 여자가 만든 케이크로 가장 적절한 것을 고르시오.

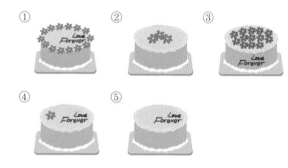

03 다음을 듣고, 인천의 내일 오후 날씨로 가장 적절한 것을 고르시오.

🇬🇧
04 대화를 듣고, 남자가 한 마지막 말의 의도로 가장 적절한 것을 고르시오.

① 사과   ② 승낙   ③ 충고
④ 거절   ⑤ 위로

05 다음을 듣고, 남자가 자신에 대해 언급하지 <u>않은</u> 것을 고르시오.

① 이름   ② 현재 거주지   ③ 이사 온 이유
④ 장래 희망   ⑤ 좋아하는 운동

06 대화를 듣고, 두 사람이 만날 시각을 고르시오.

① 9:00 a.m.   ② 10:00 a.m.   ③ 11:00 a.m.
④ 12:00 p.m.   ⑤ 1:00 p.m.

07 대화를 듣고, 여자의 장래 희망으로 가장 적절한 것을 고르시오.

① 성우   ② 프로듀서   ③ 아나운서
④ 작가   ⑤ 기자

🇬🇧
08 대화를 듣고, 남자의 심정으로 가장 적절한 것을 고르시오.

① curious   ② proud   ③ pleased
④ annoyed   ⑤ relaxed

09 대화를 듣고, 여자가 대화 직후에 할 일로 가장 적절한 것을 고르시오.

① 서점 가기   ② 옷 세탁하기
③ 책꽂이 주문하기   ④ 세탁기 옮기기
⑤ 책 빼내기

🇬🇧
10 대화를 듣고, 무엇에 관한 내용인지 가장 적절한 것을 고르시오.

① 방학 숙제   ② 장학금 신청
③ 성적 향상 비법   ④ 고등학교 진학
⑤ 온라인 강의 수강신청

11 대화를 듣고, 여자가 이용할 교통수단으로 가장 적절한 것을 고르시오.

① 지하철   ② 자전거   ③ 버스

④ 기차   ⑤ 자동차

12 대화를 듣고, 남자가 컴퓨터 회사에 전화한 이유로 가장 적절한 것을 고르시오.

① 컴퓨터 속도가 느려서

② 컴퓨터에서 소음이 발생해서

③ 컴퓨터 전원이 켜지지 않아서

④ 컴퓨터가 바이러스에 감염되어서

⑤ 컴퓨터에서 소리가 나오지 않아서

13 대화를 듣고, 두 사람이 대화하는 장소로 가장 적절한 곳을 고르시오.

① 호텔   ② 음식점   ③ 아파트

④ 백화점   ⑤ 식료품점

고난도

14 대화를 듣고, 남자가 찾고 있는 휴대전화의 위치로 가장 알맞은 곳을 고르시오.

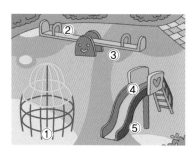

고난도

15 대화를 듣고, 여자가 남자에게 부탁한 일로 가장 적절한 것을 고르시오.

① 아침에 전화해주기   ② 알람시계 맞춰놓기

③ 여행 일정 짜기   ④ 숙소 예약하기

⑤ 해돋이 사진 찍어오기

16 대화를 듣고, 여자가 남자에게 제안한 것으로 가장 적절한 것을 고르시오.

① 서평 검색하기   ② 인터넷 서점 이용하기

③ 스마트폰 구입하기   ④ 도서관 회원 가입하기

⑤ 전자책 이용하기

17 대화를 듣고, 남자가 어제 한 일로 가장 적절한 것을 고르시오.

① 쇼핑하기   ② 체스 게임하기

③ 동물원 가기   ④ 컴퓨터 게임하기

⑤ 할머니 댁 가기

18 대화를 듣고, 여자의 직업으로 가장 적절한 것을 고르시오.

① 교사   ② 배우   ③ 디자이너

④ 매표원   ⑤ 출판사 직원

[19-20] 대화를 듣고, 남자의 마지막 말에 이어질 여자의 말로 가장 적절한 것을 고르시오.

19 Woman: _____

① No. A repairman will fix the fence.

② Don't worry, honey. It wasn't your fault.

③ I'm sorry, but I don't have time right now.

④ Sure. Hand me the hammer and those nails.

⑤ Okay, I will pick you up after I'm finished.

고난도

20 Woman: _____

① You should leave now.

② That's strange. Do you know why?

③ Wow! No wonder you can't stay awake!

④ That's okay. I finished my homework earlier today.

⑤ Sorry, I didn't realize you had other plans already.

DICTATION

일반 속도   빠른 속도

01 ◀ 지칭

다음을 듣고, 'I'가 무엇인지 가장 적절한 것을 고르시오.

①
②
③
④
⑤

M I am _____ _____ _____ _____. I don't have any fur or feathers. My skin is usually green or brown. I have _____ _____ _____ and a long tongue. I like to _____ _____ and eat insects. What am I?

02 ◀ 그림 묘사

대화를 듣고, 여자가 만든 케이크로 가장 적절한 것을 고르시오.

①
②
③
④
⑤

W Look at this cake! I _____ _____ _____.

M It's very nice. You wrote "Love Forever" on the top.

W That's right. I used liquid chocolate. And I put a flower _____ _____ _____ _____.

M It looks good. But why is there only one?

W I wanted to put a flower on the right side too. But _____ _____ _____ _____.

M That's okay. It's still awesome!

03 ◀ 날씨

다음을 듣고, 인천의 내일 오후 날씨로 가장 적절한 것을 고르시오.

①
②
③
④
⑤

W Here's tomorrow's weather. There will be snow in Seoul. But it will be sunny in Daegu. The day will _____ _____ _____ in Incheon, but it will be sunny in the afternoon. And in Busan, it will rain all day, so don't _____ _____ _____.

142

04 ◀ 의도

대화를 듣고, 남자가 한 마지막 말의
의도로 가장 적절한 것을 고르시오.

① 사과　　　② 승낙
③ 충고　　　④ 거절
⑤ 위로

M Is this your book?

W Oh! Actually, it's a library book. I _____ _____ _____.

M When did you borrow it?

W About a month ago.

M You should _____ _____ _____ to the library today.

05 ◀ 언급하지 않은 내용

다음을 듣고, 남자가 자신에 대해 언
급하지 <u>않은</u> 것을 고르시오.

① 이름　　　② 현재 거주지
③ 이사 온 이유　④ 장래 희망
⑤ 좋아하는 운동

M Hello. My name is Patrick. I moved here from Seoul because my father _____ _____. In my free time, I like keeping a blog. When _____ _____ _____, I want to be a writer. And _____ _____ _____ is soccer. I'm glad to meet everyone.

06 ◀ 시각

대화를 듣고, 두 사람이 만날 시각을
고르시오.

① 9:00 a.m.　② 10:00 a.m.
③ 11:00 a.m.　④ 12:00 p.m.
⑤ 1:00 p.m.

[Cell phone rings.]

W Hello?

M Hi. I'm calling from the _____ _____.

W Oh. You're coming tomorrow at 10:00 a.m., aren't you?

M Well, _____ _____ _____ _____ in the afternoon. So I want to come one hour earlier.

W That's fine. How long will it take?

M We can move everything _____ _____ _____.

W Great! See you tomorrow!

07 ◀ 장래 희망

대화를 듣고, 여자의 장래 희망으로
가장 적절한 것을 고르시오.

① 성우　　② 프로듀서
③ 아나운서　④ 작가
⑤ 기자

M I want to be an announcer someday. So I'm joining the school's
　 _____ _____ .

W Oh, let's _____ _____ !

M Do you want to be an announcer, too?

W No. I want to be a journalist.

M Then you should _____ _____ _____ at the school
　 magazine, instead.

W Oh! That's a great idea.

08 ◀ 심정

대화를 듣고, 남자의 심정으로 가장
적절한 것을 고르시오.

① curious　　② proud
③ pleased　　④ annoyed
⑤ relaxed

M I haven't been sleeping well these days. There's _____ _____
　 _____ from upstairs.

W Why? Are there kids running around?

M No, it's a dog. It _____ _____ _____ .

W Really? You should talk to your neighbors.

M I did that _____ _____ . But their dog still barks all the time!

09 ◀ 할 일

대화를 듣고, 여자가 대화 직후에 할
일로 가장 적절한 것을 고르시오.

① 서점 가기
② 옷 세탁하기
③ 책꽂이 주문하기
④ 세탁기 옮기기
⑤ 책 빼내기

W Are you busy?

M No. I just finished _____ _____ _____ . Do you need some
　 help?

W Yes. I want to _____ _____ _____ . But they're too heavy.

M I can help you move them. But you should remove all the books first. It
　 will _____ _____ _____ _____ .

W Okay. I'll do it right now.

144

10 ◀ 주제

대화를 듣고, 무엇에 관한 내용인지
가장 적절한 것을 고르시오.

① 방학 숙제
② 장학금 신청
③ 성적 향상 비법
④ 고등학교 진학
⑤ 온라인 강의 수강신청

W I heard _____ _____ _____ on the midterm exams. Congratulations!

M Thank you. I studied hard _____ _____ _____.

W How did you study?

M I took an online class. When I had a question, I _____ _____ _____.

W I should try that for the next exam.

11 ◀ 특정 정보

대화를 듣고, 여자가 이용할 교통수단
으로 가장 적절한 것을 고르시오.

① 지하철　　② 자전거
③ 버스　　　④ 기차
⑤ 자동차

M It's almost time to go home. Can I _____ _____ _____ the bus station?

W Actually, I'm not taking the bus today. _____ _____ _____ because of an accident.

M Oh. I can _____ _____ _____ _____ home if you'd like.

W I'll just ride a bike across the park to get home. I'd prefer to avoid the roads altogether.

12 ◀ 이유

대화를 듣고, 남자가 컴퓨터 회사에
전화한 이유로 가장 적절한 것을 고르
시오.

① 컴퓨터 속도가 느려서
② 컴퓨터에서 소음이 발생해서
③ 컴퓨터 전원이 켜지지 않아서
④ 컴퓨터가 바이러스에 감염되어서
⑤ 컴퓨터에서 소리가 나오지 않아서

[Telephone rings.]

W MG Computers. Can I help you?

M Hi. I bought one of your computers last week.

W I see. Is there _____ _____ _____ _____?

M It works very well. But it is _____ _____ _____ _____.

W Please bring it to the nearest service center.

M Okay.

13 ◀ 대화 장소

대화를 듣고, 두 사람이 대화하는 장소로 가장 적절한 곳을 고르시오.

① 호텔　　② 음식점
③ 아파트　④ 백화점
⑤ 식료품점

M Hello. Can I help you?

W Yes. Do you _____?

M Actually, we have two. They're both on the 3rd floor.

W Do they deliver?

M Well, _____ _____ _____ here?

W Yes. I'm in room 702.

M In that case, you can order room service _____ _____ _____

_____.

고난도

14 ◀ 위치

대화를 듣고, 남자가 찾고 있는 휴대 전화의 위치로 가장 알맞은 곳을 고르시오.

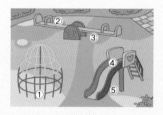

M Oh, I lost my cell phone! Can you help me find it?

W Sure. Did you look around the jungle gym?

M Yes, but there was nothing there.

W _____ _____ _____ by the see-saw for you.

M Did you find it?

W No. _____ _____ _____ go up the slide and check there? I saw that you were riding it.

M Okay. *[pause]* My cell phone isn't here either.

W Oh, look! It's _____ _____ _____!

M You're right! Thanks.

고난도

15 ◀ 부탁한 일

대화를 듣고, 여자가 남자에게 부탁한 일로 가장 적절한 것을 고르시오.

① 아침에 전화해주기
② 알람시계 맞춰놓기
③ 여행 일정 짜기
④ 숙소 예약하기
⑤ 해돋이 사진 찍어오기

[Cell phone rings.]

W Hello?

M Hi, it's Frank. Do you want to _____ _____ _____ together at the beach tomorrow?

W Oh, that sounds fun.

M Great! _____ _____ _____ _____ so we don't miss it.

W Sure. What time does the sun rise?

M At 6:35 a.m.

W That's so early. Can you call me at 5:00 a.m.? _____ _____ _____.

M Okay. I will.

16 ◄ 제안한 일

대화를 듣고, 여자가 남자에게 제안한 것으로 가장 적절한 것을 고르시오.

① 서평 검색하기
② 인터넷 서점 이용하기
③ 스마트폰 구입하기
④ 도서관 회원 가입하기
⑤ 전자책 이용하기

W You look bored, Mark. You should have brought a book to read.

M I like to read books, but they are _____ _____ _____ _____.

W Then why don't you try reading e-books? They _____ _____.

M Sounds like a great idea!

W Yeah! You can just _____ _____ onto your smartphone.

M Thank you for letting me know.

17 ◄ 한 일

대화를 듣고, 남자가 어제 한 일로 가장 적절한 것을 고르시오.

① 쇼핑하기
② 체스 게임하기
③ 동물원 가기
④ 컴퓨터 게임하기
⑤ 할머니 댁 가기

M Hi, Stella. What did you do yesterday?

W I went to the zoo. How about you?

M I visited my uncle's house.

W What did you do there?

M I _____ _____ with my cousin.

W Oh, _____ _____ _____ _____ _____?

M No. I couldn't _____ _____ _____ _____. It was fun, though.

18 ◄ 직업

대화를 듣고, 여자의 직업으로 가장 적절한 것을 고르시오.

① 교사   ② 배우
③ 디자이너   ④ 매표원
⑤ 출판사 직원

W Hi, Charlie. What's up?

M I'm not _____ _____ _____, but I'd like to write for the school newspaper.

W Great! You don't have to be _____ _____ _____ _____ to work for the newspaper.

M Really? I'm glad to hear that.

W We're meeting tomorrow at 4:00 p.m. _____ _____ _____ _____. Come join us!

19 ◀ 마지막 말에 대한 응답

대화를 듣고, 남자의 마지막 말에 이어질 여자의 말로 가장 적절한 것을 고르시오.

Woman: _____

① No. A repairman will fix the fence.
② Don't worry, honey. It wasn't your fault.
③ I'm sorry, but I don't have time right now.
④ Sure. Hand me the hammer and those nails.
⑤ Okay, I will pick you up after I'm finished.

M What are you doing, Mom?
W Do you remember when that car _____ _____ _____ the other day?
M Yes, of course I do.
W Well, I'm going to _____ _____ _____ _____ _____.
M Can I help you?
W _____

20 ◀ 마지막 말에 대한 응답

대화를 듣고, 남자의 마지막 말에 이어질 여자의 말로 가장 적절한 것을 고르시오.

Woman: _____

① You should leave now.
② That's strange. Do you know why?
③ Wow! No wonder you can't stay awake!
④ That's okay. I finished my homework earlier today.
⑤ Sorry, I didn't realize you had other plans already.

W Minsu, wake up! You _____ _____ again.
M Oh, I'm sorry.
W We need to _____ _____ _____ _____ by tonight.
M I know. But I'm really exhausted today.
W Why are you so tired? Did you study all night for an exam?
M No. Actually, I _____ _____ _____ _____ _____ at 1:00 a.m.
W _____

A

다음 영어 어휘나 표현의 뜻을 우리말로 쓰세요.

01 skin		**02** fall asleep	
03 noise		**04** bark	
05 fault		**06** broadcasting	
07 liquid		**08** tongue	
09 editor		**10** space	
11 feather		**12** journalist	
13 midterm exam		**14** traffic	
15 avoid		**16** bookshelf	

B

우리말에 맞는 영어 어휘나 표현을 [보기]에서 찾아 쓰세요.

보기	convenient	theater	oversleep	single	be supposed to-v
	all day	remove	realize	stay awake	set an alarm clock

01 온종일		**02** 깨닫다	
03 편리한		**04** 단 하나의	
05 극장		**06** 늦잠 자다	
07 치우다		**08** 자지 않고 깨어 있다	
09 ~하기로 되어 있다		**10** 알람시계를 맞추다	

01 다음을 듣고, 'this'가 가리키는 것으로 가장 적절한 것을 고르시오.

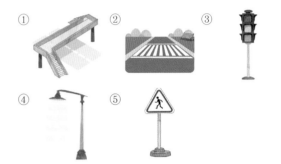

02 대화를 듣고, 두 사람이 구입할 애견 방석으로 가장 적절한 것을 고르시오.

03 다음을 듣고, 애틀랜타의 화요일 날씨로 가장 적절한 것을 고르시오.

04 대화를 듣고, 남자가 한 마지막 말의 의도로 가장 적절한 것을 고르시오.

① 감사   ② 거절   ③ 사과
④ 승낙   ⑤ 위로

05 다음을 듣고, 남자가 새 담임 교사에 대해 언급하지 않은 것을 고르시오.

① 이름   ② 담당 교과목   ③ 성격
④ 경력   ⑤ 거주지

06 대화를 듣고, 두 사람이 내일 만날 시각을 고르시오.

① 5:30 p.m.   ② 6:00 p.m.   ③ 6:30 p.m.
④ 7:00 p.m.   ⑤ 7:30 p.m.

07 대화를 듣고, 남자의 장래 희망으로 가장 적절한 것을 고르시오.

① 가수   ② 노래 강사   ③ 피아니스트
④ 작곡가   ⑤ 의상 디자이너

08 대화를 듣고, 여자의 심정으로 가장 적절한 것을 고르시오.

① 슬픔   ② 부러움   ③ 걱정스러움
④ 지루함   ⑤ 감동함

고난도

09 대화를 듣고, 여자가 대화 직후에 할 일로 가장 적절한 것을 고르시오.

① 영화 촬영하기   ② 촬영장 정리하기
③ 물 마시러 가기   ④ 화장실 가기
⑤ 인터뷰 기사 쓰기

고난도

10 대화를 듣고, 무엇에 관한 내용인지 가장 적절한 것을 고르시오.

① 내복 착용의 효과   ② 난방비 절감 요령
③ 적정 습도 유지 방법   ④ 겨울철 권장 실내 온도
⑤ 옷차림과 첫인상의 상관관계

11 대화를 듣고, 여자가 이용할 교통수단으로 가장 적절한 것을 고르시오.

① 버스   ② 기차   ③ 지하철
④ 자동차   ⑤ 자전거

🇬🇧
12 대화를 듣고, 여자가 여행을 즐기지 못한 이유로 가장 적절한 것을 고르시오.

① 날씨가 좋지 않아서   ② 휴대전화가 고장 나서
③ 숙소 시설이 열악해서   ④ 가족과 갈등이 생겨서
⑤ 몸 상태가 좋지 않아서

13 대화를 듣고, 두 사람이 대화하는 장소로 가장 적절한 곳을 고르시오.

① 미용실   ② 사진관   ③ 면접장
④ 교실   ⑤ 옷 가게

14 대화를 듣고, 꽃 가게의 위치로 가장 알맞은 곳을 고르시오.

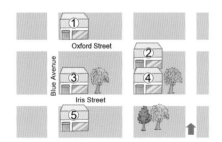

🇬🇧
15 대화를 듣고, 여자가 남자에게 부탁한 일로 가장 적절한 것을 고르시오.

① 개 산책시키기   ② 개 목욕 돕기
③ 동물병원 예약하기   ④ 욕조 골라주기
⑤ 개 사료 사 오기

🇬🇧
16 대화를 듣고, 여자가 남자에게 제안한 것으로 가장 적절한 것을 고르시오.

① 운동복 구입하기
② 헬스장 등록하기
③ 걷기 동호회 가입하기
④ 한 정거장 거리 걸어 다니기
⑤ 대중교통 이용하기

17 대화를 듣고, 두 사람이 읽고자 하는 책 종류를 고르시오.

① 역사 서적   ② 여행 서적   ③ 과학 서적
④ 아동 서적   ⑤ 예술 서적

18 대화를 듣고, 남자의 직업으로 가장 적절한 것을 고르시오.

① 지하철 기관사   ② 승무원   ③ 택시 운전사
④ 버스 운전사   ⑤ 공원 관리인

[19-20] 대화를 듣고, 여자의 마지막 말에 이어질 남자의 말로 가장 적절한 것을 고르시오.

19 Man: _____

① No, it's not available.
② Yes, that would be fine.
③ The rate is $120 a night.
④ The checkout time is 12:00 p.m.
⑤ It is served from 8:00 a.m. to 11:00 a.m.

고난도
20 Man: _____

① How many brothers do you have?
② I'm looking forward to seeing them.
③ Sorry. I don't have time to do something together today.
④ I'm sure that would make them really happy.
⑤ What do you and your friends like to do together?

DICTATION

일반 속도　빠른 속도

01 ◀ 지칭

다음을 듣고, 'this'가 가리키는 것으로 가장 적절한 것을 고르시오.

M You can find this on roads. _____ _____ _____ three colored lights: red, yellow, and green. Each color has _____ _____ _____. The red light means "stop," the yellow light means "_____ _____" and the green light means "go." What is this?

02 ◀ 그림 묘사

대화를 듣고, 두 사람이 구입할 애견 방석으로 가장 적절한 것을 고르시오.

W Hey John, let's get a new cushion for my puppy.

M That sounds like a great idea. There are a lot of cushions here.

W Which one _____ _____ _____ _____?

M How about this one? It's square and has a _____ _____.

W Well, I prefer the round one _____ _____ _____ _____ _____.

M Okay. Let's buy that one.

03 ◀ 날씨

다음을 듣고, 애틀랜타의 화요일 날씨로 가장 적절한 것을 고르시오.

W Good morning. Here is Atlanta's weather forecast. On Monday, we _____ _____ _____ throughout the day. On Tuesday, it will rain. If you planned to go on a picnic, you'd better _____ _____ until Wednesday. From Wednesday until Friday, it will be sunny.

04 ◀ 의도

대화를 듣고, 남자가 한 마지막 말의
의도로 가장 적절한 것을 고르시오.

① 감사   ② 거절
③ 사과   ④ 승낙
⑤ 위로

M Hi, Laura!

W Good morning, Bob. Tomorrow is _____ _____ _____ in New York, right?

M Yes, it is. My flight leaves at 8:00 a.m. tomorrow.

W I can _____ _____ _____ _____ to the airport if you want.

M That would be great. Thanks for _____ _____ _____.

05 ◀ 언급하지 않은 내용

다음을 듣고, 남자가 새 담임 교사에
대해 언급하지 <u>않은</u> 것을 고르시오.

① 이름   ② 담당 교과목
③ 성격   ④ 경력
⑤ 거주지

M Good morning, students. As you know, your new homeroom teacher will arrive tomorrow. Her name is Mrs. Baker. She will _____ _____. She is very _____ _____ _____. She has been teaching for fifteen years. I think you will all _____ _____ _____ from her.

06 ◀ 시각

대화를 듣고, 두 사람이 내일 만날 시
각을 고르시오.

① 5:30 p.m.   ② 6:00 p.m.
③ 6:30 p.m.   ④ 7:00 p.m.
⑤ 7:30 p.m.

M Sarah, can you still _____ _____ _____?

W We have plans for tonight?

M Yes. You suggested that we _____ _____ _____ at 6:30.

W Oh, I forgot. I'm sorry. How about tomorrow instead?

M All right. So, are you okay with 6:30?

W How about 30 minutes later? I leave work at 6:00, but there will be _____ _____ _____ _____.

M Sure.

W Where are you going, Tom?

M Hi, Jane. I'm _____ _____ _____ to my singing lessons.

W I didn't know you liked singing. Do you want to _____ _____ _____?

M Not really. My dream is to be a singing teacher.

W Oh, wow. Maybe you could teach me _____ _____ sometime!

M Your phone is vibrating, Ashley.

W Oh, it's a text message from my mom.

M _____ _____ _____ _____?

W She said that she's _____ _____ _____ for getting a job.

M That's very sweet of her.

W I know! She also wrote that she's lucky to _____ _____ _____ like me.

고난도
09 ◀ 할 일

대화를 듣고, 여자가 대화 직후에 할 일로 가장 적절한 것을 고르시오.
① 영화 촬영하기
② 촬영장 정리하기
③ 물 마시러 가기
④ 화장실 가기
⑤ 인터뷰 기사 쓰기

W Thank you for making time for this interview, Mr. Lawrence.

M It's my pleasure.

W Can you tell me about your new movie?

M Sure. I play the main character. He _____ _____ _____ in an accident.

W Wow, that's interesting. It's _____ _____ _____ _____, isn't it?

M Yes, it is.

W Sorry, but _____ _____ _____ if I get a drink of water?

M That's fine. Go ahead.

고난도

10 ◀ 주제

대화를 듣고, 무엇에 관한 내용인지 가장 적절한 것을 고르시오.

① 내복 착용의 효과
② 난방비 절감 요령
③ 적정 습도 유지 방법
④ 겨울철 권장 실내 온도
⑤ 옷차림과 첫인상의 상관관계

M You look cold, Tiffany!

W I am. I bought a new winter coat, but it doesn't _____ _____ _____ _____.

M Have you tried wearing long underwear?

W No, I haven't.

M You should! _____ _____ _____.

W Oh, does it?

M Yes. It keeps you warm by trapping your body heat. So you can also _____ _____ _____ on heating costs.

11 ◀ 특정 정보

대화를 듣고, 여자가 이용할 교통수단으로 가장 적절한 것을 고르시오.

① 버스   ② 기차
③ 지하철   ④ 자동차
⑤ 자전거

M Why are you _____ _____ _____, Natalie?

W Mom can't give me a ride to school today.

M Oh, that's right. Are you going to _____ _____ _____?

W No, I'll take the bus. It takes too long by subway. I would _____ _____ _____ three times.

M I see.

12 ◀ 이유

대화를 듣고, 여자가 여행을 즐기지 못한 이유로 가장 적절한 것을 고르시오.

① 날씨가 좋지 않아서
② 휴대전화가 고장 나서
③ 숙소 시설이 열악해서
④ 가족과 갈등이 생겨서
⑤ 몸 상태가 좋지 않아서

M Did you _____ _____ _____ _____ to Seoul last weekend, Christine?

W No, it was terrible!

M What happened? Didn't you like your hotel?

W My hotel was terrific! But I _____ _____ _____ on the first day of my visit.

M Oh, no! What did you do after _____ _____ _____?

W I just played games on my smartphone all day.

대화를 듣고, 두 사람이 대화하는 장소로 가장 적절한 곳을 고르시오.

① 미용실 ② 사진관
③ 면접장 ④ 교실
⑤ 옷 가게

M Good morning. What can I do for you today?

W I need some small photos _____ _____ _____.

M Okay. It will be $20 for ten photos.

W That's fine. Do you have a black jacket? I want to _____ _____ _____ _____ _____.

M Sure. There are several options _____ _____ _____. I'll show you.

W Thanks!

14 ◂ 위치

대화를 듣고, 꽃 가게의 위치로 가장 알맞은 곳을 고르시오.

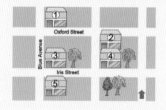

M Megan, do you know _____ _____ _____ the flower shop?

W Oh, it's _____ _____ _____. Go straight one block and then turn left on Iris Street.

M Turn left?

W Yes. Then go straight for two blocks. It will be _____ _____ _____.

M Got it. Thanks for your help!

15 ◂ 부탁한 일

대화를 듣고, 여자가 남자에게 부탁한 일로 가장 적절한 것을 고르시오.

① 개 산책시키기
② 개 목욕 돕기
③ 동물병원 예약하기
④ 욕조 골라주기
⑤ 개 사료 사 오기

W Greg, does your dog _____ _____ _____?

M Yes, she loves it. Why are you asking?

W My father brought a dog yesterday. I tried to wash him, but I couldn't.

M Why? Did he _____ _____?

W Yes! He also _____ _____ _____. Could you help me give him a bath?

M Sure, no problem.

16 ◀ 제안한 일

대회를 듣고, 여자가 남자에게 제안한 것으로 가장 적절한 것을 고르시오.

① 운동복 구입하기
② 헬스장 등록하기
③ 걷기 동호회 가입하기
④ 한 정거장 거리 걸어 다니기
⑤ 대중교통 이용하기

M Tiffany, do you think that I've _____ _____ _____?

W Yes, I think so. Your clothes _____ _____ _____ _____.

M I know. I should start exercising, but I don't have time to go to the gym.

W Then why don't you _____ _____ _____ _____ a stop early and walk home every day?

M I'll try that!

17 ◀ 특정 정보

대회를 듣고, 두 사람이 읽고자 하는 책 종류를 고르시오.

① 역사 서적   ② 여행 서적
③ 과학 서적   ④ 아동 서적
⑤ 예술 서적

M What book _____ _____ _____ _____ _____ next for our book club?

W I want to read a book about history or science.

M But we have already read those kinds of books. How about a _____ _____ _____ _____?

W What do you _____ _____ _____?

M How about a children's novel? I heard *The Giver* won several children's book awards.

W That sounds great.

18 ◀ 직업

대회를 듣고, 남자의 직업으로 가장 적절한 것을 고르시오.

① 지하철 기관사 ② 승무원
③ 택시 운전사   ④ 버스 운전사
⑤ 공원 관리인

M Good morning. _____ _____ _____ like to go?

W Central Park, please. How long will it take?

M With this traffic, _____ _____ _____ about forty minutes.

W And how much will it be?

M About $50. But it _____ _____ _____.

W All right. That's fine.

19 ◀ 마지막 말에 대한 응답

대화를 듣고, 여자의 마지막 말에 이어질 남자의 말로 가장 적절한 것을 고르시오.

Man: _____

① No, it's not available.
② Yes, that would be fine.
③ The rate is $120 a night.
④ The checkout time is 12:00 p.m.
⑤ It is served from 8:00 a.m. to 11:00 a.m.

W _____ _____ _____ _____ _____ for tonight?

M What kind of room would you like?

W A single room, please. Is breakfast included?

M All of our rooms _____ _____ _____.

W Okay. Can you tell me _____ _____ _____ _____?

M _____

고난도

20 ◀ 마지막 말에 대한 응답

대화를 듣고, 여자의 마지막 말에 이어질 남자의 말로 가장 적절한 것을 고르시오.

Man: _____

① How many brothers do you have?
② I'm looking forward to seeing them.
③ Sorry. I don't have time to do something together today.
④ I'm sure that would make them really happy.
⑤ What do you and your friends like to do together?

W What are you doing, Sean?

M I'm _____ _____ my New Year's resolutions.

W Oh, what are they?

M I want to drink less soda and _____ _____ _____.

W Sounds wonderful!

M How about you? Do you have any New Year's resolutions?

W I want to spend more time with my family. Everyone is busy with school and work, so it's _____ _____ _____ _____ together.

M _____

A 다음 영어 어휘나 표현의 뜻을 우리말로 쓰세요.

01 include

02 memory

03 resume

04 trap

05 soda

06 suggest

07 award

08 postpone

09 gain weight

10 homeroom teacher

11 sometime

12 take a bath

13 intelligent

14 text message

15 meaning

16 be proud of

B 우리말에 맞는 영어 어휘나 표현을 [보기]에서 찾아 쓰세요.

| 보기 | rate | tight | transfer | body heat | have in mind |
| | resolution | vibrate | helpful | be based on | heating cost |

01 난방비

02 꽉 조이는

03 ~에 기반을 두다

04 결심

05 기꺼이 돕는

06 환승하다

07 요금

08 체열

09 진동하다

10 ~을 염두에 두다

01 다음을 듣고, 'this'가 가리키는 것으로 가장 적절한 것을 고르시오.

①  ② ③

④   ⑤

02 대화를 듣고, 남자가 만든 화분으로 가장 적절한 것을 고르시오.

①   ②   ③

④   ⑤

03 다음을 듣고, 내일의 날씨로 가장 적절한 것을 고르시오.

①   ②   ③

④   ⑤

04 대화를 듣고, 여자가 한 마지막 말의 의도로 가장 적절한 것을 고르시오.

① 승낙   ② 충고   ③ 거절
④ 위로   ⑤ 칭찬

05 다음을 듣고, 여자가 스케이트화에 대해 언급하지 않은 것을 고르시오.

① 색상   ② 소재   ③ 사용 권장 대상
④ 가격   ⑤ 할인 행사 기간

06 대화를 듣고, 두 사람이 만날 시각을 고르시오.

① 3:30 p.m.   ② 4:00 p.m.   ③ 4:30 p.m.
④ 5:00 p.m.   ⑤ 5:30 p.m.

07 대화를 듣고, 여자의 장래 희망으로 가장 적절한 것을 고르시오.

① 건축가   ② 승무원   ③ 조종사
④ 여행 가이드   ⑤ 작곡가

08 대화를 듣고, 남자의 심정으로 가장 적절한 것을 고르시오.

① shy   ② excited   ③ indifferent
④ jealous   ⑤ nervous

09 대화를 듣고, 여자가 대화 직후에 할 일로 가장 적절한 것을 고르시오.

① 감기약 복용하기   ② 휴식 취하기
③ 병문안 가기   ④ 진료 예약하기
⑤ 약국 가기

10 대화를 듣고, 무엇에 관한 내용인지 가장 적절한 것을 고르시오.

① 청소도구 구입하기   ② 옷장 정리하기
③ 침실 청소하기   ④ 침대 설치하기
⑤ 집안일 배분하기

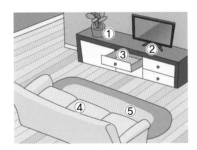

11 대화를 듣고, 두 사람이 이용할 교통수단으로 가장 적절한 것을 고르시오.

① 버스 　　② 지하철 　　③ 자전거
④ 자동차 　　⑤ 오토바이

12 대화를 듣고, 남자가 살사춤을 배우는 이유로 가장 적절한 것을 고르시오.

① 운동을 위해서
② 여자친구가 함께 배우길 원해서
③ 새로운 사람들을 만나기 위해서
④ 장기자랑에 대비하기 위해서
⑤ 내성적인 성격을 극복하기 위해서

13 대화를 듣고, 두 사람이 대화하는 장소로 가장 적절한 곳을 고르시오.

① 은행 　　② 경찰서 　　③ 버스 정류장
④ 영화관 　　⑤ 자동차 정비소

고난도
14 대화를 듣고, 남자가 찾고 있는 리모컨의 위치로 가장 알맞은 곳을 고르시오.

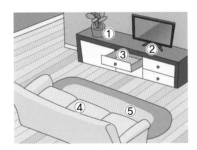

15 대화를 듣고, 남자가 여자에게 부탁한 일로 가장 적절한 것을 고르시오.

① 학교에 일찍 오기 　　② 자리 바꿔주기
③ 남자 앞자리에 앉기 　　④ 말한 내용 상기시켜주기
⑤ 칠판 필기 내용 읽어주기

16 대화를 듣고, 여자가 남자에게 제안한 것으로 가장 적절한 것을 고르시오.

① 축구 경기 관람하기 　　② 축구 규칙 익히기
③ 학교 축구부 가입하기 　　④ 옛 친구들에게 연락하기
⑤ 교내 응원단 가입하기

고난도
17 대화를 듣고, 남자가 지난 일요일에 한 일로 가장 적절한 것을 고르시오.

① 농구하기 　　② 공연 관람하기
③ 운동 경기 관람하기 　　④ 오디션 참가하기
⑤ 생일 파티에 가기

18 대화를 듣고, 여자의 직업으로 가장 적절한 것을 고르시오.

① 간호사 　　② 조련사 　　③ 약사
④ 수의사 　　⑤ 미용사

[19-20] 대화를 듣고, 남자의 마지막 말에 이어질 여자의 말로 가장 적절한 것을 고르시오.

19 Woman: _____

① That's not mine.
② It stopped raining.
③ What does it look like?
④ I looked everywhere for it.
⑤ It's okay. I'll buy another one.

고난도
20 Woman: _____

① I can pick up the pizza.
② Either one would be fine.
③ I can pay for it. It's my treat!
④ There is no soda in the fridge.
⑤ No, thanks. It has too much sugar in it.

DICTATION

정답 단서 오답 함정

일반 속도   빠른 속도

01 ◀ 지칭

다음을 듣고, 'this'가 가리키는 것으로 가장 적절한 것을 고르시오.

① ②
③ ④
⑤

W You _____ _____ _____ or hat on this. Usually, you can find this near a door. This is a tall pole. Hooks _____ _____ _____ _____. This is usually made of metal, wood, or plastic. What is this?

02 ◀ 그림 묘사

대화를 듣고, 남자가 만든 화분으로 가장 적절한 것을 고르시오

① ②
③ ④
⑤

M Do you like my flower pot? I _____ _____ _____ _____ _____.

W It's great! I like the ladybug on the flower.

M Thanks. I wanted to draw a bumblebee instead, but it was too hard.

W Are you going to _____ _____ _____ _____?

M No. I'm going to give it to my friend.

03 ◀ 날씨

다음을 듣고, 내일의 날씨로 가장 적절한 것을 고르시오.

① ②
③ ④
⑤

M Good morning! This is Anthony Brown with the weather. It will snow all day today, so _____ _____ on the roads! Tomorrow, it will be very foggy but the _____ _____ _____. The day after tomorrow, there is a 30% _____ _____ _____.

04 ◀ 의도

대화를 듣고, 여자가 한 마지막 말의
의도로 가장 적절한 것을 고르시오.

① 승낙　　　　② 충고
③ 거절　　　　④ 위로
⑤ 칭찬

M Hi, Beth. Are you ＿＿＿＿＿＿ ＿＿＿＿＿＿ ＿＿＿＿＿＿ this weekend?

W Yes, I am. ＿＿＿＿＿＿ ＿＿＿＿＿＿ ＿＿＿＿＿＿!

M Who is going to take care of your dog?

W I'm going to ask my best friend to do it. Why?

M Oh. Could I ＿＿＿＿＿＿ ＿＿＿＿＿＿ ＿＿＿＿＿＿ ＿＿＿＿＿＿ instead? I really love your dog.

W Sure! Thanks a lot.

05 ◀ 언급하지 않은 내용

다음을 듣고, 여자가 스케이트화에 대
해 언급하지 <u>않은</u> 것을 고르시오.

① 색상　　　　② 소재
③ 사용 권장 대상　④ 가격
⑤ 할인 행사 기간

W We're introducing a new style of ice skates today. They are available in white, black, and green. Only the softest leather ＿＿＿＿＿ ＿＿＿＿＿ ＿＿＿＿＿ ＿＿＿＿＿ these skates. They are perfect for beginner figure skaters. ＿＿＿＿＿ ＿＿＿＿＿ ＿＿＿＿＿ ＿＿＿＿＿ ＿＿＿＿＿ $199, you should buy a pair today!

06 ◀ 시각

대화를 듣고, 두 사람이 만날 시각을
고르시오.

① 3:30 p.m.　　② 4:00 p.m.
③ 4:30 p.m.　　④ 5:00 p.m.
⑤ 5:30 p.m.

W Hey! Can you still ＿＿＿＿＿ ＿＿＿＿＿ ＿＿＿＿＿ after school today?

M Definitely. We should study for the history test.

W Great. Let's meet at 4:00 p.m.

M I can't. I ＿＿＿＿＿ ＿＿＿＿＿ ＿＿＿＿＿ at 3:30 p.m. Can we meet at 5:30 p.m.?

W No problem. I'll see you ＿＿＿＿＿ ＿＿＿＿＿ ＿＿＿＿＿ the library.

M All right. See you then.

대화를 듣고, 여자의 장래 희망으로
가장 적절한 것을 고르시오.

① 건축가　　② 승무원
③ 조종사　　④ 여행 가이드
⑤ 작곡가

M Molly, I liked your _____ _____ _____ _____ to Italy.

W Thanks! I think the topic is really interesting.

M You _____ _____ _____.

W I do. I want to travel around the world someday.

M You should become a pilot!

W No, I don't want to fly planes. I want to _____ _____ _____ _____ the passengers by serving them food and drinks.

08 ◀ 심정

대화를 듣고, 남자의 심정으로 가장
적절한 것을 고르시오.

① shy　　　② excited
③ indifferent　④ jealous
⑤ nervous

W Hi, Tony. Did you have a good day at school?

M I did! I _____ _____ _____!

W What is it?

M I _____ _____ _____ _____ on my Spanish test!

W That's wonderful! I knew you could do it.

M Thanks!

09 ◀ 할 일

대화를 듣고, 여자가 대화 직후에 할
일로 가장 적절한 것을 고르시오.

① 감기약 복용하기
② 휴식 취하기
③ 병문안 가기
④ 진료 예약하기
⑤ 약국 가기

M Are you okay, Diane? You look tired.

W No, I'm sick. I _____ _____ _____ _____ and a sore throat.

M I'm sorry to hear that. Did you take some medicine?

W I took some this morning, but it didn't help.

M Why don't you _____ _____ _____ _____?

W Yeah… I should _____ _____ _____ now.

10 ◀ 주제

대화를 듣고, 무엇에 관한 내용인지 가장 적절한 것을 고르시오.

① 청소도구 구입하기
② 옷장 정리하기
③ 침실 청소하기
④ 침대 설치하기
⑤ 집안일 배분하기

W Oh my gosh! Your bedroom _____ _____ _____. You promised me that you would clean it.
M I know. Sorry, Mom. I'll clean it right now.
W Can you start by _____? They're all over the floor.
M Okay. I'll make my bed and _____ _____ _____ after that.
W Great.

11 ◀ 특정 정보

대화를 듣고, 두 사람이 이용할 교통수단으로 가장 적절한 것을 고르시오.

① 버스 ② 지하철
③ 자전거 ④ 자동차
⑤ 오토바이

M Kelly, is that your science project? It looks big and heavy.
W Yes, it is. _____ _____ _____.
M Can you take it on the bus _____ _____?
W Actually, I was wondering if you could give me a ride.
M My car broke down yesterday. Let's _____ _____ _____ _____.
W Okay.

12 ◀ 이유

대화를 듣고, 남자가 살사춤을 배우는 이유로 가장 적절한 것을 고르시오.

① 운동을 위해서
② 여자친구가 함께 배우길 원해서
③ 새로운 사람들을 만나기 위해서
④ 장기자랑에 대비하기 위해서
⑤ 내성적인 성격을 극복하기 위해서

W What are you doing tonight, Cory?
M I'm _____ _____ _____ _____. It starts at 7:00 p.m.
W That's great! Are you taking it _____ _____?
M No. My girlfriend wants me to take the class with her.
W Wow, I'm sure that you'll _____ _____ _____ _____!

W Hello, sir. How may I help you?

M Can I _____ _____ _____ _____, please?

W Okay. Is there anything else I can do for you?

M I also need a new debit card.

W Sure. Please _____ _____ _____ _____ first.

M Okay. _____ _____ _____ _____ _____ to get the card?

W It will take three or four days.

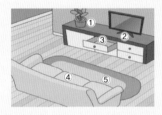
M Mom, do you know _____ _____ _____ _____ _____?

W It's always by the plant or in front of the TV, you know.

M But it's not in either of those places.

W _____ _____ _____ _____ in the drawer, then?

M There's nothing in the drawer.

W Hmm… Did you look on the sofa?

M Oh, I found it! It's on the rug. It _____ _____ _____ _____ the sofa.

15 ◀ 부탁한 일

대화를 듣고, 남자가 여자에게 부탁한 일로 가장 적절한 것을 고르시오.

① 학교에 일찍 오기
② 자리 바꿔주기
③ 남자 앞자리에 앉기
④ 말한 내용 상기시켜주기
⑤ 칠판 필기 내용 읽어주기

M Hi, Mrs. O'Brien.

W Hello, Max. Do you need something?

M Can I _____ _____ _____? I need to sit closer to the board.

W Oh, I'm sorry. I forgot that you _____ _____ _____ _____ very well. Can you _____ _____ _____ tomorrow? I'll find a new seat for you then.

M Okay. Thank you.

16 ◀ 제안한 일

대화를 듣고, 여자가 남자에게 제안한 것으로 가장 적절한 것을 고르시오.

① 축구 경기 관람하기
② 축구 규칙 익히기
③ 학교 축구부 가입하기
④ 옛 친구들에게 연락하기
⑤ 교내 응원단 가입하기

W Have you _____ _____ _____ at your new school yet, Jake?

M Not yet. I'm too shy.

W Making new friends is always difficult.

M My old friends and I _____ _____ _____ _____. I miss them.

W Why don't you _____ _____ _____ _____ _____? You can meet new people that way.

M Sounds great!

고난도

17 ◀ 한 일

대화를 듣고, 남자가 지난 일요일에 한 일로 가장 적절한 것을 고르시오.

① 농구하기
② 공연 관람하기
③ 운동 경기 관람하기
④ 오디션 참가하기
⑤ 생일 파티에 가기

W Hi, Jason. Why didn't you come to Emma's party last Sunday?

M I really wanted to go. But I just _____ _____ _____.

W Ah, now I remember. You said you _____ _____ _____ _____, didn't you?

M Well, actually, that was last Friday.

W Then what did you do?

M I _____ _____ a dance audition.

W Oh, that's so cool!

18 ◀ 직업

대화를 듣고, 여자의 직업으로 가장 적절한 것을 고르시오.

① 간호사　　② 조련사
③ 약사　　　④ 수의사
⑤ 미용사

W Hello. How may I help you?

M I made an appointment for my dog, Paris. She _____ _____ _____.

W Please come into my office. Does she _____ _____ _____?

M She scratches a lot. I think she has dry skin.

W Let me see. [pause] She has fleas. You need to _____ _____ _____ _____ with this shampoo.

M Okay. Thank you.

대화를 듣고, 남자의 마지막 말에 이어질 여자의 말로 가장 적절한 것을 고르시오.

Woman: _____

① That's not mine.
② It stopped raining.
③ What does it look like?
④ I looked everywhere for it.
⑤ It's okay. I'll buy another one.

M Haley, where is your umbrella?

W Oh, no! I guess _____ _____ _____.

M Where did you have it last?

W I had it with me while I was _____ _____ _____ _____ at the bus station.

M Oh, you probably left it there. You should go back and _____ _____ _____.

W _____

고난도

20 ◀ 마지막 말에 대한 응답

대화를 듣고, 남자의 마지막 말에 이어질 여자의 말로 가장 적절한 것을 고르시오.

Woman: _____

① I can pick up the pizza.
② Either one would be fine.
③ I can pay for it. It's my treat!
④ There is no soda in the fridge.
⑤ No, thanks. It has too much sugar in it.

M I'm going to _____ _____ _____ _____ _____. What would you like on it?

W Sausage and pepperoni, please. Those are my favorite toppings.

M But _____ _____ _____. Could you pick something else?

W Okay. What about tomatoes and spinach?

M Sure. _____ _____ _____ some soda too?

W _____

6회 어휘·표현 다지기

실전 모의고사

A

다음 영어 어휘나 표현의 뜻을 우리말로 쓰세요.

01 speech

02 sweep

03 medicine

04 promise

05 perfect score

06 leather

07 pole

08 flower pot

09 indifferent

10 scratch

11 vegetarian

12 passenger

13 someday

14 ladybug

15 by oneself

16 have a runny nose

B

우리말에 맞는 영어 어휘나 표현을 [보기]에서 찾아 쓰세요.

| 보기 | due | stick out | definitely | remote control | make one's bed |
| | mess | checkup | break down | participate in | have a sore throat |

01 툭 튀어나오다

02 ~에 참가하다

03 엉망인 상태

04 그렇고말고

05 리모컨

06 잠자리를 정돈하다

07 목이 아프다

08 고장 나다

09 건강진단

10 ~하기로 예정된[되어 있는]

점수   / 20문항

일반 속도

빠른 속도

01 다음을 듣고, 'this'가 가리키는 것으로 가장 적절한 것을 고르시오.

05 다음을 듣고, 여자가 자신에 대해 언급하지 않은 것을 고르시오.

① 이름   ② 직업   ③ 고향
④ 취미   ⑤ 반려동물

02 대화를 듣고, 남자가 만든 생일 카드로 가장 적절한 것을 고르시오.

06 대화를 듣고, 두 사람이 만날 시각을 고르시오.

① 6:10 p.m.   ② 6:20 p.m.   ③ 6:50 p.m.
④ 8:00 p.m.   ⑤ 8:20 p.m.

07 대화를 듣고, 여자의 장래 희망으로 가장 적절한 것을 고르시오.

① 여행가   ② 사진작가   ③ 모델
④ 화가   ⑤ 미술교사

08 대화를 듣고, 여자의 심정으로 가장 적절한 것을 고르시오.

① 부끄러움   ② 걱정스러움   ③ 실망스러움
④ 무관심함   ⑤ 화남

03 다음을 듣고, 베이징의 오늘 날씨로 가장 적절한 것을 고르시오.

09 대화를 듣고, 남자가 대화 직후에 할 일로 가장 적절한 것을 고르시오.

① 영화제 참석하기   ② 영화표 환불하기
③ 영화 시간 변경하기   ④ 영화표 예매하기
⑤ 영화평 작성하기

04 대화를 듣고, 여자가 한 마지막 말의 의도로 가장 적절한 것을 고르시오.

① 거절   ② 핀잔   ③ 격려
④ 사과   ⑤ 동의

10 대화를 듣고, 무엇에 관한 내용인지 가장 적절한 것을 고르시오.

① 온실 효과   ② 식물 재배   ③ 대기 오염
④ 집들이 선물   ⑤ 유기농 채소

11 대화를 듣고, 여자가 이용할 교통수단으로 가장 적절한 것을 고르시오.

① 버스   ② 비행기   ③ 기차
④ 지하철   ⑤ 자동차

12 대화를 듣고, 남자가 어제 야구 연습에 오지 못한 이유로 가장 적절한 것을 고르시오.

① 여행을 가서
② 병문안을 가서
③ 병원 진료를 받아서
④ 할아버지 댁에 다녀와서
⑤ 가족 행사에 참여해서

13 대화를 듣고, 두 사람이 대화하는 장소로 가장 적절한 곳을 고르시오.

① 카페   ② 음식점   ③ 도서관
④ 영화관   ⑤ 동물원

14 대화를 듣고, 제과점의 위치로 가장 알맞은 곳을 고르시오.

15 대화를 듣고, 여자가 남자에게 부탁한 일로 가장 적절한 것을 고르시오.

① 시계 건전지 교체하기   ② 버스표 예매하기
③ 샌드위치 만들어주기   ④ 아침에 깨워주기
⑤ 해변에 태워다 주기

16 대화를 듣고, 여자가 남자에게 제안한 것으로 가장 적절한 것을 고르시오.

① 함께 숙제하기   ② 친구들과 농구하기
③ 농구 경기 보러 가기   ④ TV 프로그램 함께 보기
⑤ 집으로 친구들 초대하기

17 대화를 듣고, 여자가 구입할 것을 고르시오.

① 커피   ② 케이크   ③ 쿠키
④ 초콜릿   ⑤ 아이스크림

18 대화를 듣고, 여자의 직업으로 가장 적절한 것을 고르시오.

① 영화배우   ② 미용사   ③ 헬스 트레이너
④ 수영선수   ⑤ 의상 디자이너

[19-20] 대화를 듣고, 여자의 마지막 말에 이어질 남자의 말로 가장 적절한 것을 고르시오.

19 Man: _____

① Let me help you.
② When is your project due?
③ Okay, thanks for your advice.
④ There are five people on my team.
⑤ I don't know what's going on here.

20 Man: _____

① I'm afraid I can't.
② It will not take long.
③ From 6:00 p.m. to 8:00 p.m.
④ I took violin lessons for five years.
⑤ I don't like playing music that much.

일반 속도   빠른 속도

01 다음을 듣고, 'this'가 가리키는 것으로 가장 적절한 것을 고르시오.

① ② ③

④ ⑤

02 대화를 듣고, 여자가 찾고 있는 목도리로 가장 적절한 것을 고르시오.

① ② ③

④ ⑤

03 다음을 듣고, 오늘 오후의 날씨로 가장 적절한 것을 고르시오.

① ② ③

④ ⑤

04 대화를 듣고, 남자가 한 마지막 말의 의도로 가장 적절한 것을 고르시오.

① 칭찬   ② 거절   ③ 축하
④ 위로   ⑤ 승낙

05 다음을 듣고, 여자가 자신에 대해 언급하지 <u>않은</u> 것을 고르시오.

① 살던 곳   ② 나이   ③ 형제자매
④ 취미   ⑤ 좋아하는 음식

06 대화를 듣고, 두 사람이 만날 시각을 고르시오.

① 5:00 p.m.   ② 5:30 p.m.   ③ 6:00 p.m.
④ 6:30 p.m.   ⑤ 8:30 p.m.

07 대화를 듣고, 남자의 장래 희망으로 가장 적절한 것을 고르시오.

① 댄서   ② 가수   ③ 교사
④ 배우   ⑤ 코미디언

08 대화를 듣고, 남자의 심정으로 가장 적절한 것을 고르시오.

① angry   ② happy   ③ peaceful
④ bored   ⑤ proud

09 대화를 듣고, 여자가 대화 직후에 할 일로 가장 적절한 것을 고르시오.

① 음식점에 전화하기   ② 예약 취소하기
③ 메뉴 고르기   ④ 음식점 검색하기
⑤ 식탁 주문하기

10 대화를 듣고, 무엇에 관한 내용인지 가장 적절한 것을 고르시오.

① 주차 단속   ② 교통사고
③ 어린이 보호구역   ④ 통학시간
⑤ 무단횡단

11 대화를 듣고, 남자가 퇴근 후에 이용할 교통수단으로 가장 적절한 것을 고르시오.

① 지하철　　② 자전거　　③ 자동차
④ 기차　　　⑤ 버스

12 대화를 듣고, 남자가 망토를 만들고 있는 이유로 가장 적절한 것을 고르시오.

① 가장무도회에 쓰기 위해서
② 교내 연극에 쓰기 위해서
③ 마술 공연에 쓰기 위해서
④ 핼러윈 파티에 쓰기 위해서
⑤ 수업 과제를 하기 위해서

13 대화를 듣고, 두 사람이 대화하는 장소로 가장 적절한 곳을 고르시오.

① 공항　　　② 호텔　　　③ 가방 가게
④ 헬스장　　⑤ 버스 정류장

14 대화를 듣고, 남자가 찾고 있는 사탕의 위치로 가장 알맞은 곳을 고르시오.

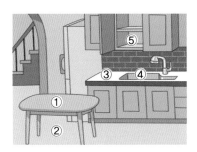

15 대화를 듣고, 여자가 남자에게 부탁한 일로 가장 적절한 것을 고르시오.

① 잔디 깎기　　　② 숙제 도와주기
③ 역사 강의하기　④ 숙제 발표하기
⑤ 저녁 식사 준비하기

16 대화를 듣고, 남자가 여자에게 제안한 것으로 가장 적절한 것을 고르시오.

① 딸에게 전화하기　　② 약 사오기
③ 병원 가기　　　　　④ 학부모와 상담하기
⑤ 휴식 취하기

17 대화를 듣고, 두 사람이 주말에 할 일로 가장 적절한 것을 고르시오.

① 꽃 사진 찍기　　② 암벽 등반하기
③ 사진 강의 듣기　④ 케이블카 타기
⑤ 꽃꽂이 배우기

18 대화를 듣고, 남자의 직업으로 가장 적절한 것을 고르시오.

① 부동산 중개업자　　② 보석 가공사
③ 옷 가게 점원　　　　④ 인테리어 디자이너
⑤ 가구 판매원

[19-20] 대화를 듣고, 남자의 마지막 말에 이어질 여자의 말로 가장 적절한 것을 고르시오.

19 Woman: _____

① What a shame!
② That's a good idea.
③ I'm glad to hear that.
④ Thank you for coming.
⑤ They're uncomfortable.

20 Woman: _____

① That's correct.
② It's too expensive.
③ I prefer watching movies.
④ Actually, it is a library book.
⑤ Reading books is my favorite hobby.

MEMO

MEMO

지은이

NE능률 영어교육연구소

NE능률 영어교육연구소는 혁신적이며 효율적인 영어 교재를 개발하고
영어 학습의 질을 한 단계 높이고자 노력하는 NE능률의 연구조직입니다.

1316 Listening 〈Level 1〉

펴 낸 이	주민홍
펴 낸 곳	서울특별시 마포구 월드컵북로 396(상암동) 누리꿈스퀘어 비즈니스타워 10층
	㈜ NE능률 (우편번호 03925)
펴 낸 날	2024년 1월 5일 개정판 제1쇄 발행
	2024년 9월 15일 제5쇄
전 화	02 2014 7114
팩 스	02 3142 0356
홈 페 이 지	www.neungyule.com
등 록 번 호	제1-68호
I S B N	979-11-253-4290-8
정 가	14,000원

NE 능률

고객센터

교재 내용 문의 : contact.nebooks.co.kr (별도의 가입 절차 없이 작성 가능)
제품 구매, 교환, 불량, 반품 문의 : 02-2014-7114
☎ 전화문의는 본사 업무시간 중에만 가능합니다.

NE능률 교재 MAP

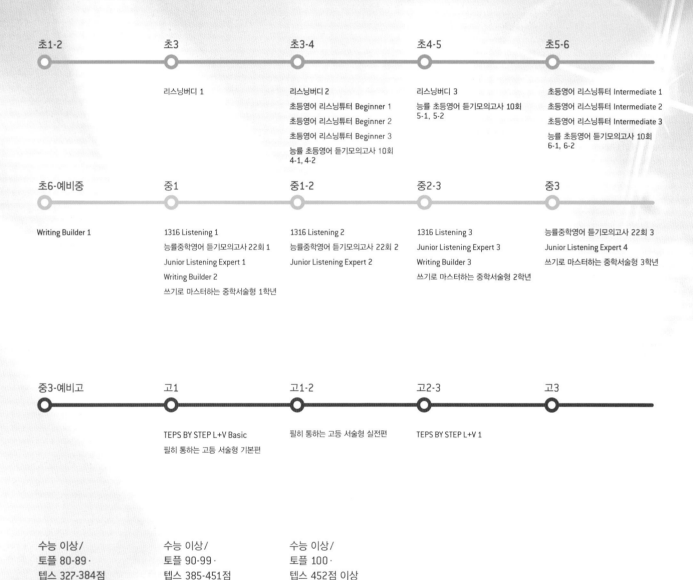

아래 교재 MAP을 참고하여 본인의 현재 혹은 목표 수준에 따라 교재를 선택하세요.
NE능률 교재들과 함께 영어실력을 쑥쑥~ 올려보세요!
MP3 등 교재 부가 학습 서비스 및 자세한 교재 정보는 www.nebooks.co.kr 에서 확인하세요.

듣기
말하기
쓰기

초1-2	초3	초3-4	초4-5	초5-6
	리스닝버디 1	리스닝버디 2 초등영어 리스닝튜터 Beginner 1 초등영어 리스닝튜터 Beginner 2 초등영어 리스닝튜터 Beginner 3 능률 초등영어 듣기모의고사 10회 4-1, 4-2	리스닝버디 3 능률 초등영어 듣기모의고사 10회 5-1, 5-2	초등영어 리스닝튜터 Intermediate 1 초등영어 리스닝튜터 Intermediate 2 초등영어 리스닝튜터 Intermediate 3 능률 초등영어 듣기모의고사 10회 6-1, 6-2

초6-예비중	중1	중1-2	중2-3	중3
Writing Builder 1	1316 Listening 1 능률중학영어 듣기모의고사 22회 1 Junior Listening Expert 1 Writing Builder 2 쓰기로 마스터하는 중학서술형 1학년	1316 Listening 2 능률중학영어 듣기모의고사 22회 2 Junior Listening Expert 2	1316 Listening 3 Junior Listening Expert 3 Writing Builder 3 쓰기로 마스터하는 중학서술형 2학년	능률중학영어 듣기모의고사 22회 3 Junior Listening Expert 4 쓰기로 마스터하는 중학서술형 3학년

중3-예비고	고1	고1-2	고2-3	고3
	TEPS BY STEP L+V Basic 필히 통하는 고등 서술형 기본편	필히 통하는 고등 서술형 실전편	TEPS BY STEP L+V 1	

수능 이상/ 토플 80-89· 텝스 327-384점	수능 이상/ 토플 90-99· 텝스 385-451점	수능 이상/ 토플 100· 텝스 452점 이상		
TEPS BY STEP L+V 2 RADIX TOEFL Blue Label Listening 1 RADIX TOEFL Blue Label Listening 2	RADIX TOEFL Black Label Listening 1	TEPS BY STEP L+V 3 RADIX TOEFL Black Label Listening 2		

기초부터 실전까지 중학 듣기 완성

1316

1316 LISTENING
정답 및 해설

LEVEL
1

NE
능률

기초부터 실전까지 중학 듣기 완성

1316 LISTENING

정답 및 해설

LEVEL
1

UNIT 1 그림 묘사 · 위치

주요 어휘·표현 미리보기

p. 10

01 [b] nearby
02 [e] corner
03 [f] Go straight
04 [a] in front of
05 [h] on the right side
06 [d] across from
07 [c] next to
08 [g] Make a right

LISTENING PRACTICE

pp. 12-14

01 ⑤	02 ③	03 ④	04 ⑤	05 ③	06 ②
07 ②	08 ④	09 ③	10 ①	11 ②	12 ④

01 ⑤

M I ordered a birthday cake from the bakery. It's big and round.
W Does it have any flowers on it?
M Just one big one.
W Does it say "Happy Birthday" on it?
M No. It doesn't have any words on it.
W Well, it sounds great anyway.

남 나 제과점에서 생일 케이크를 하나 주문했어. 크고 둥근 모양이야.
여 그 위에 꽃이 있니?
남 큰 것이 딱 하나 있어.
여 위에 "Happy Birthday"라고 쓰여 있니?
남 아니. 위에 아무 말도 안 쓰여 있어.
여 음, 그래도 멋진 것 같아.

|어휘| order [동] 주문하다 bakery [명] 제과점, 빵집 word [명] 단어, 말 sound [동] ~처럼 들리다

02 ③

W My puppy is in the dog park. He's playing with the other dogs!
M Which one is he? Does he have pointy ears?
W No. His ears are long, and they hang down.
M I think I see him. He has a short tail, doesn't he?
W Yes! And he has short legs too.

여 내 강아지는 강아지 공원에 있어. 다른 개들과 놀고 있지!
남 어떤 게 네 강아지야? 귀가 뾰족하니?
여 아니. 귀가 길고 늘어져 있어.
남 보이는 것 같아. 꼬리가 짧은 강아지지, 그렇지?
여 응! 다리도 짧아.

|해설| 귀가 뾰족하지 않고 길고 늘어져 있으며, 꼬리와 다리가 짧은 강아지라고 했다.

|어휘| pointy [형] 끝이 뾰족한 hang down 늘어지다 tail [명] 꼬리

03 ④

M Excuse me. Is there a bookstore nearby?
W Yes. Just walk down Smith Street and make a right on First Avenue.
M Okay. Is it easy to find?
W Yes. It's on the right side of the street and across from a park.
M Great. Thanks for your help.

남 실례합니다. 근처에 서점이 있나요?
여 네. Smith 가를 걸어 내려가서 1번가에서 우회전하세요.
남 알겠습니다. 찾기 쉽나요?
여 네. 그 거리의 우측에 있고 공원 맞은편이에요.
남 좋아요. 도와주셔서 감사합니다.

|어휘| nearby [부] 근처에 walk down 걸어 내려가다 make a right 우회전하다 find [동] 찾다 on the right side 우측에 across from ~의 바로 맞은편에

04 ⑤

W Uh-oh. I can't find my library card.
M Didn't you just put it on the table?
W No, I didn't. I thought I put it on the bookshelf. But it's not there.
M Hmm… Did you look on the sofa?
W Yes, I checked the sofa. But my card's not there.
M How about beside the trash can?
W Let me see. Nope! It's not there either.
M Oh, there's something under this cushion!
W That's my library card! Thank you.

여 이런. 내 도서관 카드를 찾을 수가 없어.

남 방금 테이블 위에 놓지 않았어?
여 아니. 책꽂이 위에 뒀다고 생각했어. 하지만 거기에 없네.
남 음… 소파 위에 봤니?
여 응, 소파를 확인했어. 하지만 내 카드는 거기 없어.
남 쓰레기통 옆은 어때?
여 어디 보자. 아니야! 거기에도 없어.
남 아, 이 쿠션 밑에 뭔가 있어!
여 그게 내 도서관 카드야! 고마워.

|어휘| library card 도서관 카드 bookshelf [명] 책꽂이 check [동] 확인하다 beside [전] ~ 옆에 trash can 쓰레기통

05 ③

M What pretty nails!
W Thanks. I painted them myself.
M Really? I thought you went to a nail shop.
W No. I painted my favorite flowers on them.
M I like the butterfly on the flower in the middle.
W Thanks. At first, painting my nails was difficult, but now I enjoy it.

남 손톱 예쁘네!
여 고마워. 내가 직접 그렸어.
남 정말? 나는 네가 네일 숍에 간 줄 알았어.
여 아니야. 손톱에 내가 매우 좋아하는 꽃을 그렸어.
남 가운데 꽃에 앉아 있는 나비가 마음에 든다.
여 고마워. 처음에는 손톱을 칠하는 게 어려웠는데, 지금은 그것을 즐기고 있어.

|해설| 꽃 위에 나비가 있는 손톱 무늬다.

|어휘| nail [명] 손톱 paint [동] (그림물감으로) 그리다 favorite [형] 매우 좋아하는 in the middle 가운데에

06 ②

M Is this your new novel, *Moonlight*?
W Yes. What do you think of the round moon on the cover?
M I like it. And there are three stars under it.
W That's right. And the book's title is above the moon.
M It looks terrific. I can't wait to read it.

남 이게 네 새 소설 〈달빛〉이니?
여 응. 표지에 있는 둥근 달 어때?
남 마음에 들어. 그 아래에 별도 세 개 있네.
여 맞아. 그리고 달 위에 책 제목이 있어.
남 아주 좋아 보여. 빨리 읽고 싶다.

|어휘| novel [명] 소설 cover [명] 표지 title [명] 제목 terrific [형] 아주 좋은

07 ②

W Excuse me. Is there a dry cleaner's around here?
M Well, you have to go straight and make a left on Green Street.
W I see.
M Then make a right on James Road. The dry cleaner's is on the right.
W Great! Thanks for your help!

여 실례합니다. 이 근처에 세탁소가 있나요?
남 음, 쭉 가서 Green 가에서 좌회전하셔야 합니다.
여 그렇군요.
남 그러고 나서 James 로에서 우회전하세요. 세탁소는 우측에 있습니다.
여 좋습니다! 도와주셔서 감사해요!

|어휘| dry cleaner's 세탁소 straight [부] 똑바로

08 ④

W What are you doing, Nick?
M I'm looking for my watch. But I can't find it.
W Did you look on your bed?
M Yes, but it's not there. I checked on my desk and under the chair too. But I still can't find it.
W Oh, look! Isn't that your watch on the bookshelf?
M It is! Thanks.

여 뭐 하고 있어, Nick?
남 내 시계를 찾고 있어. 하지만 찾을 수가 없네.
여 침대 위를 봤니?
남 응, 그런데 거기 없어. 내 책상 위랑 의자 아래도 확인했어. 그런데 아직도 못 찾겠어.
여 오, 봐! 책꽂이 위에 있는 것이 네 시계 아니니?
남 맞아! 고마워.

|어휘| look for ~을 찾다 still [부] 아직(도), 여전히

09 ③

[Cell phone rings.]
M Hello?
W Hi, it's me. I'm on your street. Which house is yours?
M It has two floors. And there are three windows on the top floor.
W Okay. Are there two trees in front of it?

M No, there's only one tree. And there's a driveway on the right.
W Is there a car parked in the driveway?
M Yes, there is!
W Aha! I see it!

[휴대전화벨이 울린다.]
남 여보세요?
여 안녕, 나야. (너희 집이 있는) 거리에 있어. 어떤 집이 너희 집이니?
남 이층집이야. 그리고 2층에 창문이 세 개 있어.
여 알겠어. 집 앞에 나무가 두 그루 있니?
남 아니, 한 그루밖에 없어. 그리고 오른쪽에 진입로가 있어.
여 진입로에 차가 주차되어 있니?
남 응, 그래!
여 아하! 보인다!

|해설| 이층집이고 2층에 창문 세 개, 집 앞에 나무 한 그루가 있으며, 진입로에 주차되어 있는 차가 있다고 했다.

|어휘| street [명] 거리, -가 floor [명] 층 top [형] 맨 위의 in front of ~의 앞에 driveway [명] 진입로, 차도 park [동] 주차하다

10 ①

W What do you think of this jacket?
M It's nice. I like the three big buttons.
W Me too. And it also has a belt.
M But it's very long. Do you think it will be comfortable?
W Yes. And it will keep me warm.

여 이 재킷 어때?
남 멋지네. 큰 단추 세 개가 마음에 들어.
여 나도 그래. 벨트도 달려 있어.
남 그런데 굉장히 기네. 편할 것 같니?
여 응. 따뜻하기도 할 거야.

|어휘| jacket [명] 재킷, 상의 button [명] 단추 belt [명] 벨트, 허리띠 comfortable [형] 편한 warm [형] 따뜻한

11 ②

M Excuse me. Is this Third Street?
W No. Walk straight until you see a pizza place on the corner. That's Third Street.
M I see. Someone said there's a supermarket on Third Street.
W That's right. Make a left at the pizza place and you'll see it.
M Is it next to the pizza place?
W No, it's not. It's across from a bakery.
M Thanks for your help.
W You're welcome.

남 실례합니다. 여기가 3번가인가요?
여 아니요. 모퉁이에 피자 가게가 보일 때까지 쭉 걸어가세요. 거기가 3번가예요.
남 알겠습니다. 누가 3번가에 슈퍼마켓이 있다고 하던데요.
여 맞아요. 피자 가게에서 좌회전하시면 보일 거예요.
남 피자 가게 옆인가요?
여 아니요. 제과점 맞은편이에요.
남 도와주셔서 감사해요.
여 별말씀을요.

|해설| 피자 가게 옆이 아니라 제과점 맞은편에 슈퍼마켓이 있다고 했다.

|어휘| corner [명] 모퉁이 next to ~ 옆에

12 ④

W Hey, Jack. Would you help me find my earphone, please?
M Oh, you dropped it around here?
W Yes. But I can't find it.
M Did you look around the exercise balls?
W Yes. It's not there. I also checked the area in front of the mirror. But I still can't find it.
M All right. Then why don't we check around the treadmill?
W Okay. *[pause]* Oh, I found it! It's on the floor between the exercise bike and the treadmill.

여 얘, Jack. 내 이어폰 찾는 것 좀 도와줄래?
남 아, 이 근처에 떨어뜨렸니?
여 응. 그런데 못 찾겠어.
남 운동용 공 주변을 봤니?
여 응. 거기에 없어. 거울 앞 부분도 확인했고. 그런데 아직도 못 찾겠어.
남 좋아. 그럼 러닝머신 주변을 확인해보는 게 어때?
여 알았어. [잠시 후] 아, 찾았다! 운동용 자전거와 러닝머신 사이의 바닥에 있네.

|어휘| drop [동] 떨어뜨리다 exercise [명] 운동 area [명] 구역, 부분 mirror [명] 거울 treadmill [명] 러닝머신 floor [명] 바닥 between [전] 사이에 bike [명] 자전거

어휘·표현 다지기 p. 19

A

01	주문하다	02	손톱
03	운동	04	따뜻한
05	거리, -가	06	편한
07	~ 옆에	08	꼬리
09	진입로, 차도	10	가운데에
11	세탁소	12	~을 찾다
13	떨어뜨리다	14	사이에
15	단추	16	제과점, 빵집

B

01	walk down	02	hang down
03	find	04	area
05	pointy	06	trash can
07	park	08	sound
09	word	10	floor

UNIT 2 의도·이유

주요 어휘·표현 미리보기 p. 20

01	[a] feel bad	02	[g] ready for
03	[d] has trouble	04	[f] interested in
05	[b] see a movie	06	[h] something wrong
07	[c] until midnight	08	[e] Why don't you

LISTENING PRACTICE pp. 22-23

01 ③	02 ②	03 ⑤	04 ②	05 ④
06 ⑤	07 ②	08 ④	09 ①	10 ④

01 ③

M How was your day at school, Anna?
W It was terrible. I made a mistake on a test.
M Don't be too upset, honey. Everyone makes mistakes.
W I feel bad about it.
M You will do fine next time.

남 Anna, 오늘 학교에서 어땠니?
여 끔찍했어요. 시험에서 실수했어요.
남 너무 속상해하지 말아라, 얘야. 누구나 실수를 해.
여 그것 때문에 기분이 안 좋아요.
남 다음번에는 잘할 거야.

|어휘| terrible [형] 끔찍한 make a mistake 실수하다 upset [형] 속상한 feel bad 낙담하다 next time 다음번

02 ②

W Oh no! I can't believe it!
M What's wrong?
W I was writing my research paper, and the computer suddenly turned off. I can't turn it back on.
M Uh-oh. You have to finish your paper by tomorrow, don't you?
W That's right. Hey, you know a lot about computers, right? Can you give me a hand?

여 아, 안 돼! 믿을 수가 없어!
남 무슨 일이야?
여 내가 학기 말 리포트를 쓰고 있었는데 컴퓨터가 갑자기 꺼졌어. 다시 켤 수가 없어.
남 아, 이런. 너 내일까지 리포트를 끝내야 하지 않아?
여 맞아. 아, 너 컴퓨터에 대해 많이 알지? 나 좀 도와줄래?

|어휘| believe [동] 믿다 wrong [형] 잘못된 research paper 학기 말 리포트 suddenly [부] 갑자기 turn off (전원이) 꺼지다 finish [동] 끝내다 a lot 많이 give a hand 도움을 주다

03 ⑤

W What are you doing?
M I'm reading a book for homework.
W Oh. Well, I got two free movie tickets. Would you like to see a movie tonight?
M Sorry, I can't. I have to visit my uncle.
W Maybe next time, then.
M Sure. Enjoy the movie!

여 뭐 하고 있니?
남 숙제 때문에 책을 읽고 있어.
여 아. 있지, 나 무료 영화표 두 장이 생겼어. 오늘 밤에 영화 볼래?
남 미안, 못 볼 것 같아. 삼촌을 뵈러 가야 해.
여 그럼 다음에 가자.
남 그래. 영화 잘 봐!

|어휘| homework [명] 숙제 free [형] 무료의 see a movie 영화를 보다 visit [동] 방문하다 maybe [부] 아마

04 ②

W What's the matter? You don't look well.
M I just got back from a restaurant.
W Oh. Was the food bad?
M No. But I think I left my watch there.
W You should call the restaurant!
M I did. They said they don't have it.

여 무슨 일이야? 안색이 안 좋아 보이네.
남 나 식당에서 막 돌아왔어.
여 아. 음식이 형편없었어?
남 아니. 그런데 나 거기에 시계를 놓고 온 것 같아.
여 식당에 전화해 봐야지!
남 했지. 안 가지고 있대.

|어휘| matter [명] 문제 leave [동] 두고 오다[가다] watch [명] 시계

05 ④

M Are you ready to study for the test together?
W Well… Do you mind if I get some coffee first?
M No. You look tired.
W Yes, I went to see a play yesterday. I didn't get home until midnight.
M I understand. But don't drink too much coffee.
W Why not?
M You'll have trouble sleeping tonight.
W Good point. I'll only have one cup.

남 시험공부 같이 할 준비 되었니?
여 음… 나 커피 먼저 마셔도 될까?
남 물론이지. 너 피곤해 보여.
여 응, 나 어제 연극 보러 갔거든. 자정이 되어서야 집에 왔어.
남 그렇구나. 하지만 커피 너무 많이 마시지 마.
여 왜?
남 오늘 밤에 자기 어려울 거야.
여 좋은 지적이야. 딱 한 잔만 마실게.

|해설| 여자는 자신이 피곤한 이유를 연극을 보고 집에 늦게 왔기 때문이라고 말하고 있다.

|어휘| Do you mind if ~? ~해도 될까요? tired [형] 피곤한 midnight [명] 자정 have trouble v-ing ~하는 데 어려움이 있다

06 ⑤

W Do you have any plans this weekend?
M I'm going to see a jazz concert with Cathy.
W Really? Is there a good jazz band in our town?
M Yes. They're new, but I heard they're really good.
W Really? I want to hear them play.
M Why don't you come with us?

여 이번 주말에 무슨 계획 있니?
남 Cathy랑 재즈 콘서트 보러 갈 거야.
여 정말? 우리 동네에 괜찮은 재즈 밴드가 있니?
남 응. 그들은 신인인데도, 정말 잘한다고 들었어.
여 그래? 그들이 연주하는 걸 듣고 싶다.
남 우리랑 같이 가는 게 어때?

|어휘| plan [명] 계획 jazz [명] 재즈 Why don't you ~? ~하는 것이 어때?

07 ②

W I'm here! What are you doing?
M Hi. I'm just watching the baseball game.
W But you invited me over to play a board game.
M Yes, but I forgot about the baseball game. Let's watch it together.
W I'm not interested in baseball. I'll come over another time.

여 나 왔어! 뭐 하니?
남 안녕. 그냥 야구 경기 보고 있어.
여 하지만 네가 보드게임 하자고 나 초대했잖아.
남 그래. 그런데 야구 경기를 깜박했네. 같이 경기 보자.
여 나는 야구에 관심 없어. 다음에 들를게.

|해설| 여자는 야구에 관심이 없다며 같이 야구 경기를 보자는 남자의 제안을 거절하고 있다.

|어휘| invite ~ over ~을 자기 집으로 초대하다 board game 보드게임 forget [동] 잊다 be interested in ~에 관심이 있다 come over ~에 들르다 another time 언제 다시 한번

08 ④

W Excuse me.
M Yes, ma'am? How is your food?
W There's something wrong. I didn't order this.
M Oh, I'm sorry. What did you order?
W I wanted the shrimp. But this is beef!
M I'm sorry. I'll be right back with your order.

여 실례합니다.
남 네, 손님? 음식 어떠세요?
여 뭐가 잘못된 것 같아요. 저 이거 주문 안 했어요.
남 아, 죄송합니다. 무엇을 주문하셨나요?
여 저는 새우를 원했는데요. 하지만 이건 소고기예요!
남 죄송합니다. 주문하신 것 가지고 바로 돌아오겠습니다.

|어휘| order [동] 주문하다 [명] 주문 shrimp [명] 새우 beef [명] 소고기

09 ①

W Hi, Tony! Why didn't you come to the party yesterday? Did you forget about it?
M No. I really wanted to go, but I had to stay in bed.
W Why?
M I ate too much ice cream. So I had a stomachache.
W Oh, that's too bad. Are you okay now?
M Yes, but it really hurt.

여 안녕, Tony! 어제 왜 파티에 안 왔니? 그걸 깜박했니?
남 아니. 정말 가고 싶었지만, 계속 누워 있어야 했어.
여 왜?
남 아이스크림을 너무 많이 먹었거든. 그래서 배탈이 났었어.
여 아, 너무 안됐다. 지금은 괜찮아?
남 응, 하지만 정말 아팠어.

|어휘| stay in bed 침대에 머무르다 stomachache [명] 배탈, 복통 hurt [동] 아프다

10 ④

W Where have you been?
M I was at the mall. I just got back.
W The mall? Didn't you buy new shoes there yesterday?
M Yes. But they were two different sizes!
W You're kidding!
M No. I was pretty annoyed. I took them back.
W That's too bad. Anyway, are you ready for dinner?
M Sure. Let's go to my favorite Chinese restaurant.
W Okay.

여 너 어디 있었니?
남 쇼핑몰에 있었어. 방금 돌아왔어.
여 쇼핑몰? 어제 거기서 새 신발 사지 않았어?
남 응. 하지만 두 짝이 서로 다른 치수였어!
여 농담이겠지!
남 아니야. 나 정말 짜증 났었어. 그걸 반품했어.
여 안타깝네. 그건 그렇고, 저녁 먹을 준비는 됐니?
남 물론이지. 내가 정말 좋아하는 중식당에 가자.
여 좋아.

|어휘| mall [명] 쇼핑몰 pretty [부] 상당히, 꽤 annoyed [형] 짜증이 난 take ~ back ~을 돌려주다[반품하다] anyway [부] 그건 그렇고 be ready for ~을 위한 준비가 되다

어휘·표현 다지기 p. 27

A

01	잘못된	02	다음번
03	그건 그렇고	04	끔찍한
05	아마	06	속상한
07	잊다	08	계획
09	끝내다	10	많이
11	갑자기	12	짜증이 난
13	실수하다	14	방문하다
15	피곤한	16	배탈, 복통

B

01	give a hand	02	pretty
03	hurt	04	Do you mind if ~?
05	take ~ back	06	matter
07	turn off	08	stay in bed
09	another time	10	homework

UNIT 3 언급하지 않은 내용

주요 어휘·표현 미리보기 p. 28

01	ⓑ on sale	02	ⓓ weighs
03	ⓕ misses	04	ⓒ available
05	ⓗ rent a car	06	ⓐ terrific
07	ⓖ good at	08	ⓔ was born

LISTENING PRACTICE pp. 30-31

01 ②	02 ③	03 ④	04 ③	05 ⑤
06 ④	07 ⑤	08 ②	09 ②	10 ⑤

01 ②

M Welcome to Eastern Hotel! This beautiful hotel is just two years old. It has 120 rooms, two terrific restaurants, and three nice swimming pools. You can stay in a room for just $70 a night.

남 Eastern 호텔에 오신 것을 환영합니다! 이 아름다운 호텔은 지어진 지 2년밖에 되지 않았습니다. 120개의 객실, 두 곳의 훌륭한 식당과 세 개의 멋진 수영장을 갖추고 있습니다. 여러분은 1박에 단 70달러로 객실에 묵으실 수 있습니다.

|어휘| terrific [형] 훌륭한 swimming pool 수영장 stay [동] 묵다

02 ③

M The X87 laptop computer is on sale! You can get 25% off the regular price. It is available in black or silver. It is 33 centimeters wide and weighs less than one kilogram. Get one today!

남 X87 노트북 컴퓨터가 할인 중입니다! 정가에서 25%를 할인받으실 수 있습니다. 검은색이나 은색으로 구매하실 수 있습니다. 33cm의 너비에 무게는 1kg이 채 되지 않습니다. 오늘 구매하세요!

|어휘| laptop (computer) 노트북 컴퓨터 on sale 할인 판매 중인 regular price 정가 available [형] 구할 수 있는 wide [형] 폭이 ~인 weigh [동] 무게가 ~이다

03 ④

W Mike was born in Sydney, but he lives in Tokyo now. He is majoring in Japanese history there. His hobby is watching movies, so he often goes to the theater with his friends. Mike is happy with his life in Tokyo, but he misses his parents in Sydney.

여 Mike는 시드니에서 태어났지만, 지금은 도쿄에서 삽니다. 그는 그곳에서 일본 역사학을 전공하고 있습니다. 그의 취미는 영화 보기라서, 그는 친구들과 함께 자주 극장에 갑니다. Mike는 도쿄에서의 자신의 삶에 만족하지만, 시드니에 계신 부모님을 그리워합니다.

|어휘| be born 태어나다 major in ~을 전공하다 history [명] 역사 miss [동] 그리워하다

04 ③

M Hello! Let me introduce myself. My name is Kim Minjun. I live in Daegu. I am a student at Daegu Middle School. My favorite subject is science. And I want to be a scientist. Thank you for listening.

남 안녕하세요! 제 소개를 하겠습니다. 제 이름은 김민준입니다. 저는 대구에 삽니다. 대구중학교 학생입니다. 제가 가장 좋아하는 과목은 과학입니다. 그리고 저는 과학자가 되고 싶습니다. 들어주셔서 감사합니다.

|어휘| introduce [동] 소개하다 favorite [형] 매우 좋아하는 subject [명] 과목 scientist [명] 과학자

05 ⑤

W Our class will go to Sokcho for a camping trip. We will leave on September 9 and return on the 11. The cost will be $100. We will travel by bus. At the campsite, we will play games and sing around the campfire. Please bring warm clothes!

여 우리 반은 캠핑 여행으로 속초에 갈 예정입니다. 우리는 9월 9일에 떠나서 11일에 돌아올 것입니다. 비용은 100달러가 될 것입니다. 우리는 버스로 이동할 예정입니다. 야영지에서, 우리는 게임을 하고 모닥불 주위에서 노래할 것입니다. 따뜻한 옷을 가져오세요!

|어휘| cost [명] 비용 travel [동] 이동하다 campsite [명] 야영지 campfire [명] 모닥불 bring [동] 가져오다 clothes [명] 옷

06 ④

M Attention, please. We're looking for a missing child. Her name is Kim Jimin, and she is four years old. She has long hair and is wearing a yellow T-shirt. She is from Korea, but she speaks English. If you find her, please take her to the information center.

남 주목해 주세요. 미아를 찾고 있습니다. 아이의 이름은 김지민이고, 네 살입니다. 아이는 머리가 길고 노란색 티셔츠를 입고 있습니다. 아이는 한국 출신이지만, 영어를 합니다. 아이를 발견하시면, 안내소로 데려다주시기 바랍니다.

|어휘| missing child 미아 information center 안내소

07 ⑤

M Good evening. Today's special guest is Emily Henderson. She is a singer-songwriter from Canada. Her favorite musical genre is jazz. She is very good at playing the guitar. She started playing the guitar when she was eleven. Tonight, she will perform her new song for us.

남 안녕하세요. 오늘의 특별 손님은 Emily Henderson입니다. 그녀는 캐나다 출신의 가수 겸 작곡가입니다. 그녀가 가장 좋아하는 음악 장르는 재즈입니다. 그녀는 기타 연주에 매우 능숙합니다. 그녀는 11살때 기타를 치기 시작했습니다. 오늘 밤, 그녀가 우리를 위해 신곡을 연주할 것입니다.

|어휘| singer-songwriter [명] 싱어송라이터(가수 겸 작곡가) jazz [명] 재즈 be good at v-ing ~하는 데 능숙하다 perform [동] 연주하다

08 ②

M Today I am going to read my essay for you. I wrote it for my English homework. It took me two hours to write it. The topic is polar bears. I chose this topic because I care about animals and the environment.

남 오늘 저는 여러분을 위해 제 과제를 읽도록 하겠습니다. 저는 영어 숙제를 위해 이것을 작성했습니다. 작성하는 데 2시간이 걸렸습니다. 주제는 북극곰입니다. 저는 동물과 환경에 관심을 가지고 있어서 이 주제를 선택했습니다.

|어휘| essay [명] 과제물 topic [명] 주제 polar bear 북극곰 choose [동] 선택하다 care about ~에 관심을 가지다 environment [명] 환경

09 ②

W I'd like to tell you about my aunt. She is my role model. Her name is Lucy, and she is my father's younger sister. She is 35 years old, and she is a doctor. She works in a big hospital. I don't see her often because she lives in London. I want to be just like her when I grow up.

여 저는 여러분에게 제 고모에 대해 말씀드리고 싶습니다. 고모는 제 역할 모델입니다. 고모의 성함은 Lucy이고, 제 아버지의 여동생입니다. 고모는 35세이시고, 의사이십니다. 큰 병원에서 일하십니다. 고모는 런던에 사셔서 자주 뵙지는 못합니다. 저는 자라서 고모처럼 되고 싶습니다.

|어휘| role model 역할 모델 grow up 자라다

10 ⑤

M Do you need to rent a car? Then take a look at this red one. It is only $40 per day, and it has room for up to five people. This attractive red car is comfortable and very fast. It can go 160 kilometers per hour! Why don't you take it on a test drive?

남 차를 빌려야 하세요? 그러면 이 빨간 차를 봐주세요. 하루에 겨우 40달러인데다, 5명까지 탈 수 있는 공간도 있습니다. 이 멋진 빨간 차는 편안하고 매우 빠릅니다. 시속 160킬로미터로 달릴 수 있습니다! 한번 시승해 보지 않으실래요?

|어휘| rent [동] 빌리다 take a look at ~을 보다 per [전] ~당 room [명] 공간 up to ~까지 attractive [형] 매력적인, 멋진 comfortable [형] 편안한 test drive 시승, 시운전

어휘·표현 다지기

p. 35

A

01	미아	02	선택하다
03	자라다	04	~을 전공하다
05	~을 보다	06	매력적인, 멋진
07	수영장	08	주제
09	노트북 컴퓨터	10	폭이 ~인
11	북극곰	12	과학자
13	소개하다	14	역사
15	역할 모델	16	가져오다

B

01	per	02	campsite
03	cost	04	subject
05	information center	06	perform
07	regular price	08	travel
09	essay	10	care about

UNIT 4 시각·대화 장소

주요 어휘·표현 미리보기

p. 36

01	ⓐ join	02	ⓓ opened an account
03	ⓒ destination	04	ⓗ Would you like
05	ⓖ immediately	06	ⓕ pack
07	ⓑ stop by	08	ⓔ had better hurry

LISTENING PRACTICE

pp. 38-39

01 ④	02 ⑤	03 ③	04 ③	05 ⑤
06 ③	07 ①	08 ④	09 ②	10 ⑤

01 ④

W Are you going to pick me up after volleyball practice, Dad?

M Yes. Let's meet in front of your school at five o'clock.

W Practice doesn't end until 5:30, Dad. And I need time to change my clothes.

M So how about 5:45?

W That's much better. I'll see you then.

M Enjoy your practice!

여 아빠, 배구 연습 후에 저 데리러 와주실 거예요?

남 그래. 5시에 너희 학교 앞에서 만나자.

여 연습은 5시 30분이 돼야 끝나요, 아빠. 그리고 옷 갈아입을 시간도 필요해요.

남 그러면 5시 45분 어때?

여 그게 훨씬 좋겠네요. 그때 뵐게요.

남 연습 잘하고!

|어휘| pick ~ up ~을 데리러 가다   volleyball 몡 배구   practice 몡 연습   in front of ~ 앞에서   not ~ until ... …에서야 비로소 ~하다   end 통 끝나다   change 통 (옷을) 갈아입다

02 ⑤

M I'm going to the new cartoon museum tomorrow. Would you like to come?

W Sure. Where is it?

M It's about thirty minutes away. It opens at 9:00 a.m.

W Why don't we meet at ten?

M We'll probably be there for a while. We should have lunch before we go.

W How about noon, then?

M Sounds good.

남 나는 내일 새로 연 만화 박물관에 갈 거야. 너도 갈래?

여 그래. 어디 있는데?

남 30분 정도 떨어진 곳에 있어. 거기는 오전 9시에 문을 열어.

여 10시에 만나는 게 어때?

남 우리는 아마도 거기에 한참 있을 거야. 가기 전에 점심을 먹어야 해.

여 그럼 정오는 어때?

남 좋아.

|어휘| cartoon 몡 만화   Would you like to-v ~? ~하시겠어요?   probably 뷰 아마   noon 몡 정오

03 ③

W I'm going to go swimming this afternoon. Would you like to join me?

M Sure, that sounds great.

W What time shall we meet?

M How about 2:30 at the gym?

W No, it's already two o'clock. I need more time to pack.

M Then how about meeting in forty minutes?

W Sounds good.

여 나 오늘 오후에 수영하러 가려고 해. 나랑 같이 갈래?

남 그래, 그거 좋지.

여 몇 시에 만날까?

남 2시 30분에 체육관에서 만나는 게 어때?

여 아니, 지금 벌써 2시야. 난 짐을 챙길 시간이 더 필요해.

남 그럼 40분 후에 만나는 게 어때?

여 좋아.

|해설| 현재 시각은 2시이며, 남자가 40분 후에 만나자고 했으므로, 두 사람이 만날 시각은 2시 40분이다.

|어휘| join 통 함께 하다   gym 몡 체육관   pack 통 (짐을) 챙기다

04 ③

M Excuse me. I can't find my boarding gate.

W What's your destination?

M I'm flying to Tokyo.

W I see. You need to go to Gate 5 immediately.

M What time does boarding start?

W It starts at one o'clock.

M It's only 12:30 now. I still have thirty minutes.

W Actually, you must be at the gate at least twenty minutes before boarding.

M Oh! I had better hurry.

남 실례합니다. 저 탑승구를 못 찾겠어요.

여 목적지가 어디인가요?

남 저는 도쿄에 가요.

여 그렇군요. 즉시 5번 게이트로 가셔야 합니다.

남 탑승은 언제 시작되나요?

여 1시에 시작합니다.

남 이제 겨우 12시 30분이네요. 아직 30분 남았군요.

여 사실, 최소한 탑승 20분 전에는 게이트에 가 계셔야 해요.

남 아! 서두르는 편이 좋겠어요.

|어휘| boarding gate 탑승구   destination 몡 목적지   immediately 뷰 즉시   boarding 몡 탑승   at least 적어도, 최소한   had better ~하는 편이 좋다   hurry 통 서두르다

05 ⑤

M May I help you?

W Yes. When is *Beauty and the Beast* showing?

M There's a show starting at five. But you'd have to sit in the front row.

W When is the next show?

M It starts at 5:45. It's the 3D version, but there are many seats left.

W Okay. I'll take two tickets.

남 도와드릴까요?
여 네. 〈미녀와 야수〉가 언제 상영되나요?
남 5시에 시작하는 영화가 있어요. 그런데 앞줄에 앉으셔야 하겠네요.
여 다음 영화는 언제인가요?
남 5시 45분에 시작합니다. 3D 판이긴 한데, 남은 좌석이 많아요.
여 좋아요. 표 두 장 주세요.

|어휘| show [동] 상영되다 [명] 공연, 영화 in the front row 앞줄에 version [명] -판 seat [명] 좌석

06 ③

M Are you going to Minsu's birthday party tomorrow?
W Yes. How about you?
M I plan on going, too. But I haven't bought a gift yet.
W I haven't either. Let's stop by the mall before going to the party.
M Good idea! It starts at seven.
W Shall we meet at the mall at 4:30?
M That's too early. How about an hour later?
W Sounds good. See you then.

남 너 내일 민수 생일 파티에 갈 거니?
여 응. 너는?
남 나도 가려고 해. 근데 아직 선물을 못 샀어.
여 나도 못 샀어. 우리 파티 가기 전에 쇼핑몰에 들르자.
남 좋은 생각이야! 파티는 7시에 시작해.
여 쇼핑몰에서 4시 30분에 만날까?
남 그건 너무 일러. 한 시간 더 늦게는 어때?
여 좋아. 그때 보자.

|해설| 4시 30분보다 한 시간 더 늦게 만나기로 했으므로, 두 사람은 5시 30분에 만날 것이다.

|어휘| plan on v-ing ~할 계획이다 stop by ~에 잠시 들르다 early [형] 빠른, 이른

07 ①

M Would you like to go to Wednesday's soccer game with me?
W I'd love to. What time does it start?
M At six. Let's meet at 5:30 at World Cup Stadium Station.
W How about thirty minutes earlier?
M Thirty minutes? Why?
W It will take a while to walk to the stadium.
M Okay. See you then.

남 나랑 수요일에 하는 축구 경기에 갈래?
여 그러고 싶어. 몇 시에 시작하니?
남 6시에. 월드컵경기장역에서 5시 30분에 만나자.
여 30분 더 이른 시각은 어때?
남 30분? 왜?
여 경기장까지 걸어가는 데 시간이 꽤 걸릴 거야.
남 좋아. 그때 보자.

|어휘| stadium [명] 경기장 station [명] 역 take a while 시간이 꽤 걸리다

08 ④

W I left my bag on the subway. Do you have it?
M What does it look like?
W It's small and black. And there's a laptop in it.
M Let's see... What's your name? There's a bag with a name tag on it.
W It's Emily.
M You're lucky. Here's your bag. Try not to forget it again.

여 제가 지하철에 가방을 두고 내렸는데요. 여기에 가방이 있나요?
남 어떻게 생겼죠?
여 작고 검은색이에요. 그리고 안에 노트북 컴퓨터가 들어 있어요.
남 어디 한번 봅시다… 성함이 어떻게 되세요? 여기 이름표가 있는 가방이 있네요.
여 Emily예요.
남 운이 좋으시네요. 가방 여기 있습니다. 다시는 잃어버리지 마세요.

|어휘| leave [동] 두고 오다 subway [명] 지하철 name tag 이름표 lucky [형] 운이 좋은

09 ②

M How may I help you?
W I'd like to open an account.
M Please fill out this form.
W Okay. Do I have to put some money in the account now?
M No, you don't. I just need that form and your ID card.
W Here they are.

남 무엇을 도와드릴까요?
여 계좌를 개설하고 싶은데요.
남 이 양식을 작성해주세요.
여 알겠습니다. 지금 계좌에 돈을 입금해야 하나요?
남 아니요, 그러실 필요 없습니다. 그 양식과 신분증만 필요해요.
여 여기 있습니다.

|어휘| open an account 계좌를 개설하다 fill out ~을 작성하다 form [명] 양식 ID card 신분증

10 ⑤

M Hello. Can you drive forward a bit?
W Okay.
M Perfect. How much gas would you like?
W Can you fill it up, please?
M Okay. *[pause]* Your tank is full. It's 50,000 won. How would you like to pay?
W By credit card.
M All right. Please sign here.

남 안녕하세요. 조금 더 앞으로 오시겠어요?
여 네.
남 좋습니다. 기름을 얼마나 넣어드릴까요?
여 가득 채워 주시겠어요?
남 네. [잠시 후] (연료) 탱크가 가득 찼습니다. 50,000원입니다. 어떻게 지불하시겠어요?
여 신용카드로요.
남 알겠습니다. 여기 사인해주세요.

|해설| 'gas', 'fill it up', 'Your tank is full.' 등의 표현으로 보아, 주유소에서 일어나는 대화임을 알 수 있다.

|어휘| forward [부] 앞으로 fill up ~을 가득 채우다 pay [동] 지불하다 credit card 신용카드 sign [동] 서명하다, 사인하다

어휘·표현 다지기 p. 43

A

01 경기장	02 신분증
03 앞으로	04 만화
05 역	06 체육관
07 배구	08 이름표
09 ~ 앞에서	10 탑승구
11 적어도, 최소한	12 서명하다, 사인하다
13 신용카드	14 지불하다
15 정오	16 앞줄에

B

01 change	02 subway
03 leave	04 probably
05 hurry	06 practice
07 end	08 take a while
09 fill out	10 fill up

UNIT 5 장래 희망·직업

주요 어휘·표현 미리보기 p. 44

01 [e] take care of	02 [b] in the future
03 [c] get your hair cut	04 [d] pick up
05 [a] in your free time	06 [g] May I see
07 [f] work out	08 [h] inspired

LISTENING PRACTICE pp. 46-47

01 ②	02 ④	03 ②	04 ④	05 ③
06 ⑤	07 ③	08 ②	09 ③	10 ③

01 ②

M What do you do in your free time?
W I like playing computer games.
M Do you want to be a pro gamer in the future?
W No. It's just a hobby. I want to be a pilot.
M Wow! You could fly around the world!
W That's right.

남 넌 시간이 날 때 뭐 하니?
여 나는 컴퓨터 게임하는 걸 좋아해.
남 미래에 프로게이머가 되고 싶니?
여 아니. 그건 그냥 취미야. 나는 조종사가 되고 싶어.
남 와! 너는 세계를 비행할 수 있겠구나!
여 그렇지.

|어휘| in one's free time 시간이 날 때 pro [형] 프로의 in the future 장차, 미래에 hobby [명] 취미 pilot [명] 조종사 fly [동] 비행하다, 날다

02 ④

W What are you doing, David?
M I'm reading a book about Antoni Gaudí.
W Who is he?
M He was one of the greatest architects in the world.
W Are you interested in architecture?
M Yes. I want to be like him in the future.

여 뭐 하고 있니, David?
남 안토니 가우디에 관한 책을 읽고 있어.

여 그 사람이 누군데?
남 세계에서 가장 위대한 건축가들 중 한 명이었어.
여 너 건축에 관심 있니?
남 응. 나는 장래에 그와 같이 되고 싶어.

|어휘| architect [명] 건축가 interested in ~에 관심이 있는 architecture [명] 건축

03 ②

M Oh! It's two o'clock. I'm going to the gym.
W Again? You work out a lot.
M I do. Why don't you come with me?
W No, thanks. I'm going to the movie theater.
M You seem to really enjoy films.
W Yes. Actually, I hope to make my own movies someday. I want to entertain people.
M You want to be a director?
W That's right! And watching comedies inspires me.

남 아! 2시네. 나 헬스장에 갈 거야.
여 또? 너 운동 많이 한다.
남 그렇지. 나랑 같이 가지 않을래?
여 아니, 괜찮아. 나는 영화관에 갈 거야.
남 너는 영화를 정말 즐기는 것 같아.
여 맞아. 사실, 언젠가 나만의 영화를 만들기를 바라고 있어. 나는 사람들을 즐겁게 하고 싶어.
남 감독이 되고 싶은 거야?
여 맞아! 코미디를 보는 것도 나에게 영감을 줘.

|어휘| gym [명] 헬스장 work out 운동하다 movie theater 영화관 someday [부] 언젠가 entertain [동] 즐겁게 하다 director [명] 감독 inspire [동] 영감을 주다, 고무하다

04 ④

W Tim, are you going to the airport again?
M Yes. I need to pick up a group of people from Thailand.
W Will you show them around the city?
M Yes. I'll take them to some museums and palaces.
W You have such a great job.
M I like it. I get to tell people all about Korean culture.

여 Tim, 또 공항 가는 거야?
남 응. 태국에서 온 사람들 한 무리를 마중 나가야 해.
여 그 사람들에게 도시를 구경시켜 줄 거니?
남 응. 몇몇 박물관과 궁에 데려갈 거야.
여 너 정말 멋진 직업을 가졌구나.
남 난 그 직업이 좋아. 사람들에게 한국 문화에 대한 모든 것을 알려주게 되니까.

|해설| 남자는 외국에서 온 사람들을 공항에 마중 나가고 시내를 구경시켜주는 일을 하므로 여행 가이드일 것이다.

|어휘| pick up ~을 (차로) 마중 나가다 show ~ around ~에게 구경시켜주다 museum [명] 박물관 palace [명] 궁전 get to-v ~하게 되다 culture [명] 문화

05 ③

W Excuse me. May I see your driver's license?
M Okay. Here you are. But what did I do wrong?
W You were driving over the speed limit. The speed limit here is sixty-five kilometers per hour, but you were doing almost eighty.
M Oh, I am sorry. I didn't know.
W I'll have to give you a ticket for speeding.

여 실례합니다. 운전면허증을 볼 수 있을까요?
남 네. 여기 있습니다. 그런데 제가 뭘 잘못했나요?
여 제한 속도를 초과해서 운전하셨습니다. 이곳의 제한 속도는 시속 65km인데, 운전자분은 거의 시속 80km로 달리셨어요.
남 아, 죄송합니다. 몰랐어요.
여 속도위반 딱지를 드려야겠네요.

|해설| 여자가 속도위반을 한 남자에게 운전면허증을 보여달라고 하는 것으로 보아, 교통경찰임을 알 수 있다.

|어휘| driver's license 운전면허증 speed limit 제한 속도 per [전] ~당 ticket [명] (벌금) 딱지 speeding [명] 속도위반

06 ⑤

W What's your favorite food?
M Well, I can't just pick one. I really love eating all foods.
W Me too. That's why I want to be a chef.
M That sounds awesome.
W Do you want to be a chef, too?
M I don't think I'm good at cooking. I want to be a food critic.

여 네가 제일 좋아하는 음식은 뭐야?
남 글쎄, 하나만 고를 수 없어. 나는 모든 음식 먹는 것을 정말 좋아해.
여 나도 그래. 그게 내가 요리사가 되고 싶은 이유야.
남 그거 굉장한데.
여 너도 요리사가 되고 싶니?
남 난 요리하는 데 능숙하지 않은 것 같아. 난 음식 평론가가 되고 싶어.

|어휘| pick [동] 고르다 chef [명] 요리사 awesome [형] 굉장한 critic [명] 평론가, 비평가

07 ③

W I'm going to the animal hospital near our school.
M Why are you going there?
W I'm a volunteer. I feed the dogs and clean their cages.
M You must really love taking care of animals.
W I do. I want to be a zookeeper when I grow up.
M That sounds really interesting!

여 나는 우리 학교 근처의 동물병원에 갈 거야.
남 거기 왜 가는데?
여 내가 자원봉사자거든. 개에게 먹이를 주고 우리를 청소해.
남 너는 동물 돌보는 걸 정말 좋아하나 보다.
여 맞아. 나는 커서 동물원 사육사가 되고 싶어.
남 그거 정말 재미있겠다!

|어휘| animal hospital 동물병원 volunteer [명] 자원봉사자 feed [동] 먹이를 주다 cage [명] 우리 take care of ~을 돌보다 zookeeper [명] 동물원 사육사

08 ②

W Did you get your hair cut, Ken?
M Yes. What do you think?
W The style is great! You look like a model.
M Thanks! I have to go to an audition tomorrow.
W What is it for?
M A new TV show. It's called *Beach Police*.
W Would you play the main character?
M No. A big star will play him. I'd play his best friend.
W Well, I hope you are successful.

여 머리 잘랐니, Ken?
남 응. 어때?
여 스타일 멋지다! 모델처럼 보여.
남 고마워! 내일 오디션에 가야 하거든.
여 뭘 위한 건데?
남 새로운 TV 프로그램. 〈해양 경찰〉이라는 제목이야.
여 주인공 역할을 맡게 되는 거야?
남 아니. 대스타가 주인공 역할을 맡을 거야. 나는 그의 가장 친한 친구 역을 할 거고.
여 음, 네가 합격하길 바랄게.

|해설| 남자가 내일 TV 프로그램 오디션을 보러 간다는 말로 미루어 보아, 직업이 배우임을 알 수 있다.

|어휘| get one's hair cut 머리를 자르다 audition [명] 오디션 play [동] (영화 등에서) 연기하다 main character 주인공 successful [형] 합격한

09 ③

W Hello! How may I help you?
M I'm thinking about buying a new car. What do you recommend?
W This is our best-selling model. It can fit four people.
M It looks great! Is it available in blue?
W I'm afraid not. It only comes in black and grey.
M I see. Can I look at them now?
W Sure. This way, please.

여 안녕하세요! 무엇을 도와 드릴까요?
남 새 차를 사려고 생각 중인데요. 무엇을 추천하시나요?
여 이게 가장 잘 팔리는 모델입니다. 네 명이 탈 수 있어요.
남 아주 좋아 보이는데요! 파란색도 있나요?
여 유감스럽게도 없습니다. 검은색과 회색으로만 나오거든요.
남 알겠습니다. 지금 차를 볼 수 있을까요?
여 물론입니다. 이쪽으로 오시죠.

|해설| 가장 잘 팔리는 모델의 차를 추천하며 탑승 가능 인원수와 색상을 설명하는 것으로 보아, 여자는 자동차 판매원임을 알 수 있다.

|어휘| recommend [동] 추천하다 best-selling [형] 가장 많이 팔리는 fit [동] 맞다, 적합하다 available [형] 구할 수 있는

10 ③

M Hello. What would you like to order?
W I would like the tomato pasta and a seafood salad.
M Okay. Do you want anything to drink?
W Can I use these coupons for free drinks?
M Yes, you can.
W Great! Two glasses of lemonade, please.
M All right. Here are some breadsticks.
W Thanks.

남 안녕하세요. 무엇을 주문하시겠습니까?
여 토마토 파스타와 해산물 샐러드 주세요.
남 네. 음료수 드시겠습니까?
여 이 무료 음료 쿠폰 사용할 수 있나요?
남 네, 사용 가능합니다.
여 잘됐네요! 레모네이드 두 잔 주세요.
남 알겠습니다. 여기 막대 빵 있습니다.
여 감사합니다.

|어휘| order [동] 주문하다 seafood [명] 해산물 free [형] 무료의

어휘·표현 다지기

p. 51

A

01	우리	02	즐겁게 하다
03	감독	04	제한 속도
05	자원봉사자	06	취미
07	박물관	08	주인공
09	운전면허증	10	문화
11	영화관	12	추천하다
13	요리사	14	궁전
15	가장 많이 팔리는	16	조종사

B

01	speeding	02	awesome
03	successful	04	ticket
05	pick	06	architecture
07	zookeeper	08	critic
09	fit	10	play

UNIT 6 심정

주요 어휘·표현 미리보기

p. 52

01	[d] waiting for	02	[f] on time
03	[e] can't believe	04	[a] make friends
05	[h] had fun	06	[c] a birthday present
07	[g] Have you been	08	[b] gets well

LISTENING PRACTICE

pp. 54-55

01 ③	02 ④	03 ⑤	04 ④	05 ③
06 ②	07 ①	08 ⑤	09 ②	10 ④

01 ③

W Hi, Jimmy. How do you like your new school?
M Well, my classes are interesting, and my teachers are nice.
W That's great.
M I guess. But I don't have any friends here.
W Oh, I see. You'll make friends soon.
M I hope so. I miss my old classmates.

여 안녕, Jimmy. 새로운 학교는 어때?
남 음, 수업도 재미있고 선생님들도 좋으셔.
여 잘됐다.
남 그렇지. 그런데 이곳에 아직 친구가 없어.
여 아, 그렇구나. 곧 친구들을 사귀게 될 거야.
남 그러길 바라는데. 예전 반 친구들이 그리워.

|어휘| interesting [형] 재미있는, 흥미로운 nice [형] 좋은, 친절한 make a friend 친구를 사귀다 miss [동] 그리워하다 classmate [명] 반 친구

02 ④

M I have a birthday present for you.
W Thanks, Dad. What is it?
M Open the envelope and find out.
W Wow, it's a ticket to *Dream Girls*! I really wanted to see this musical. Thank you.
M I'm glad you like it.

남 너를 위한 생일 선물이 있단다.
여 고마워요, 아빠. 그게 뭐예요?
남 봉투를 열어서 알아내렴.
여 와, 〈드림걸즈〉 표잖아요! 이 뮤지컬 정말 보고 싶었어요. 감사해요.
남 네가 마음에 들어 하니 기쁘구나.

|어휘| present [명] 선물 envelope [명] 봉투 find out 알아내다

03 ⑤

W Hey, Eddie, what's wrong? You haven't smiled all day.
M My grandma is very sick. She is in the hospital now.
W Oh, really? That's too bad.
M I was at the hospital all day yesterday.
W I hope she gets well soon.
M Thanks. I really hope so, too.

여 얘, Eddie, 무슨 일이니? 온종일 웃지도 않고.
남 할머니께서 많이 편찮으시거든. 지금 입원 중이셔.
여 아, 그래? 정말 안됐다.
남 어제 난 온종일 병원에 있었어.
여 할머니께서 건강을 곧 회복하시길 바랄게.
남 고마워. 나도 정말 그러시길 바라고 있어.

|어휘| all day 온종일 be in the hospital 입원 중이다 get well 건강을 회복하다 soon [부] 곧, 빨리

04 ④

M Hey, Minsun. What are you doing here?
W I'm waiting for the bus. But I've already waited for thirty minutes.
M Thirty minutes? I can't believe it!
W I'm going to be late for my appointment.
M How about taking the subway instead? It usually runs on time.
W I think I should. I hate the bus!

남 안녕, 민선아. 여기서 뭐 해?
여 버스를 기다리는 중이야. 그런데 벌써 30분 동안이나 기다렸어.
남 30분이나? 믿을 수 없어!
여 약속에 늦을 것 같아.
남 대신에 지하철을 타는 게 어때? 지하철은 보통 정시 운행을 하잖아.
여 그래야겠다. 버스 정말 싫어!

|어휘| wait for ~을 기다리다 believe [동] 믿다 appointment [명] 약속 instead [부] 대신에 run [동] 운행하다 on time 시간을 어기지 않고, 정각에 hate [동] 몹시 싫어하다

05 ③

M What are you reading, Mina?
W It's a sad book about a famous woman.
M Really? What happened to her?
W She was a great scientist, but she died young. It's a great book. I'm so happy that I found it.
M I'd like to learn more about her. Can I read it when you're finished?
W Yes, you can.

남 미나야, 뭐 읽고 있어?
여 유명한 여인에 대한 슬픈 책이야.
남 정말? 그녀에게 무슨 일이 있었는데?
여 그녀는 위대한 과학자였는데, 젊은 나이에 죽었어. 이거 정말 좋은 책이야. 이 책을 발견해서 매우 기뻐.
남 그녀에 대해 더 알고 싶어. 너 끝나면 내가 읽어도 될까?
여 그래, 그렇게 해.

|해설| 남자는 여자가 읽고 있는 책에 관심을 보이고 있다.

|어휘| sad [형] 슬픈 famous [형] 유명한 happen [동] 일어나다, 발생하다 die [동] 죽다 finished [형] 끝난

06 ②

M Haru, I heard you're going on a school trip to Jeju.
W Yes, we're going next week. I can't wait!
M Have you been there before?
W No, but my parents said that it is a beautiful island.
M Well, I hope you have fun.
W I will. I'm really looking forward to the trip!

남 하루야, 너 제주도로 수학여행 간다고 들었어.
여 응, 다음 주에 가. 기다려져!
남 전에 거기 가본 적 있어?
여 아니, 하지만 우리 부모님이 아름다운 섬이라고 말씀하셨어.
남 그래, 재미있게 놀길 바랄게.
여 그래야지. 수학여행이 정말 기대돼!

|어휘| school trip 수학여행 can't wait 기다려지다 have you been (to) ~? ~에 가본 적 있니? island [명] 섬 have fun 재미있게 놀다 look forward to ~을 고대하다

07 ①

W I'm glad that test is finally over. Let's go have lunch!
M I don't feel like eating.
W Is something wrong?
M I think I might have done poorly on the test.
W Don't be silly. You always get high scores.
M Maybe not this time. That test was hard.
W I'm confident that you did well.
M I hope you're right.

여 시험이 드디어 끝나서 기분 좋다. 점심 먹으러 가자!
남 나는 먹고 싶지 않아.
여 무슨 일 있어?
남 나 시험 망쳤을지도 몰라.
여 어리석은 소리 하지 마. 너는 항상 높은 점수를 받잖아.
남 이번에는 아마 아닐 거야. 시험이 어려웠어.
여 난 네가 잘 봤을 거라고 확신해.
남 네 말이 맞았으면 좋겠다.

|해설| 남자는 시험을 못 본 것 같다는 생각에 걱정하고 있다.

|어휘| be over 끝나다 finally [부] 드디어 feel like v-ing ~하고 싶다 poorly [부] 형편없이 silly [형] 어리석은 score [명] 점수 maybe [부] 아마 hard [형] 어려운 confident [형] 확신하는, 자신감 있는 do well 잘 하다 right [형] 맞는

08 ⑤

W That painting of a sad clown is mine.
M You painted that? It's very good.
W Thanks. It's my best painting ever.
M What will you do with it?
W I will hang it on the wall so everyone can see it.

여 저 슬픈 듯한 광대 그림은 내 거야.
남 네가 저걸 그렸다고? 아주 좋은데.
여 고마워. 그게 내가 지금껏 그린 그림 중에 제일 잘 그린 거야.
남 그걸로 뭘 할 거야?
여 벽에 걸어서 모든 사람이 볼 수 있게 할 거야.

|어휘| painting [명] 그림 sad [형] 슬픈 듯한 clown [명] 광대 paint [동] 그리다 hang [동] 걸다 wall [명] 벽

09 ②

W Aren't you going to Mark's house tonight?
M No. He's not my friend anymore.
W What happened? You said he's funny and interesting.
M He is. But he lied to me.
W Oh. Well, maybe he'll apologize.
M I don't care. I'm not talking to him.

여 너 오늘 밤에 Mark네 집에 안 가니?
남 안 가요. 그 애는 더는 제 친구가 아니에요.
여 무슨 일 있었어? 그 친구가 웃기고 재미있다고 했었잖아.
남 맞아요. 하지만 그 애가 저한테 거짓말을 했어요.
여 아. 그럼, 그 애가 사과할지도 몰라.
남 상관없어요. 그 애랑 말 안 할 거예요.

|어휘| anymore [부] 이제, 더 이상 funny [형] 웃긴 lie [동] 거짓말하다 apologize [동] 사과하다 care [동] 상관하다

10 ④

M You went to the amusement park yesterday, didn't you?
W Yes. How did you know?
M Your sister said you were excited to ride the roller coaster.
W I was. But the roller coaster was closed for repairs.
M Really? Well, were the other rides fun?
W They were okay. But I really wanted to ride the roller coaster.

남 너 어제 놀이공원에 갔지?
여 맞아. 어떻게 알았어?
남 네 여동생이 네가 롤러코스터 타게 돼서 신이 났다고 말해줬어.
여 그랬지. 하지만 롤러코스터가 수리 때문에 문을 닫았더라고.
남 정말? 음, 다른 놀이 기구는 재미있었니?
여 괜찮았어. 하지만 나는 정말 롤러코스터를 타고 싶었어.

|어휘| amusement park 놀이공원 excited [형] 신이 난 ride [동] 타다 [명] 놀이 기구 closed [형] 문을 닫은 repair [명] 수리 fun [형] 재미있는

어휘·표현 다지기

p. 59

A

01	반 친구	02	어리석은
03	이제, 더 이상	04	광대
05	확신하는, 자신감 있는	06	벽
07	약속	08	재미있는, 흥미로운
09	그림	10	신이 난
11	수학여행	12	봉투
13	유명한	14	타다, 놀이 기구
15	섬	16	일어나다, 발생하다

B

01	find out	02	look forward to
03	be in the hospital	04	care
05	hang	06	closed
07	poorly	08	feel like v-ing
09	lie	10	score

UNIT 7 할 일·한 일

주요 어휘·표현 미리보기

p. 60

01	ⓓ spend the day	02	ⓗ on my way to
03	ⓐ Get moving	04	ⓖ late for
05	ⓒ take this photo	06	ⓔ was canceled
07	ⓑ cousins	08	ⓕ go shopping

LISTENING PRACTICE

pp. 62-63

01 ①	02 ③	03 ⑤	04 ①	05 ④
06 ③	07 ④	08 ②	09 ⑤	10 ①

01 ①

W Are you busy now?
M No, I just finished my homework.
W Good. Let's start the housework and finish before Dad gets home.
M Okay, Mom. I'll do the dishes and wash the clothes.
W Okay. I'll clean the living room.

M Dad will be very surprised.
W Yes, he will. Let's get moving!

여 지금 바쁘니?
남 아니요, 방금 숙제 끝냈어요.
여 좋아. 집안일을 시작해서 아빠가 집에 도착하시기 전에 끝내자.
남 알겠어요, 엄마. 제가 설거지하고 빨래를 할게요.
여 그래. 나는 거실을 청소할게.
남 아빠가 정말 놀라시겠어요.
여 그래, 그러실 거야. 빨리 시작하자!

|어휘| busy [형] 바쁜 housework [명] 집안일 do the dishes 설거지하다 living room 거실 surprised [형] 놀란 get moving 빨리 시작하다[움직이다]

02 ③

[Cell phone rings.]
W Hello?
M It's Jake. I'm sorry, but I can't come to your wedding tomorrow.
W Why not? I really want to see you.
M Unfortunately, my flight was canceled because of the bad weather.
W Oh no! What about driving?
M My car is in the repair shop.
W Why don't you take the train?
M Will it get there in time?
W I'm not sure. I don't know the schedule.
M I'll check online and then call you back.

[휴대전화벨이 울린다.]
여 여보세요?
남 나 Jake야. 미안한데, 나 내일 네 결혼식에 못 가겠어.
여 왜? 너 정말 보고 싶은데.
남 유감스럽게도, 악천후로 내 항공편이 취소되었어.
여 아 이럴 수가! 운전해서 오지 그래?
남 내 차가 정비소에 있어.
여 기차를 타는 건 어때?
남 기차가 시간 맞춰 거기 도착할까?
여 잘 모르겠어. 내가 (기차) 시간표를 몰라서.
남 내가 온라인으로 확인해보고 다시 전화할게.

|해설| 여자가 기차 시간표를 모른다고 하자, 남자가 온라인으로 확인하겠다고 했다.

|어휘| wedding [명] 결혼식 unfortunately [부] 유감스럽게도, 불행하게도 flight [명] 항공편 cancel [동] 취소하다 repair shop 정비소, 수리점 in time 시간 맞춰

03 ⑤

M Hi, Amanda. I saw you walking down Main Street yesterday.
W Oh, you did? I was on my way to Hannah's place.
M Oh, I haven't seen her in a while. Did you two have lunch together?
W No. I mostly helped her pack her things. She's moving to Atlanta tomorrow.
M Oh, I didn't know that. I'll miss her.
W Me too.

남 안녕, Amanda. 어제 네가 Main 가를 걸어가는 걸 봤어.
여 아, 그랬어? Hannah의 집에 가는 길이었어.
남 아, 한동안 그 애를 못 봤네. 너희 둘이 함께 점심 먹었니?
여 아니. 난 주로 그 애가 짐 싸는 것을 도와줬어. 내일 애틀랜타로 이사하거든.
남 아, 몰랐어. 그 애가 보고 싶을 거야.
여 나도.

|어휘| on one's way to ~로 가는 길[도중]에 in a while 한동안 mostly [부] 주로 pack [동] (짐을) 싸다 move [동] 이사하다

04 ①

W Hey, did you have fun at the amusement park yesterday?
M Actually, I didn't go.
W Oh, didn't you say you were going to go with Jack?
M I did. But Jack got sick yesterday. So he had to see a doctor.
W I'm sorry to hear that.
M Yeah. So I just stayed home and watched TV.

여 얘, 어제 놀이공원에서 재미있었니?
남 실은 난 가지 않았어.
여 아, Jack과 갈 거라고 하지 않았어?
남 그랬지. 그런데 Jack이 어제 아팠어. 그래서 의사에게 진찰을 받아야 했어.
여 안됐구나.
남 응. 그래서 난 그냥 집에 있으면서 TV를 봤어.

|어휘| have fun 재미있다, 즐겁게 지내다 amusement park 놀이공원 see a doctor 의사의 진찰을 받다 stay [동] 머물다

05 ④

W Hey, look at this. I took this photo last Saturday.
M Wow, this parrot in the photo is cute! Did you go to the zoo?

W No, I visited a special café. There were several parrots, and I could even feed them!
M That sounds amazing. I'd like to visit that café sometime too.
W Then let's go together next time.

여 얘, 이것 좀 봐. 지난 토요일에 이 사진을 찍었어.
남 와, 사진 속 앵무새가 귀여워! 동물원에 갔었니?
여 아니, 특별한 카페를 방문했어. 앵무새가 몇 마리 있어서, 먹이도 줄 수 있었어!
남 굉장해. 나도 언젠가 그 카페에 가보고 싶어.
여 그럼 다음에 같이 가자.

|어휘| take a photo 사진을 찍다 parrot [명] 앵무새 several [형] 몇몇의 amazing [형] 놀라운 sometime [부] 언젠가

06 ③

W I'm going to spend the day at the beach on Saturday!
M Sounds great. But I thought you had a violin lesson on Saturday.
W No, that's on Sunday.
M Oh, I see.
W What will you do this weekend?
M Unfortunately, I have to study for a big test.

여 나 토요일에 해변에서 하루를 보낼 거야!
남 그거 괜찮다. 하지만 난 네가 토요일에 바이올린 수업이 있는 줄 알았는데.
여 아니, 그건 일요일이야.
남 아, 그렇구나.
여 넌 이번 주말에 뭐 할 거야?
남 유감스럽게도, 난 중요한 시험이 있어서 공부해야 해.

|어휘| spend [동] (시간·돈 등을) 쓰다 beach [명] 해변 lesson [명] 수업

07 ④

W This is a great app!
M What does it do?
W It tells me exactly when the bus will arrive.
M I need that app. I often miss the bus and get to school late.
W You can download it for free.
M I'll do that now. And I'll never be late for school again.

여 이거 괜찮은 앱이다!
남 뭐 하는 앱인데?
여 버스가 언제 도착할지 정확히 알려줘.
남 나 그 앱 필요해. 내가 버스를 자주 놓쳐서 학교에 늦게 도착하거든.
여 이거 무료로 내려받을 수 있어.
남 지금 할래. 그리고 다시는 지각하지 않을 거야.

|어휘| app [명] 응용 프로그램(= application), 앱 exactly [부] 정확하게 arrive [동] 도착하다 miss [동] 놓치다 download [동] (데이터를) 내려받다 for free 무료로 late for ~에 늦은[지각한]

08 ②

M Honey, how about going shopping together?
W Okay. Are there any sales at the department store?
M Yes. Spring is coming, so winter clothes are 40% off.
W Wow! I can buy a sweater for my ski trip.
M That's a good idea.
W But can we go later? I need to return some library books first.
M Sure. I'll wait for you.
W Great. I'll be back in about an hour.
M No problem.

남 여보, 함께 쇼핑하러 가는 게 어때요?
여 그래요. 백화점에서 할인 판매 중인 게 있나요?
남 네. 봄이 오고 있어서, 겨울옷을 40% 할인 판매하고 있어요.
여 와! 스키 여행용으로 스웨터 한 벌을 살 수 있겠네요.
남 그거 좋은 생각이네요.
여 하지만 우리 나중에 가도 될까요? 도서관 책을 먼저 반납해야 해서요.
남 그래요. 기다릴게요.
여 좋아요. 한 시간쯤 뒤에 올게요.
남 알겠어요.

|해설| 여자는 먼저 도서관에 책을 반납한 뒤에 쇼핑을 가자고 했다.

|어휘| go shopping 쇼핑하러 가다 department store 백화점 off [부] 할인되어 return [동] 반납하다

09 ⑤

M Hi, Irene. What did you do last Saturday?
W I saw *Matilda*. It was really good.
M *Matilda*? Do you mean the movie?
W No, the musical. How about you, Mike? What did you do?
M I went to an aquarium with my parents.
W Sounds fun!

남 안녕, Irene. 지난 토요일에 뭘 했니?

여 〈마틸다〉를 봤어. 정말 좋았어.
남 〈마틸다〉? 영화 말하는 거야?
여 아니, 뮤지컬. 너는 어때, Mike? 넌 뭘 했니?
남 부모님과 함께 수족관에 갔어.
여 재밌었겠다!

|어휘| mean [동] 의미하다 musical [명] 뮤지컬 aquarium [명] 수족관

10 ①

M Did you have a nice weekend?
W Yes, I did. I went to the beach with my cousins.
M You must have had fun!
W Yeah. We swam in the sea and made a big sandcastle. Did you go somewhere nice too?
M Yes, I went camping with my family.
W Oh, that sounds lovely!

남 주말 잘 보냈어?
여 응. 난 사촌들과 해변에 갔었어.
남 재미있었겠다!
여 응. 우리는 바다에서 수영을 하고 큰 모래성을 만들었어. 너도 좋은 곳에 갔었니?
남 응, 나는 가족과 함께 캠핑을 갔어.
여 오, 멋지다!

|어휘| cousin [명] 사촌 sandcastle [명] 모래성 somewhere [부] 어딘가에 go camping 캠핑 가다 lovely [형] 멋진

어휘·표현 다지기

p. 67

A

01	놀란	02	머물다
03	도착하다	04	해변
05	시간 맞춰	06	수업
07	주로	08	앵무새
09	집안일	10	거실
11	정확하게	12	바쁜
13	정비소, 수리점	14	수족관
15	설거지하다	16	모래성

B

01	amusement park	02	department store
03	move	04	off
05	flight	06	see a doctor
07	miss	08	somewhere
09	download	10	unfortunately

UNIT 8 지칭·주제/화제

주요 어휘·표현 미리보기

p. 68

01	[h] made of	02	[b] weather
03	[f] how to	04	[a] a kind of
05	[d] feed	06	[g] good for
07	[c] wash	08	[e] useful

LISTENING PRACTICE

pp. 70-71

01 ①	02 ②	03 ④	04 ③	05 ④
06 ③	07 ②	08 ⑤	09 ①	10 ③

01 ①

M You can see this in homes, offices and schools. This is a kind of furniture. People sit at this when they are doing work or studying. This sometimes has drawers. There are often books or a computer on top of this. What is this?

남 여러분은 이것을 가정, 사무실 그리고 학교에서 볼 수 있습니다. 이것은 가구의 일종입니다. 사람들은 일하거나 공부할 때 이것에 앉습니다. 이것은 가끔 서랍이 있기도 합니다. 이것 위에는 종종 책이나 컴퓨터가 있습니다. 이것은 무엇일까요?

|어휘| office [명] 사무실 a kind of 일종의 furniture [명] 가구 drawer [명] 서랍 on top of ~의 위에

02 ②

W I live in China. My ears and feet are black, and I have black circles around my eyes. The rest of my body is white. I like to eat bamboo, and I live in the mountains. What am I?

여 나는 중국에 삽니다. 귀와 발은 검은색이고, 눈 주위에는 검은색 원이 있습니다. 몸의 나머지는 흰색입니다. 나는 대나무 먹는 것을 좋아하며, 산에 삽니다. 나는 누구일까요?

|어휘| circle [명] 원, 동그라미 rest [명] 나머지 bamboo [명] 대나무

03 ④

W You <u>look tired</u>, David.

M Yes, I have to walk my dog every morning.

W I don't have to walk my cat. But I <u>have to feed her</u>.

M I feed my dog three times a day. And I wash him too.

W Now I understand <u>why you're tired</u>.

여 너 피곤해 보여, David.

남 응, 나 매일 아침 우리 개를 산책시켜야 해서.

여 난 우리 고양이를 산책시킬 필요 없는데. 하지만 먹이를 줘야 해.

남 난 하루에 세 번 우리 개에게 먹이를 줘. 그리고 목욕도 시켜.

여 이제 네가 왜 피곤한지 알겠다.

|해설| 두 사람은 산책시키고, 먹이를 주고, 목욕시키는 반려동물 돌보기에 대해 이야기하고 있다.

|어휘| tired 휑 피곤한 walk 통 (동물을) 산책시키다 feed 통 먹이를 주다 wash 통 씻기다 understand 통 이해하다

04 ③

M I saw an earthquake <u>on the news</u>. It looked scary.

W What should we do if one occurs?

M We should hide under some furniture. And we shouldn't use anything electrical.

W <u>That makes sense</u>. What else?

M We shouldn't use elevators. We should <u>take the stairs</u> instead.

남 나 뉴스에서 지진을 봤어. 무서워 보였어.

여 만약에 지진이 일어나면 우리는 어떻게 해야 하지?

남 가구 아래에 숨어야 해. 그리고 전기를 이용하는 어떤 것도 사용해서는 안 돼.

여 이해가 되네. 또 뭐 다른 건?

남 엘리베이터를 사용하면 안 돼. 대신에 계단을 이용해야 해.

|어휘| earthquake 명 지진 scary 휑 무서운 occur 통 일어나다, 발생하다 hide 통 숨다 electrical 휑 전기의, 전기를 이용하는 make sense 말이 되다, 이해가 되다 elevator 명 엘리베이터 stairs 명 계단 instead 분 대신에

05 ④

W Did you <u>have a nice time</u> at the swimming pool?

M Actually, a young girl fell in. She couldn't swim.

W That's terrible! Is she okay?

M Yes. A man pulled her from the pool and <u>gave her first aid</u>. He saved her life.

W That's great. First aid is very useful.

M Yes. We really need to learn <u>how to perform</u> it.

W I agree.

여 수영장에서 재미있는 시간 보냈니?

남 실은, 어떤 어린 여자아이가 물에 빠졌어. 그 아이가 수영을 못하더라고.

여 큰일이네! 그 아이는 괜찮아?

남 응. 한 남자가 수영장에서 그 아이를 끌어올려서 응급 처치를 했어. 그가 아이의 생명을 구했지.

여 멋지다. 응급 처치가 아주 유용하네.

남 맞아. 우리는 그것을 어떻게 하는지 정말 배워야 할 필요가 있어.

여 동의해.

|해설| 물에 빠진 여자아이가 응급 처치 덕분에 목숨을 건진 일화가 언급되고 있다.

|어휘| fall 통 떨어지다, 빠지다 terrible 휑 끔찍한 pull 통 끌어당기다, 잡아당기다 first aid 응급 처치 save 통 (생명 등을) 구하다 useful 휑 유용한 learn 통 배우다 how to-v ~하는 방법, 어떻게 ~하는지 perform 통 행하다

06 ③

W You can carry this. When you close this, it is <u>long and thin</u>. But this <u>gets bigger</u> when you open it. This is useful if you don't want to <u>get wet</u> when the weather is bad. What is this?

여 여러분은 이것을 가지고 다닐 수 있습니다. 이것을 접으면, 길고 가늡니다. 하지만 이것을 펴면 더 커집니다. 이것은 날씨가 나쁠 때 여러분이 젖고 싶지 않다면 유용합니다. 이것은 무엇일까요?

|어휘| carry 통 가지고 다니다 close 통 접다, 닫다 thin 휑 얇은, 가는 wet 휑 젖은 weather 명 날씨

07 ②

W You can find this <u>in a kitchen</u>. This is small, and it is usually <u>made of</u> metal or wood. One end is shaped like a small bowl. You can hold this in your hand and use it to <u>pick up food</u>. What is this?

여 여러분은 이것을 부엌에서 찾을 수 있습니다. 이것은 작고, 대개 금속이나 나무로 만들어집니다. 한쪽 끝은 우묵하고 작은 그릇 같은 모양입니다. 여러분은 이것을 손에 쥐고, 그것을 사용해 음식을 집을 수 있습니다. 이것은 무엇일까요?

|어휘| usually 분 대개, 보통 be made of ~로 만들어지다 metal 명 금속 wood 명 나무 end 명 끝 shaped like ~와 같은 모양을 한 bowl 명 (우묵한) 그릇 hold 통 쥐다 pick up ~을 집어 들다

08 ⑤

W People use this when they are traveling. You must use this in cars and on airplanes. You find this on some buses too. This has two thin parts. They can be connected by a metal or plastic part in the middle. This keeps people safe if there is an accident. What is this?

여 사람들은 이동할 때 이것을 사용합니다. 여러분은 자동차와 비행기 안에서 이것을 사용해야 합니다. 일부 버스에서도 이것이 보입니다. 이것은 두 개의 얇은 부분이 있습니다. 그것들은 가운데의 금속이나 플라스틱 부분으로 연결될 수 있습니다. 이것은 사고가 나면 사람들을 안전하게 지켜줍니다. 이것은 무엇일까요?

|해설| 자동차나 비행기 안에서 사용하는 것으로 금속이나 플라스틱으로 두 부분이 연결되며, 사람을 사고로부터 보호하는 것은 안전띠이다.

|어휘| travel [동] 이동하다 connect [동] 연결하다 keep ~ safe ~을 안전하게 지키다 accident [명] 사고

09 ①

W Hi, Matthew! What are you doing on Saturday?
M I'm not sure yet. I usually spend time with my friends.
W What do you and your friends usually do together on weekends?
M We like to play computer games and watch movies. How about you?
W I go grocery shopping with my husband every Saturday. I also take piano lessons on Sundays.

여 안녕, Matthew! 토요일에 뭐 할 거야?
남 아직 잘 모르겠어. 나는 보통 친구들과 시간을 보내.
여 너랑 네 친구들은 보통 주말에 함께 뭘 하니?
남 우리는 컴퓨터 게임을 하고 영화 보는 것을 좋아해. 너는 어때?
여 나는 매주 토요일에 남편하고 장보러 가. 일요일에는 피아노 수업도 받아.

|어휘| grocery shopping 장보기 husband [명] 남편

10 ③

W Those cars are so quiet! I didn't even hear them.
M That's because they run on electricity, not gasoline.
W I see. That must be very good for the environment.
M It is. But some people don't like them because they are slow.
W That doesn't matter. I want to buy one someday.

여 저 차들은 정말 조용하다! 난 심지어 아무 소리도 못 들었어.
남 그건 저 차들이 휘발유가 아니라 전기로 작동해서 그래.
여 그렇구나. 환경에 정말 좋을 것 같아.
남 그렇지. 하지만 어떤 사람들은 느려서 좋아하지 않아.
여 그건 중요하지 않아. 언젠가 한 대 사고 싶어.

|어휘| quiet [형] 조용한 run [동] 작동하다 electricity [명] 전기 gasoline [명] 휘발유 be good for ~에 좋다 environment [명] 환경 matter [동] 중요하다 someday [부] 언젠가

어휘·표현 다지기

p. 75

A

01 가구	02 배우다
03 지진	04 서랍
05 응급 처치	06 연결하다
07 ~의 위에	08 금속
09 전기	10 무서운
11 사무실	12 얇은, 가는
13 사고	14 환경
15 이해하다	16 대나무

B

01 carry	02 hold
03 pull	04 stairs
05 pick up	06 make sense
07 matter	08 save
09 walk	10 occur

UNIT 9 특정 정보

주요 어휘·표현 미리보기

p. 76

01 ⓑ takes too long	02 ⓖ drove
03 ⓔ look good on	04 ⓕ continue
05 ⓐ get to	06 ⓒ woke up
07 ⓗ idea	08 ⓓ take

LISTENING PRACTICE

pp. 78-79

01 ③	02 ④	03 ③	04 ②	05 ⑤
06 ④	07 ②	08 ②	09 ③	10 ②

01 ③

M Good morning! This is your daily weather report. It's snowing right now, but the snow will change to rain this evening. Tomorrow it will be windy in the morning but cold and sunny in the afternoon.

남 좋은 아침입니다! 일일 일기 예보입니다. 현재 눈이 오고 있지만, 이 눈은 오늘 저녁에 비로 바뀔 것입니다. 내일은 아침에 바람이 불겠지만, 오후에는 추운 가운데 맑겠습니다.

|어휘| weather report 일기 예보 change [동] 변하다 windy [형] 바람이 부는

02 ④

M Hello, everyone! I'm Alan Johnson, and here is tomorrow's weather forecast for Seoul. It will be sunny in the morning, but it will become cloudy in the afternoon. Rain will start late in the evening and continue all night. So don't forget your umbrella!

남 안녕하세요, 여러분! 저는 Alan Johnson이고, 내일 서울의 일기 예보입니다. 아침에는 화창하겠지만, 오후에는 흐려지겠습니다. 저녁 늦게는 비가 시작되어 밤새 계속되겠습니다. 그러니 우산 잊지 마세요!

|어휘| weather forecast 일기 예보 continue [동] 계속되다 forget [동] 잊다

03 ③

M Where are you going, Kimberly?
W I'm going to the mall. I need some new shoes.
M Are you going to take the subway?
W Yes. I usually take the bus, but it's too slow.
M Can I go with you?
W Sure! That would be great!

남 어디 가니, Kimberly?
여 쇼핑몰에 가는 중이야. 새 신발이 필요하거든.
남 지하철 탈 거니?
여 응. 난 보통 버스를 타는데, 너무 느려.
남 같이 갈까?
여 그래! 그럼 좋겠다!

|해설| 여자는 버스가 너무 느려서 지하철을 탈 것이라고 했다.

|어휘| mall [명] 쇼핑몰 take the subway 지하철을 타다 usually [부] 보통 slow [형] 느린

04 ②

W Hi, Matt. I didn't see you on the school bus yesterday.
M That's because I woke up late and missed it.
W Oh no. Did your father drive you to school?
M No, he was too busy. I had to take a taxi.
W That's too bad.

여 안녕, Matt. 너 어제 통학 버스에서 안 보이더라.
남 왜냐하면 늦게 일어나서 버스를 놓쳤거든.
여 아, 저런. 너희 아버지께서 학교까지 태워다주셨니?
남 아니, 아버지는 너무 바쁘셨어. 난 택시를 타야 했어.
여 안됐네.

|어휘| wake up (잠에서) 깨다 miss [동] 놓치다 drive [동] 태워다 주다 busy [형] 바쁜

05 ⑤

W Come over here, Derek. What do you think of this scarf?
M I like it a lot. It's the same color as my shirt.
W Yes, but it's too expensive. I'll just get this hat instead.
M It looks good on you!
W Thanks! You should get one too.

여 Derek, 이리로 와봐. 이 스카프 어때?
남 정말 마음에 들어. 내 셔츠랑 같은 색이네.
여 응, 그런데 너무 비싸. 대신 이 모자를 사야겠어.
남 그거 너한테 잘 어울린다!
여 고마워! 너도 하나 사.

|해설| 여자는 마음에 드는 스카프가 너무 비싸서 대신 모자를 사기로 했다.

|어휘| scarf [명] 스카프, 목도리 same [형] 같은 expensive [형] 비싼 instead [부] 대신에 look good on ~와 잘 어울리다

06 ④

W Good morning. I'm Tina Wilson. Here is the ABC weather forecast. Today we'll have heavy rain with strong winds all day. Please remember to take an umbrella with you. Tomorrow, it will be foggy in the morning. But by the afternoon, it will be nice and sunny. The sunny weather will continue the next day as well.

여 좋은 아침입니다. Tina Wilson입니다. ABC 일기 예보를 전해드립니다. 오늘은 종일 강한 바람을 동반한 폭우가 쏟아질 예정입니다. 우산 챙기는 걸 기억하세요. 내일은 아침에 안개가 끼겠습니다. 하지만 오후 경에는 매우 맑겠습니다. 맑은 날씨는 다음 날에도 계속되겠습니다.

|어휘| heavy rain 폭우 strong [형] 강한 remember [동] 기억하다 foggy [형] 안개가 낀 as well 역시, 또한

07 ②

W I'm Diana Lee, and here is the national weather report. There are sunny skies over Seoul and Incheon today, but the weather is very different in Daegu. Heavy rain started this morning and is expected to continue all day. It will be cloudy in Busan, but it won't rain. And Jeju will experience high winds because of a storm.

여 저는 Diana Lee이며, 전국의 일기 예보를 알려드리겠습니다. 오늘 서울과 인천 하늘은 맑지만, 대구의 날씨는 매우 다릅니다. 오늘 아침에 폭우가 시작되었으며 종일 계속될 예정입니다. 부산은 구름이 끼겠지만, 비는 오지 않겠습니다. 그리고 제주는 폭풍으로 인한 강풍을 겪겠습니다.

|어휘| national [형] 전국적인 different [형] 다른 be expected to-v ~하기로 예상되다 experience [동] 경험하다 high wind 강풍 storm [명] 폭풍

08 ②

W Have a good day today, Joey.
M You too, Laura. Don't forget your subway card. I'll put it on your desk.
W Thanks, but I don't need it today.
M Why not? Will one of your coworkers pick you up instead?
W No, I'm going to walk to work. I need some exercise.
M Oh, okay.

여 오늘 좋은 하루 보내요, Joey.
남 당신도요, Laura. 지하철 카드 잊지 마요. 책상 위에 둘게요.
여 고마워요, 그런데 오늘은 그거 필요 없어요.
남 왜 필요 없어요? 대신 당신 직장 동료 중 한 명이 당신을 태우러 오나요?
여 아니요, 저 오늘 회사에 걸어갈 거예요. 운동이 좀 필요해서요.
남 아, 알았어요.

|해설| 여자는 운동 목적으로 회사까지 걸어가겠다고 했다.

|어휘| coworker [명] 직장 동료 pick up ~을 태우러 가다 exercise [명] 운동

09 ③

M Let's go to the festival in Toronto next week!
W All right. We can take my car.
M No, it would take too long to drive there.
W Then why don't we take the train? It's faster than driving.
M That's true. But flying is the fastest way to get to Toronto.
W Yes, but it's also the most expensive way. My idea is better.
M I guess you're right.

남 다음 주에 토론토에서 하는 축제에 가자!
여 좋아. 내 차 타고 가면 되겠다.
남 아니야, 거기에 운전해서 가면 너무 오래 걸릴 거야.
여 그러면 기차를 타는 게 어때? 운전하는 것보다 더 빠르잖아.
남 맞아. 하지만 비행기를 타는 게 토론토에 가는 가장 빠른 방법이지.
여 그래, 하지만 가장 비싼 방법이기도 하지. 내 생각이 나아.
남 네 말이 맞는 것 같다.

|해설| 여자가 제안한 기차 타기에 남자가 동의하고 있다.

|어휘| festival [명] 축제 fly [동] 비행기를 타고 가다 way [명] 방법 get to ~에 도착하다 idea [명] 생각 better [형] 더 좋은, 나은

10 ②

M I want to bake a cake. Let's go to the market.
W Okay. You'll need sugar and flour.
M I'll get some sugar, but I already have lots of flour.
W You'll need eggs too.
M Don't worry. I have plenty of eggs.
W I can't wait to taste your cake!

남 나 케이크 굽고 싶어. 시장에 가자.
여 좋아. 설탕이랑 밀가루가 필요할 거야.
남 설탕은 살 거지만 밀가루는 이미 많이 있어.
여 계란도 필요할 거야.
남 걱정하지 마. 계란 많이 있어.
여 네 케이크 빨리 맛보고 싶다!

|어휘| bake [동] 굽다 market [명] 시장 sugar [명] 설탕 flour [명] 밀가루 already [부] 이미 lots of 많은 worry [동] 걱정하다 plenty of 많은 taste [동] 맛보다

어휘·표현 다지기

p. 83

A

01 쇼핑몰
02 폭풍
03 다른
04 축제
05 시장
06 바람이 부는
07 방법
08 기억하다
09 역시, 또한
10 대신에
11 변하다
12 보통
13 강한
14 일기 예보
15 굽다
16 밀가루

B

01 plenty of
02 experience
03 foggy
04 high wind
05 expensive
06 coworker
07 heavy rain
08 national
09 same
10 be expected to-v

UNIT 10 부탁·제안한 일

주요 어휘·표현 미리보기

p. 84

01 ⓖ take a walk
02 ⓓ a piece of
03 ⓑ graduated from
04 ⓔ go out
05 ⓗ look down
06 ⓒ add
07 ⓐ shut
08 ⓕ give it a try

LISTENING PRACTICE

pp. 86-87

01 ③	02 ⑤	03 ③	04 ④	05 ①
06 ③	07 ④	08 ②	09 ①	10 ④

01 ③

M Is something wrong, Lisa?
W Yes. It's too cold in here. I'm freezing.
M Yes, it is a little cold. Would you like to borrow a sweater?
W No. But the window is open. Could you shut it?
M Sure. Sorry about that.

남 무슨 일 있니, Lisa?
여 응. 여기 너무 추워. 꽁꽁 얼게 추워.
남 그러게, 좀 춥네. 스웨터 빌릴래?
여 아니. 그런데 창문이 열려 있네. 닫아줄 수 있니?
남 물론이지. 미안해.

|어휘| freezing [형] 꽁꽁 얼게 추운 borrow [동] 빌리다 sweater [명] 스웨터 shut [동] 닫다

02 ⑤

W Jake, are you playing phone games?
M No! I'm reading an e-book.
W Oh, okay. Will you go out after you finish?
M I don't have any plans. Why?
W I have to pick up your sister, but a delivery man is coming soon.
M Did you order something for Dad's birthday?
W Yes. Can you get the package when it arrives?
M Sure, Mom. And I'll hide it in the closet.
W Thanks, honey!

여 Jake, 너 핸드폰 게임하고 있니?
남 아니요! 전자책 읽는 중이에요.
여 아, 그렇구나. 마치고 외출할 거니?
남 아무 계획 없는데요. 왜요?
여 내가 네 여동생을 데리러 가야 하는데, 배달원이 곧 오실 거거든.
남 아빠 생신을 위해 무언가 주문하셨어요?
여 응. 택배 도착하면 좀 받아줄 수 있니?
남 물론이죠, 엄마. 그리고 그거 옷장에 숨길게요.
여 고맙다, 얘야!

|어휘| go out 외출하다 pick up ~을 태우러 가다 delivery man 상품 배달원 package [명] 소포 hide [동] 숨기다 closet [명] 옷장

03 ③

M What are you doing with that bread?
W I'm making a sandwich. Can you give me a piece of ham?
M Sure. Here you are.
W Thanks. Now, I'll just cut two slices of cheese. And I'm finished! Here! You can have half!
M Thanks. But can you add more cheese for me?
W Sure!

남 그 빵으로 뭐 하는 중이야?
여 샌드위치를 만들고 있어. 햄 한 조각 건네줄래?
남 그래. 여기 있어.

여 고마워. 이제 치즈 두 조각을 자를 거야. 그러면 끝이야! 여기! 절반 먹어!

남 고마워. 그런데 나 치즈 좀 더 넣어줄래?

여 그래!

|어휘| a piece of 하나의, 한 조각의   slice 명 (음식을 얇게 썬) 조각   finished 형 끝난   half 명 절반   add 동 더하다, 추가하다

04 ④

W What's wrong, Mark? You look down.

M Some students keep bullying me these days.

W Oh. Would you like me to talk to them?

M No! That would just make it worse.

W How about talking to your teacher? She might be able to help.

M Okay. I'll give it a try, Mom.

여 무슨 일이니, Mark? 너 우울해 보인다.

남 몇몇 학생들이 요즘 저를 계속 괴롭혀요.

여 아. 내가 그 애들에게 이야기해볼까?

남 아니요! 그건 상황을 더 악화시키기만 할 거예요.

여 너희 선생님께 말씀드리는 건 어때? 도와주실 수 있을지도 몰라.

남 알겠어요. 한번 해 볼게요, 엄마.

|어휘| look down 우울해 보이다   bully 동 괴롭히다   make worse 악화시키다   give it a try 한번 (시도)해 보다

05 ①

W Alex is graduating from middle school tomorrow. What will you get him?

M I already bought his present. It's a new wallet. What about you?

W I haven't gotten him anything. I don't have any good ideas.

M Why don't you buy him some new school clothes?

W That's a good idea. Thanks!

여 Alex가 내일 중학교를 졸업해요. 그 애한테 뭘 줄 거예요?

남 나는 이미 선물을 샀어요. 새 지갑으로요. 당신은요?

여 나는 아무것도 못 샀어요. 좋은 생각이 안 나네요.

남 새 학생복을 좀 사주는 건 어때요?

여 그거 좋은 생각이네요. 고마워요!

|어휘| graduate from ~을 졸업하다   present 명 선물   wallet 명 지갑   school clothes 학생복

06 ③

M I'm going on vacation tomorrow.

W That's great! Do you need a ride to the airport?

M No, but I need someone to watch Fluffy.

W Fluffy? Is that your cat?

M Yes, can you feed her and play with her?

W Sure! I'd be glad to.

남 나 내일 휴가 가.

여 멋지다! 공항까지 태워줄 필요 있니?

남 아냐, 그런데 나 Fluffy를 잠깐 봐줄 사람이 필요해.

여 Fluffy? 네 고양이니?

남 응, 고양이한테 먹이 주고 놀아줄 수 있니?

여 물론이지! 기꺼이 그렇게 할게.

|어휘| go on vacation 휴가를 가다   ride 명 타기, 태워주기   watch 동 (잠깐 동안) 봐주다   feed 동 먹이를 주다

07 ④

W Edward, can you do me a favor?

M Well, I don't have much time. My class starts in five minutes.

W It won't take long. I just need a book from the top shelf.

M Oh! You can't reach it?

W No, I can't. Could you get it for me?

M No problem.

여 Edward, 내 부탁 좀 들어줄래?

남 음, 나 시간이 많지 않아. 5분 뒤에 수업이 시작해.

여 오래 걸리지 않을 거야. 나는 그냥 책장 맨 위 칸에 있는 책이 필요해.

남 아! 너 그게 손에 안 닿아?

여 응, 안 닿아. 나한테 그 책 좀 가져다줄래?

남 알겠어.

|어휘| do ~ a favor ~의 부탁을 들어주다   take long 오래 걸리다   shelf 명 책꽂이, (책장의) 칸, 선반   reach 동 (손이) 닿다

08 ②

M Do we have any onions?

W No. We used the last ones yesterday.

M I was going to make dinner, but I need onions.

W Would you like me to go to the store and get some?

M No, it's raining too hard.

W Why don't you just have something delivered from the restaurant around the corner?

M Good idea. I can cook tomorrow night.

남 우리 양파 좀 있어요?
여 아니요. 어제 마지막 남은 걸 썼어요.
남 내가 저녁 식사를 준비하려고 했는데, 양파가 필요해서요.
여 내가 가게에 가서 좀 사 올까요?
남 아니요, 비가 너무 많이 오잖아요.
여 그냥 코앞에 있는 식당에서 뭔가 시켜먹는 게 어때요?
남 좋은 생각이에요. 요리는 내일 밤에 해도 되니까요.

|어휘| onion [명] 양파 last [형] 마지막 (남은) make dinner 저녁 식사를 준비하다 hard [부] 심하게, 많이 deliver [동] 배달하다 around the corner 코앞에 있는

09 ①

M How's your essay going?
W Terrible. I can't think of any new ideas.
M Why don't you take a walk? It will refresh your brain.
W Really? Okay. Do you want to come with me?
M No, thanks. I have to do my laundry.
W All right. Thanks for the suggestion.

남 과제는 어떻게 되어 가니?
여 큰일이야. 새로운 생각이 전혀 떠오르지 않아.
남 산책을 하는 건 어때? 그게 머리를 상쾌하게 할 거야.
여 정말? 그래. 나랑 같이 갈래?
남 아니, 난 됐어. 빨래해야 해.
여 알겠어. 제안 고마워.

|어휘| essay [명] 과제, 에세이 terrible [형] 끔찍한 take a walk 산책하다 refresh [동] 상쾌하게 하다 do laundry 빨래하다 suggestion [명] 제안

10 ④

W I borrowed Holly's camera and accidentally broke it.
M She must be angry.
W She is. I would buy her a new one, but I can't afford it. I don't know what to do.
M Why don't you just tell her that you're sorry?
W You're right. I should.
M It was an accident, so she'll probably forgive you.

여 내가 Holly의 카메라를 빌렸는데 뜻하지 않게 잘못해서 고장 냈어.
남 그 애가 화났겠는데.
여 그렇지. Holly한테 새것을 사주려는데, 내가 형편이 안 돼. 뭘 해야 할지 모르겠어.
남 그냥 그 애한테 미안하다고 말하는 게 어때?
여 네 말이 맞아. 그래야지.
남 그건 우연한 사고였으니까, 그 애가 아마 용서해줄 거야.

|어휘| accidentally [부] 뜻하지 않게 잘못하여 afford [동] 여유[형편]가 되다 accident [명] (우연한) 사고[사건] forgive [동] 용서하다

어휘·표현 다지기 p. 91

A

01	제안	02	빨래하다
03	지갑	04	책꽂이, (책장의) 칸, 선반
05	절반	06	숨기다
07	옷장	08	소포
09	빌리다	10	배달하다
11	오래 걸리다	12	심하게, 많이
13	용서하다	14	괴롭히다
15	여유[형편]가 되다	16	저녁 식사를 준비하다

B

01	freezing	02	slice
03	pick up	04	reach
05	refresh	06	go on vacation
07	watch	08	accidentally
09	do ~ a favor	10	make worse

UNIT 11 마지막 말에 대한 응답

주요 어휘·표현 미리보기 p. 92

01	ⓖ far away	02	ⓑ apologize
03	ⓗ smells good	04	ⓒ sold out
05	ⓐ looks sad	06	ⓔ fixed
07	ⓓ cost	08	ⓕ urgent

LISTENING PRACTICE pp. 94-95

01 ②	02 ④	03 ②	04 ⑤	05 ①
06 ④	07 ③	08 ②	09 ④	10 ⑤

01 ②

M What's wrong, Marie? You look sad.
W Today is a special day, but you forgot.
M What day is it?
W It's my birthday!
M I didn't really forget. Here are some flowers.
W What a surprise!

① It was yesterday.
③ When is your birthday?
④ You don't have to apologize.
⑤ Why don't you buy them?

남 무슨 일이야, Marie? 슬퍼 보여.
여 오늘 특별한 날인데, 네가 잊어버렸어.
남 무슨 날인데?
여 내 생일이잖아!
남 사실은 잊지 않았어. 여기 꽃이야.
여 깜짝이야!

① 그건 어제였어.
③ 네 생일은 언제니?
④ 너는 사과할 필요 없어.
⑤ 그것들을 사지 그러니?

|어휘| sad [형] 슬픈 special [형] 특별한 **[문제]** surprise [명] 놀라운 일[소식] apologize [동] 사과하다

02 ④

M Sumi! You're home!
W It's good to see you, Junwoo. I'm finally back in Seoul.
M Why did you come back early?
W Because my work schedule changed.
M I see. Did you have a good time there?
W Yes, I did. But I missed you a lot.

① I came here at 5:00 p.m.
② I'm too busy to go back.
③ No, I'm going there next week.
⑤ I went there with my family.

남 수미야! 집에 왔구나!
여 너 보니까 좋다, 준우야. 나 드디어 서울에 돌아왔어.
남 왜 일찍 돌아왔어?
여 업무 일정이 바뀌었거든.
남 그렇구나. 그곳에서는 즐거운 시간 보냈니?
여 응, 그랬어. 하지만 네가 매우 그리웠어.

① 나는 오후 5시에 여기에 왔어.
② 나는 너무 바빠서 돌아갈 수 없어.
③ 아니, 나는 다음 주에 거기에 갈 거야.
⑤ 나는 그곳에 우리 가족과 함께 갔어.

|어휘| finally [부] 마침내 early [부] 일찍 schedule [명] 일정 have a good time 즐거운 시간을 보내다 **[문제]** go back 돌아가다 miss [동] 그립다

03 ②

M Do you take the bus to school?
W No, I walk to school. My home isn't very far away.
M How lucky you are!
W How do you get to school?
M By bus, and it takes a long time.
W How long does it take?
M It takes fifty minutes.

① Yes, it is very far.
③ School begins at nine o'clock.
④ No, I don't take a bus.
⑤ Only when I am late.

남 너는 학교에 버스 타고 가니?
여 아니, 난 학교에 걸어가. 우리 집은 그리 멀지 않거든.
남 너는 정말 운이 좋구나!
여 너는 학교에 어떻게 가?
남 버스 타고 가는데, 시간이 오래 걸려.
여 얼마나 걸리는데?
남 50분 걸려.

① 응, 굉장히 멀어.
③ 학교는 9시에 시작해.
④ 아니, 난 버스를 타지 않아.
⑤ 내가 늦을 때만.

|해설| 학교에 가는 데 시간이 얼마나 걸리는지 물었으므로, 소요 시간을 말하는 ②가 가장 적절하다.

|어휘| far away 먼, 멀리 떨어진 lucky [형] 행운의 get to ~에 가다[도착하다] **[문제]** begin [동] 시작하다

04 ⑤

W Do you like the opera, Harry?
M No, I don't. Actually, I hate it. I think it's boring.
W Oh. I have two tickets to the opera for tonight.
M Really? Who are you going with?
W Well, I was going to ask you to go with me.
M Sorry, I'm not interested.

① I'm afraid the tickets are sold out.

② That show was amazing.
③ Okay, I'll see you then.
④ How much do they cost?

여 Harry, 오페라 좋아하니?
남 아니, 안 좋아해. 사실, 싫어해. 지루한 것 같아.
여 아. 오늘 밤에 하는 오페라 티켓이 두 장 있는데.
남 정말? 누구랑 가는데?
여 음, 나는 너에게 같이 가자고 하려고 했지.
남 미안해, 나는 관심이 없어.

① 유감이지만 티켓이 매진된 것 같아.
② 그 공연은 멋졌어.
③ 좋아, 그때 봐.
④ 그것들은 얼마니?

|어휘| boring [형] 지루한 **[문제]** I'm afraid (that) 유감이지만 ~이다 sold out 표가 매진된 amazing [형] 멋진, 놀라운 cost [동] (값이) ~이다 interested [형] 관심 있어 하는

05 ①

W What are you doing, Steven?
M I'm getting ready to go out.
W Oh! Where are you going?
M My friend's house. Did you need something?
W Yes. Can I borrow your computer again?
M Again? Didn't you get yours fixed?
W Not yet. I've been too busy.
M Well, you can't keep using mine.
W But it's really urgent. Please?
M Okay, but this is the last time.

② No, I don't have one anymore.
③ Sure, you can come with me.
④ Sorry, but I don't know how.
⑤ Yes, I will fix it tomorrow.

여 뭐 하니, Steven?
남 외출할 준비하고 있어.
여 아! 어디 가는데?
남 친구 집에. 뭐 필요한 것 있었어?
여 응. 네 컴퓨터 한 번 더 빌릴 수 있을까?
남 또? 네 것 수리 안 맡겼어?
여 아직. 너무 바빴어.
남 음, 네가 내 것을 계속 쓸 순 없는데.
여 하지만 정말 급해. 응?
남 알았어, 하지만 이번이 마지막이야.

② 아니, 이제는 하나도 없어.
③ 물론이지, 너 나랑 같이 가도 돼.
④ 미안하지만, 나는 어떻게 하는지 몰라.
⑤ 그래, 내가 내일 그거 고칠게.

|해설| 남자는 컴퓨터를 빌려주는 것을 주저하지만 여자가 계속 부탁하고 있는 상황이다.

|어휘| get ready to-v ~할 준비를 하다 get ~ fixed ~을 수리 맡기다 urgent [형] 급한 **[문제]** fix [동] 고치다

06 ④

W May I take your order?
M Yes, I'll have the corn salad and the steak.
W How would you like your steak?
M Well-done, please.
W And anything to drink?
M Just a glass of water, please.

① I ate some cookies already.
② No, I don't have anything.
③ Soda is not a healthy drink.
⑤ Yes, I ordered a salad and a steak.

여 주문하시겠습니까?
남 네, 콘 샐러드와 스테이크로 할게요.
여 스테이크는 어떻게 해드릴까요?
남 완전히 익혀 주세요.
여 마실 것은 어떻게 하시겠습니까?
남 그냥 물 한 잔 주세요.

① 저는 이미 쿠키를 좀 먹었어요.
② 아니요, 저는 아무것도 없어요.
③ 탄산음료는 건강에 좋은 음료가 아니에요.
⑤ 네, 저는 샐러드와 스테이크를 주문했어요.

|해설| 음료는 무엇을 주문하겠냐는 질문에 물을 달라고 하는 대답이 자연스럽다.

|어휘| well-done [형] (고기가) 잘 익은 **[문제]** already [부] 이미 soda [명] 탄산음료 healthy [형] 건강에 좋은 a glass of ~ 한 잔

07 ③

W I guess I should be going.
M Yes. We'll be boarding soon.
W Enjoy your flight. And be careful, honey.
M Don't worry, Mom. I'll be fine.
W How will you get to your dormitory in Vancouver?
M Someone from the school will pick me up at the airport.
W How will I know that you arrived safely?
M I will call you when I get there.

① They sent me an email.
② Let me check the schedule.
④ You're a very careful driver.
⑤ My flight arrives at 9:30 p.m.

여 나 가봐야 할 것 같구나.
남 네. 저희 곧 탑승할 거예요.
여 즐거운 비행 되길 바란다. 그리고 조심하고, 얘야.
남 걱정하지 마세요, 엄마. 잘 지낼 거예요.
여 밴쿠버에 있는 기숙사까지는 어떻게 갈 거니?
남 학교에서 나오신 분이 공항에 저를 태우러 와주실 거예요.
여 네가 안전하게 도착했다는 걸 내가 어떻게 알 수 있을까?
남 제가 그곳에 도착하면 전화 드릴게요.

① 그들이 제게 이메일을 보냈어요.
② 일정을 확인해볼게요.
④ 운전을 매우 조심스럽게 하시네요.
⑤ 제 비행기는 밤 9시 30분에 도착해요.

|해설| 여자는 남자가 잘 도착했는지 알고 싶어 하므로, 도착하면 전화하겠다는 응답이 가장 적절하다.

|어휘| board [동] 탑승하다 dormitory [명] 기숙사 pick up ~을 태우러 오다 **[문제]** careful [형] 조심하는

08 ②

W What's that smell?
M I think it's chicken.
W Is Mom cooking for the party?
M Yes, she is.
W It smells really good. Maybe she'll let us have some.
M Didn't you just have a big lunch?
W Yes, but I'm still hungry.

① Thanks, but I'm full.
③ I will have chicken for lunch.
④ Yes, this new restaurant is excellent.
⑤ No, we're going to be late for the party.

여 저 냄새는 뭐지?
남 닭고기인 것 같아.
여 엄마가 파티를 위해 요리하고 계시나?
남 응, 맞아.
여 냄새가 정말 좋다. 아마 엄마가 우리에게 좀 먹으라고 하시겠지.
남 너 방금 점심 푸짐하게 먹지 않았니?
여 응, 하지만 난 아직도 배가 고파.

① 고맙지만, 난 배불러.
③ 나는 점심으로 닭고기를 먹을 거야.
④ 그래, 새로 생긴 이 식당은 훌륭하네.
⑤ 아니야, 우리는 파티에 늦을 거야.

|해설| 방금 점심을 푸짐하게 먹지 않았냐는 남자의 질문에 아직도 배가 고프다는 대답이 가장 자연스럽다.

|어휘| smell [명] 냄새 [동] 냄새가 나다 have a big lunch 점심을 푸짐하게 먹다 **[문제]** still [부] 아직도, 여전히 excellent [형] 훌륭한

09 ④

W Hey, Jason. Could you help me carry this box?
M Sure. Where are you going?
W I'm going to the bus stop.
M Oh, are you going home now?
W Yes, I am.
M Then I'll give you a ride home. I'm going in the same direction.
W That would be great. Thanks.

① It's my pleasure.
② Okay, I'll ask someone else.
③ Sorry, but I have to go now.
⑤ Walk two blocks and turn left.

여 얘, Jason. 이 상자 나르는 것 좀 도와줄래?
남 그래. 어디 가는 거야?
여 버스 정류장에 가고 있어.
남 아, 너 지금 집에 가는 거니?
여 응, 맞아.
남 그러면 내가 차로 집까지 태워줄게. 나도 같은 방향으로 가거든.
여 그거 좋겠다. 고마워.

① 천만에.
② 그래, 내가 다른 누군가에게 물어볼게.
③ 미안한데, 내가 지금 가봐야 해.
⑤ 두 블록을 걸어가서 왼쪽으로 돌아.

|해설| 상자 나르는 것을 도와달라는 여자의 요청에 남자가 집까지 태워주겠다고 했으므로, 고맙다는 응답이 이어지는 것이 자연스럽다.

|어휘| help [동] 돕다 carry [동] 나르다 give a ride ~을 태워주다 direction [명] 방향

10 ⑤

W Summer vacation is coming.
M Yes, it is. Do you have any plans?
W My family is going to visit my uncle's house in Sydney.
M Wow, that will be fun.
W Yes, I am very excited.
M When will you go there?
W We'll leave next Wednesday.

① We'll go there by plane.
② Let's meet at five o'clock.
③ You can go there, too.
④ I've never been there before.

여 여름방학이 다가오고 있어.
남 그래, 맞아. 무슨 계획 있니?
여 우리 가족은 시드니에 있는 삼촌 댁을 방문할 거야.
남 와, 그거 재미있겠다.
여 응, 정말 신나.
남 거기 언제 가는데?
여 우리는 다음 주 수요일에 출발할 거야.

① 우리는 그곳에 비행기로 갈 거야.
② 5시에 만나자.
③ 너도 그곳에 가도 돼.
④ 나는 그곳에 한 번도 가본 적이 없어.

|해설| 언제 갈지 물었으므로, 출발하는 때를 말하는 ⑤가 가장 적절하다.

|어휘| vacation 몡 방학 [문제] leave 동 떠나다, 출발하다

p. 99

어휘·표현 다지기

A

01 조심하는	02 방향
03 멋진, 놀라운	04 ~ 한 잔
05 일찍	06 행운의
07 시작하다	08 관심 있어 하는
09 특별한	10 일정
11 돌아가다	12 기숙사
13 돕다	14 지루한
15 마침내	16 ~할 준비를 하다

B

01 surprise	02 I'm afraid (that)
03 excellent	04 healthy
05 get to	06 have a good time
07 have a big lunch	08 give a ride
09 board	10 well-done

주요 어휘·표현 미리보기
p. 100

01 ⓓ share		02 ⓗ in third grade	
03 ⓖ can't wait to		04 ⓔ free	
05 ⓐ lost		06 ⓕ have to return	
07 ⓑ younger than		08 ⓒ decided to	

LISTENING PRACTICE
pp. 102-103

01 ③	02 ⑤	03 ④	04 ④	05 ⑤
06 ③	07 ④	08 ③	09 ⑤	10 ⑤

01 ③

M Hi, Emily. Are you free this Saturday?
W Yes, what's up?
M It's my birthday. I want you to come to my party.
W Thanks for the invite. How many people will there be?
M I invited eight friends including you. Please come to my house at 2:00 p.m.
W Okay. See you then.

남 안녕, Emily. 너 이번 주 토요일에 시간 있니?
여 응, 무슨 일인데?
남 그날이 내 생일이거든. 네가 내 파티에 와주면 좋겠어.
여 초대해 줘서 고마워. 파티에 몇 명이나 올 거야?
남 너를 포함해서 친구 여덟 명을 초대했어. 오후 2시에 우리 집으로 와줘.
여 알았어. 그때 보자.

|해설| 남자는 여자를 포함하여 8명의 친구를 초대했다고 했다.

|어휘| free 혱 다른 약속이 없는, 한가한 invite 몡 초대 동 초대하다 including 전 ~을 포함하여

02 ⑤

M We are going to the amusement park for a field trip this Friday! I'm so excited!
W Me too. We will go there by bus, won't we?
M Yes. We have to be at school by 8:30. Then we will take a bus together.

W Cool. Should we bring our lunch boxes?
M If you want to. But you can just buy some food there.
W All right. I can't wait to go!

남 우리 이번 주 금요일에 놀이공원으로 현장 학습을 갈 거야! 너무 신이 나!
여 나도 그래. 우리는 그곳에 버스를 타고 갈 거야, 그렇지?
남 맞아. 8시 30분까지 학교에 가야 해. 그러고 나서 우리는 함께 버스를 탈 거야.
여 좋아. 우리 도시락을 가져가야 하니?
남 원한다면. 하지만 그냥 거기서 음식을 살 수도 있어.
여 알겠어. 빨리 가고 싶어!

|해설| 도시락을 싸와도 좋지만 그곳에서 음식을 살 수도 있다고 했다.

|어휘| amusement park 놀이공원 field trip 현장 학습 excited [형] 신이 난 lunch box 도시락 can't wait to-v 빨리 ~하고 싶다

03 ④

W Do you have any pets, Danny?
M Actually, I have three pets, a puppy and two cats.
W That's awesome! Do they get along with each other?
M Yes. My dog, Larry, is very friendly. My cats, Coco and Choco, are a bit shy, but they like Larry.
W How old are they?
M Larry is three years old, and Coco and Choco are four years old.
W Oh, I want to see them.
M Come over anytime. They all love visitors.

여 너 반려동물 있니, Danny?
남 사실, 나는 세 마리의 반려동물, 개 한 마리랑 고양이 두 마리가 있어.
여 굉장해! 그들은 서로 잘 지내니?
남 응. 나의 개 Larry는 매우 다정해. 나의 고양이 Coco와 Choco는 약간 수줍음을 타지만, Larry를 좋아해.
여 그들은 몇 살이니?
남 Larry는 세 살이고, Coco와 Choco는 네 살이야.
여 아, 보고 싶다.
남 언제든지 와. 그들 모두 손님들을 아주 좋아해.

|해설| 개는 3살이고 고양이들은 4살이라고 했으므로, 고양이들이 개보다 나이가 많다.

|어휘| pet [명] 반려동물 actually [부] 사실은 awesome [형] 굉장한 get along with ~와 살 지내다 each other 서로 friendly [형] 친절한, 다정한 a bit 조금, 약간 shy [형] 수줍음을 많이 타는 come over (~의 집에) 들르다 anytime [부] 언제든지 visitor [명] 방문객, 손님

04 ④

W Who is the boy in this picture? Is he your classmate?
M No, he is my cousin, Andrew. He is a year younger than me.
W Really? But he seems very tall.
M Yeah. He is about 180 cm.
W Wow. Does he like to play soccer like you?
M Not really. He likes to read books. He wants to be a writer in the future.

여 이 사진 속 남자 아이는 누구야? 너희 반 친구니?
남 아니, 그는 내 사촌 Andrew야. 나보다 한 살 어려.
여 정말? 하지만 키가 엄청 커 보여.
남 그래. 키가 거의 180cm거든.
여 와. 그 애도 너처럼 축구하는 걸 좋아하니?
남 그렇진 않아. 그 애는 책 읽는 것을 좋아해. 장래에 작가가 되고 싶어 하지.

|어휘| classmate [명] 반 친구 cousin [명] 사촌 younger [형] 더 어린 seem [동] ~처럼 보이다 writer [명] 작가 in the future 장래에, 미래에

05 ⑤

M Why are there white sneakers in this box?
W I ordered them online, but I have to return them.
M Why?
W They're too big. I usually wear size 8. But those are size 10.
M Then why did you order such big shoes?
W I ordered size 8. But they sent me the wrong ones.
M Oh, in that case, they'll probably exchange them for free.

남 왜 이 상자에 흰색 운동화가 있어?
여 내가 인터넷으로 주문했는데, 반품해야 해.
남 왜?
여 너무 커. 나는 보통 8사이즈를 신어. 하지만 그건 10사이즈거든.
남 그럼 왜 그렇게 큰 신발을 주문했어?
여 난 8사이즈를 주문했어. 하지만 나에게 잘못된 신발을 보냈어.
남 아, 그런 경우에는 아마 무료로 교환해 줄 거야.

|해설| 여자는 보통 본인이 신던 사이즈를 주문했지만 다른 사이즈의 신발을 받았다고 했다.

|어휘| sneaker [명] 운동화 order [동] 주문하다 return [동] 반품하다 usually [부] 대개, 보통 wrong [형] 잘못된 in that case 그런 경우에는 exchange [동] 교환하다 for free 무료로

06 ③

M Where are you going this vacation? Are you going to Seattle again?
W No, I decided to go to Hawaii this time.
M Sounds cool. When are you leaving?
W Next Friday. I'll be there for a week.
M Do you have any plans?
W I'll stay at a hotel near the beach and learn to surf.
M That sounds really fun.

남 이번 방학 때 어디 갈 거야? 또 시애틀에 갈 거니?
여 아니, 이번에는 하와이에 가기로 했어.
남 멋진데. 언제 떠나?
여 다음 주 금요일. 일주일 동안 거기 있을 거야.
남 무슨 계획 있어?
여 해변 가까운 호텔에 묵으면서 서핑하는 걸 배울 거야.
남 그거 정말 재미있겠다.

|해설| 여자는 일주일 동안 하와이에 있을 것이라고 했다.

|어휘| decide [동] 결정하다 stay [동] 묵다, 숙박하다 near [전] ~에서 가까이 learn [동] 배우다 surf 파도타기[서핑]를 하다

07 ④

W Wow, your room is very tidy. Do you share it with your brother?
M Yes. That's why there are two desks here.
W I see. But there's only one bed.
M Right. But it's big enough for both of us.
W And you guys must like books. I see a lot of books on the bookshelf.
M Yes. We really do.

여 와, 네 방 정말 깔끔하구나. 네 남동생과 방을 함께 쓰니?
남 응. 그래서 여기 책상이 두 개 있지.
여 그렇구나. 하지만 침대는 하나뿐이네.
남 맞아. 근데 우리 둘한테 충분히 커.
여 그리고 너희들은 틀림없이 책을 좋아하겠구나. 책꽂이에 많은 책들이 보여.
남 응. 정말 좋아해.

|해설| 침대가 하나뿐이지만 매우 크다고 했다.

|어휘| tidy [형] 깔끔한 share [동] 함께 쓰다 enough [부] (~할 만큼) 충분히 both of ~의 양쪽 모두 must [조] 틀림없이 ~일 것이다 bookshelf [명] 책꽂이

08 ③

W Uh-oh. I think I lost my pencil case.
M What does it look like? Let me help you find it.
W It's red and made of cloth.
M Okay. Is it big?
W It's not that big. And it only has a few pencils in it.
M All right. Did you write your name on it?
W Yes. And I also drew a flower next to my name.

여 이런. 나 필통을 잃어버린 것 같아.
남 어떻게 생겼어? 내가 찾는 걸 도와줄게.
여 빨간색이고 천으로 만든 거야.
남 알겠어. 그거 크니?
여 그렇게 크진 않아. 그리고 그 안에 연필 약간만 있어.
남 좋아. 거기에 네 이름을 썼니?
여 응. 그리고 내 이름 옆에 꽃도 그렸어.

|해설| 필통에는 연필이 약간 있다고 했다.

|어휘| lose [동] 잃어버리다 pencil case 필통 made of ~로 만든 cloth [명] 옷감, 천 a few 약간의, 소수의 draw [동] 그리다

09 ⑤

W How many people are there in your family?
M There are five people in my family: Mom, Dad, my brother, my sister, and me.
W How old are your siblings? Are you the youngest?
M No, my older brother is twenty-four, and my younger sister is nine. She's in third grade.
W What does your brother do?
M He's a college student. He studies math and wants to be a math teacher.
W Cool.

여 너희 가족은 몇 명이니?
남 우리 가족은 엄마, 아빠, 형, 여동생, 그리고 나, 이렇게 5명이야.
여 형제자매는 몇 살이야? 네가 막내니?
남 아니, 형은 24살이고, 여동생은 9살이야. 그 애는 3학년이지.
여 네 형은 무슨 일을 해?
남 형은 대학생이야. 수학을 공부하고 있고 수학 선생님이 되기를 원하고 있어.
여 멋지다.

|해설| 남자의 형은 대학생으로, 수학 선생님이 되고 싶어 한다고 했다.

|어휘| sibling [명] 형제자매 grade [명] 학년 college [명] 대학

10 ⑤

M Hi, Judy. Have you been to Taste of Venice?
W No, I haven't. What is that?
M It's an Italian restaurant on Main Street. It opened last week.
W Oh, I didn't know that. Have you been there yet?
M Yes. I had dinner there yesterday. Everything tasted great.
W I'll try going there tomorrow, then.
M Unfortunately, it's closed on Sundays.
W Oh, thanks for letting me know. I'll visit next Monday, then.

남 안녕, Judy. 너 Taste of Venice에 가본 적 있니?
여 아니, 없어. 그게 뭔데?
남 Main 가에 있는 이탈리아 음식점이야. 지난주에 문을 열었어.
여 아, 그건 몰랐네. 벌써 거기 가봤니?
남 응. 어제 거기서 저녁 먹었어. 모든 게 맛있었어.
여 그럼 내일 한번 가봐야겠다.
남 안타깝게도 일요일에는 문을 닫아.
여 아, 알려줘서 고마워. 그럼 다음 주 월요일에 가야겠다.

|해설| 식당이 일요일에는 문을 닫아서 여자가 월요일에 방문해보겠다고 했다.

|어휘| bowl [명] 그릇 taste [동] 맛이 ~하다 try v-ing 한번 해보다 unfortunately [부] 안타깝게도 closed [형] 문을 닫은

어휘·표현 다지기

p. 107

A

01 그릇
02 그리다
03 대학
04 깔끔한
05 옷감, 천
06 ~에서 가까이
07 ~의 양쪽 모두
08 언제든지
09 신이 난
10 서로
11 방문객, 손님
12 작가
13 교환하다
14 초대, 초대하다
15 ~을 포함하여
16 그런 경우에는

B

01 taste
02 actually
03 sibling
04 a few
05 field trip
06 come over
07 sneaker
08 get along with
09 for free
10 enough

실전 모의고사 1회

pp. 110-111

01 ④	02 ②	03 ③	04 ①	05 ③
06 ②	07 ④	08 ⑤	09 ④	10 ③
11 ①	12 ⑤	13 ③	14 ⑤	15 ②
16 ③	17 ⑤	18 ③	19 ③	20 ①

01 ④

W I have light brown fur all over my body. I also have strong back legs and a long tail. My back legs help me jump and kick, while I use my tail to keep my balance. I carry my baby in a small pouch. I live in Australia. What am I?

여 나는 온몸에 밝은 갈색 털이 있습니다. 나는 강한 뒷다리와 긴 꼬리도 가지고 있습니다. 내가 균형을 유지하기 위해 꼬리를 사용하는 반면, 뒷다리는 내가 뛰어오르고 발차기를 하는 데 도움을 줍니다. 나는 작은 주머니에 새끼를 넣고 다닙니다. 나는 호주에 삽니다. 나는 누구일까요?

|어휘| light [형] 밝은 fur [명] 털 strong [형] 강한 back [형] 뒤(쪽)의 tail [명] 꼬리 kick [동] (다리를) 차올리다 keep one's balance 균형을 잡다 carry [동] 가지고 다니다 pouch [명] 주머니

02 ②

W What are you reading, Tom?
M It's a book on insects. It's called *Insects and You*.
W Oh, okay. I like the picture of the fly below the title.
M Actually, that's a bumblebee.
W Really? I guess I don't know much about bugs.
M Then you should read this book!

여 뭐 읽고 있니, Tom?
남 곤충에 관한 책이야. 〈Insects and You〉라고 해.
여 아, 그렇구나. 나는 제목 밑에 파리 한 마리가 있는 그림이 마음에 드네.
남 사실, 그거 꿀벌이야.
여 정말? 나는 벌레에 관해서는 잘 모르는 것 같아.
남 그러면 너 이 책 읽어야겠다!

|어휘| insect [명] 곤충 fly [명] 파리 below [전] ~ 밑에 title [명] 제목 bumblebee [명] 꿀벌 bug [명] 벌레

03 ③

M Hello, this is Ethan Holmes from Channel 4 News with the weather. On Monday, it will be windy for most of the day. The skies will be clear on Tuesday, but it will rain on Wednesday. The temperature will rise on Thursday, and it will be cloudy in the afternoon.

남 안녕하세요, 저는 Channel 4 News에서 날씨를 전해드릴 Ethan Holmes입니다. 월요일에는 대체로 바람이 불겠습니다. 화요일에는 하늘이 맑겠지만, 수요일에는 비가 오겠습니다. 목요일에는 기온이 올라가겠으며, 오후에는 구름이 끼겠습니다.

|어휘| windy [형] 바람이 부는 clear [형] 화창한 temperature [명] 기온 rise [동] (기온 등이) 올라가다

04 ①

W I can't believe this!
M What is it, Maggie? Is something wrong?
W Samantha didn't invite me to her pool party.
M What makes you think that?
W She passed out invitations at school today, but she didn't give me one.
M Don't worry. Maybe she will give you one tomorrow.

여 믿을 수가 없어!
남 무슨 일이야, Maggie? 뭐가 잘못됐니?
여 Samantha가 수영장 파티에 나를 초대하지 않았어.
남 왜 그렇게 생각하는데?
여 그 애가 오늘 학교에서 초대장을 나눠줬는데, 나에게는 주지 않았어.
남 걱정하지 마. 아마 그 애가 내일 너에게 줄 거야.

|해설| 남자는 파티 초대장을 받지 못한 여자에게 걱정하지 말라며 위로하고 있다.

|어휘| invite [동] 초대하다 pool [명] 수영장 pass out ~을 나눠주다 invitation [명] 초대장

05 ③

W This is my older brother, Max. He is twenty-four years old. He is a wedding photographer. In his free time, Max likes to take kickboxing lessons and spend time with his friends. He and I like to play computer games together. He is very friendly and outgoing.

여 이 사람은 제 오빠 Max입니다. 오빠는 스물네 살입니다. 결혼식 전문 사진사죠. 시간이 날 때, 오빠는 킥복싱 수업을 듣고 친구들과 시간을 보내는 것을 좋아합니다. 오빠와 저는 함께 컴퓨터 게임하는 것을 좋아하죠. 오빠는 정말 상냥하고 외향적입니다.

|어휘| photographer [명] 사진사 kickboxing [명] 킥복싱 spend [동] 시간을 보내다 friendly [형] 상냥한, 친절한 outgoing [형] 외향적인

06 ②

[Cell phone rings.]

W Hello?

M Hi, Jasmine. This is Brandon. Do you want to go to a concert tonight in Lake Park?

W Sure! When does it start?

M It starts at 8:30. But I want to get there early.

W All right. It's 5:30 now. Let's meet in half an hour.

M Okay, I'll pick you up at your house.

W All right. See you then.

[휴대전화벨이 울린다.]

여 여보세요?

남 안녕, Jasmine. 나 Brandon이야. 너 오늘 밤 Lake Park에서 하는 콘서트에 가고 싶니?

여 물론이지! 언제 시작하는데?

남 8시 30분에 시작해. 그런데 난 거기에 일찍 가고 싶어.

여 알았어. 지금 5시 30분이네. 30분 후에 보자.

남 좋아, 내가 너희 집으로 데리러 갈게.

여 그래. 그때 보자.

|해설| 여자가 지금 5시 30분이고 30분 후에 만나자고 했다.

|어휘| half an hour 30분

07 ④

M What are you watching, Debbie?

W I'm watching a travel show on Spain. I'm going there next month.

M Really? That's great! What will you do there?

W I have so many ideas! Take a look at my travel plans!

M Wow! They look so professional. You should be a tour guide.

W Thanks. I want to be one someday.

남 너 뭐 보니, Debbie?

여 스페인에 관한 여행 프로그램을 보고 있어. 나 다음 달에 그곳에 가거든.

남 정말? 그거 멋지다! 거기서 뭐 할 건데?

여 정말 많은 아이디어가 있어! 내 여행 계획을 봐!

남 와! 이거 아주 전문적으로 보이는데. 너 여행 가이드가 되어야겠어.

여 고마워. 언젠가 여행 가이드가 되고 싶어.

|어휘| travel [명] 여행 take a look at ~을 보다 professional [형] 전문적인

08 ⑤

M Kate, don't forget that you have a dentist appointment tomorrow.

W I don't want to go.

M Why? Last week you said you had a cavity.

W I know. But I'm scared of the dentist.

M Don't worry. It will be okay.

남 Kate, 내일 치과 예약 있는 거 잊지 마.

여 저 가고 싶지 않아요.

남 왜? 너 지난주에 충치 있다고 했잖니.

여 맞아요. 하지만 치과는 무서워요.

남 걱정하지 마. 괜찮을 거란다.

|어휘| dentist [명] 치과 의사, 치과 appointment [명] (만날) 예약, 약속 cavity [명] 충치 be scared of ~을 두려워하다

09 ④

[Cell phone rings.]

W Hey, Derek! What's up?

M Hey, Tiffany! I just talked to Mom this morning.

W Oh, really? How is she?

M Today is her and Dad's 40th anniversary. I totally forgot!

W So did I. I'll pick up some flowers on my way to their house. Could you pick up a cake?

M Sure. I'll get one right now.

[휴대전화벨이 울린다.]

여 안녕, Derek! 무슨 일이야?

남 안녕, Tiffany! 나 오늘 아침에 엄마랑 이야기했거든.

여 아, 정말? 엄마는 어떠셔?

남 오늘이 엄마와 아빠의 40주년이야. 나 완전히 깜박한 것 있지!

여 나도 그랬어. 내가 부모님 댁에 가는 길에 꽃을 좀 사 갈게. 너는 케이크 사 올 수 있니?

남 물론이지. 지금 당장 살게.

|어휘| anniversary [명] 기념일 totally [부] 완전히 forget [동] 잊다 pick up ~을 사 오다[가다] on one's way to ~로 가는 길에

10 ③

W Hi, Bill. What are you doing?
M I'm planning a trip to Canada.
W Wow! When are you leaving?
M This summer. We're going to go camping for a week. Do you have any plans?
W Yes, I signed up for a ballet class. I can't wait!

여 안녕, Bill. 뭐 하고 있어?
남 캐나다 여행 계획을 세우고 있어.
여 와! 언제 떠날 건데?
남 이번 여름에. 우리는 일주일 동안 캠핑을 갈 거야. 너는 계획 있니?
여 응, 나는 발레 수업을 등록했어. 기다려져!

|어휘| plan [동] 계획을 세우다 [명] 계획 trip [명] 여행 go camping 캠핑을 가다 sign up for ~을 등록하다 ballet [명] 발레 can't wait 기다려지다

11 ①

[Cell phone rings.]
M Hello?
W It's me. I'm finally in Seoul. It was a long flight.
M I can't wait to see you. But it's 1:00 a.m. It's too late for the bus.
W Yes, but maybe the subway is still running.
M Let me check online. *[pause]* Nope. It stopped at 12:00 a.m.
W Then I'll catch a taxi.

[휴대전화벨이 울린다.]
남 여보세요?
여 나야. 드디어 서울에 왔어. 긴 비행이었어.
남 빨리 보고 싶다. 하지만 새벽 1시야. 버스 타기에는 너무 늦었네.
여 응, 그런데 아마 지하철은 아직 다닐 거야.
남 온라인으로 알아볼게. [잠시 후] 아니야. 밤 12시에 끊겼네.
여 그러면 택시 잡을게.

|어휘| finally [부] 드디어 flight [명] 비행 late [형] 늦은 maybe [부] 아마도 still [부] 아직, 여전히 run [동] 운행하다 check [동] 알아보다, 확인하다 catch a taxi 택시를 잡다

12 ⑤

[Telephone rings.]
M Hello, this is Sunnyhill Hotel. How may I help you?
W Hi, this is Erica Marshall. I reserved a twin room for two nights from June 25 to June 27.
M Yes, I remember.
W My friend can't go on the trip, so I need a single room, instead.
M Okay. I'll make the change to your reservation.

[전화벨이 울린다.]
남 안녕하세요. Sunnyhill 호텔입니다. 무엇을 도와드릴까요?
여 안녕하세요. 저는 Erica Marshall이에요. 제가 6월 25일부터 27일까지 2인실을 이틀 밤 예약했는데요.
남 네, 기억납니다.
여 제 친구가 여행을 갈 수 없어서, 대신 1인실이 필요해요.
남 알겠습니다. 예약 내용을 변경해 드릴게요.

|어휘| reserve [동] 예약하다 twin room 1인용 침대(single bed)가 2개 있는 방 single room 1인용 침실 make a change 변경하다

13 ③

M How can I help you?
W Do you have a book called *Charlotte's Web*?
M Yes. Would you like to check it out?
W Yes, please. How long can I keep it?
M Up to two weeks. Can I see your student ID card?
W Here it is.

남 무엇을 도와드릴까요?
여 〈샬롯의 거미줄〉이라는 책 있나요?
남 네. 그 책을 대출하고 싶으세요?
여 네, 해주세요. 얼마 동안 대출 가능한가요?
남 2주일까지요. 학생증 좀 볼 수 있을까요?
여 여기 있습니다.

|어휘| check out (책 등을) 대출하다 up to ~까지 student ID card 학생증

14 ⑤

W Excuse me, I'm lost. Could you help me? I'm looking for the police station.
M Sure. Go straight for 30 meters and turn right at the bank.
W Okay.
M The police station is on the right side of the street, next to the convenience store.
W Thanks for your help!

여 실례합니다만, 제가 길을 잃었어요. 도와주실 수 있나요? 저는 경찰서를 찾고 있어요.
남 물론이죠. 30m를 똑바로 가셔서 은행에서 우회전하세요.

여 네.
남 경찰서는 길 오른편, 편의점 옆에 있어요.
여 도와주셔서 감사합니다!

|어휘| lost [형] 길을 잃은 go straight 똑바로 가다 turn right 우회전하다 convenience store 편의점

15 ②

W I think we're ready for the party.
M I still need to buy a cake.
W Oh, I can pick one up. Don't worry.
M Thanks, but it's okay. I can do it.
W Okay. Is there anything else I can do?
M Can you bring some chairs from upstairs? We need three more.
W Sure.

여 우리 파티할 준비가 된 것 같아.
남 나 아직 케이크를 사야 해.
여 아, 내가 하나 사 올 수 있어. 걱정하지 마.
남 고맙지만 괜찮아. 내가 할 수 있어.
여 그래. 내가 할 수 있는 다른 일이 있을까?
남 위층에서 의자 좀 가지고 올 수 있어? 우리 세 개가 더 필요해.
여 물론이지.

|어휘| upstairs [명] 위층

16 ③

M Why didn't you have any lunch today?
W I don't want to gain weight, so I'm trying to eat less.
M That's not healthy. Why don't you start exercising?
W I don't like exercising. It's boring.
M You should join a jogging club! It will be fun, and you'll make new friends.
W That's a great idea!

남 왜 오늘 점심을 전혀 안 먹었니?
여 체중이 늘어나는 걸 원치 않아서, 덜 먹으려고 하고 있어.
남 그건 건강에 좋지 않아. 운동을 시작하는 건 어때?
여 나는 운동하는 걸 좋아하지 않아. 그건 지루해.
남 너 조깅 동호회에 가입해야겠다! 재미도 있고, 새로운 친구도 사귀게 될 거야.
여 그거 멋진 생각인데!

|해설| 남자는 운동하는 것이 지루하다는 여자에게 조깅 동호회에 가입할 것을 권하고 있다.

|어휘| gain weight 체중이 늘다 healthy [형] 건강에 좋은, 건강한 boring [형] 지루한 make a friend 친구를 사귀다

17 ⑤

M Where are you going, Mia? You just got home.
W I'm going to the bus station.
M Are you meeting a friend there?
W No, Dad. I'm going to look for my glove. I think I dropped it around there.
M Oh, no. I hope you find it. Those are your favorite gloves.

남 Mia, 너 어디 가니? 집에 방금 왔잖아.
여 버스 정류장에 가요.
남 거기서 친구 만나니?
여 아니요, 아빠. 장갑 찾으러 가요. 거기 주변에 떨어뜨린 것 같아요.
남 아, 저런. 찾기를 바란다. 그거 네가 무척 좋아하는 장갑이잖니.

|어휘| bus station 버스 정류장 glove [명] 장갑 drop [동] 떨어뜨리다 find [동] 찾다 favorite [형] 매우 좋아하는

18 ③

W How is your new job so far, David?
M I like it, but it can be stressful sometimes.
W What are some of your duties?
M I take the customers' orders, and then I tell them to the cook.
W Does anyone help you serve the dishes to the customers?
M Sometimes. But I usually do it myself.

여 새 일은 지금까지 어때, David?
남 좋은데, 가끔 스트레스가 많아.
여 네 업무가 뭔데?
남 손님들의 주문을 받고, 그러고 나서 그걸 요리사에게 말해줘.
여 네가 손님에게 음식을 내가는 걸 누군가가 도와주니?
남 가끔. 하지만 보통 내가 직접 해.

|어휘| so far 지금까지 stressful [형] 스트레스가 많은 sometimes [부] 때때로, 가끔 duty [명] 직무, 업무 take an order 주문을 받다 customer [명] 손님, 고객 serve [동] (음식 등을) 제공하다 usually [부] 보통, 대개

19 ③

W I'm really tired today.
M Why? Are you having trouble sleeping?
W No, I stayed up until 1:00 a.m. last night.
M Oh. Were you studying for the English test?
W No! I forgot all about the test!
M Then what were you doing?

W I was watching a movie.

① I studied all night.
② I won't be late again.
④ I go to sleep at 10:00 p.m. every night.
⑤ I usually go to sleep later on the weekends.

여 나 오늘 정말 피곤해.
남 왜? 자는 데 어려움이 있니?
여 아니, 나 어젯밤에 새벽 1시까지 깨어 있었어.
남 아. 영어 시험공부를 하고 있었던 거야?
여 아니! 나 시험에 대해서는 완전히 잊고 있었어!
남 그러면 뭐 하고 있었는데?
여 영화 보고 있었어.

① 나 밤새도록 공부했어.
② 다시는 안 늦을게.
④ 나는 매일 밤 10시에 자.
⑤ 나는 보통 주말에는 더 늦게 자.

|어휘| tired [형] 피곤한 have trouble v-ing ~하는 데 어려움이 있다 stay up (평상시보다 더 늦게까지) 안 자고 깨어 있다 until [전] ~까지

20 ①

M What are you going to do this Sunday?
W Nothing special.
M I'm going to a bookstore downtown. Do you want to join me?
W Sure. I want to buy some comic books.
M Great! Would you like to meet for lunch first?
W Okay. Let's get sushi!

② Let's meet at three o'clock.
③ I'm sorry, but I'm busy on Sunday.
④ I think we should take the subway.
⑤ What kind of books do you like to read?

남 이번 일요일에 뭐 할 거야?
여 특별한 건 없어.
남 나는 시내에 있는 서점에 갈 거야. 나랑 같이 갈래?
여 좋지. 나는 만화책을 좀 사고 싶어.
남 잘됐네! 먼저 만나서 점심 먹을까?
여 그래. 초밥 먹자!

② 3시 정각에 만나자.
③ 미안한데, 나는 일요일에 바빠.
④ 우리 지하철을 타야 할 것 같아.
⑤ 어떤 종류의 책을 읽는 것을 좋아하니?

|해설| 남자가 먼저 만나서 점심을 먹자고 하는 말에 가장 어울리는 대답은 'Okay. Let's get sushi!'이다.

|어휘| special [형] 특별한 bookstore [명] 서점 downtown [부] 시내에 comic book 만화책 [문제] busy [형] 바쁜

어휘·표현 다지기

p. 119

A

01 상냥한, 친절한	02 ~ 밑에
03 아직, 여전히	04 ~까지
05 시내에	06 털
07 주머니	08 스트레스가 많은
09 완전히	10 초대장
11 손님, 고객	12 균형을 잡다
13 기념일	14 예약하다
15 기온	16 전문적인

B

01 upstairs	02 glove
03 half an hour	04 outgoing
05 rise	06 convenience store
07 check out	08 pass out
09 serve	10 sign up for

실전 모의고사 2회

pp. 120-121

01 ⑤	02 ④	03 ④	04 ①	05 ②
06 ③	07 ②	08 ②	09 ④	10 ①
11 ③	12 ②	13 ①	14 ⑤	15 ⑤
16 ③	17 ②	18 ①	19 ①	20 ③

01 ⑤

M This egg-shaped fruit is often grown in New Zealand. The outside of this is brown and covered with short hairs. We must remove this part before we eat this. Inside, this is usually green, although it is sometimes yellow. There are many small, black seeds in the center. What is this?

남 이 달걀 모양의 과일은 흔히 뉴질랜드에서 재배됩니다. 이것의 겉면은 갈색이며 짧은 털로 덮여 있습니다. 우리는 이것을 먹기 전에 이 부분을 제거해야 합니다. 속은, 가끔 노란색이긴 하지만, 대개는 초록색입니다. 중앙에는 작고 검은 씨가 많습니다. 이것은 무엇일까요?

|어휘| grow [동] 자라다, 재배하다 outside [명] 겉(면) be

covered with ~로 덮이다   hair 몡 털   remove 동 제거하다
inside 믱 안[속/내부]에   seed 몡 씨

02 ④

M   Did you buy a new umbrella, Ashley?

W   No, it was a gift from my friend.

M   The elephant on the umbrella is so cute. It looks like
it is holding bananas.

W   It is actually holding flowers! Also, I really like the
balloons above it.

M   It's a lovely design.

남   너 새 우산 샀니, Ashley?

여   아니, 친구가 준 선물이야.

남   우산에 있는 코끼리가 매우 귀엽다. 마치 바나나를 들고 있는 것처
럼 보여.

여   그거 사실 꽃을 들고 있는 거야! 그리고 그 위에 있는 풍선들이 정
말 마음에 들어.

남   매력적인 디자인이네.

|어휘| hold 동 들고 있다   above 전 ~보다 위에   lovely 형 사랑
스러운, 매력적인

03 ④

W   Good morning! This is Sandra Collins with the
weather report. It will be cloudy for most of the
day today, and there is a 40% chance of rain this
afternoon. Tomorrow, it is going to snow all day. You
should try to stay inside.

여   안녕하세요! 저는 일기 예보를 전해드릴 Sandra Collins입니다.
오늘은 대체로 구름이 끼겠으며, 오후에는 비 올 가능성이 40%
있습니다. 내일은 종일 눈이 내리겠습니다. 실내에 머무시는 것이
좋겠습니다.

|어휘| chance 몡 가능성   stay 동 머무르다

04 ①

W   What are you doing this weekend, Jason?

M   I don't have any plans yet. What about you?

W   I'm going to a musical. I won two free tickets
yesterday!

M   Oh, wow! I'm sure you'll have a great time.

W   You like musicals too, right? Would you be able to go
with me?

M   I'd love to.

여   이번 주말에 뭐 하니, Jason?

남   아직 아무 계획 없어. 너는?

여   나는 뮤지컬 보러 가. 어제 무료 티켓 두 장을 얻었거든!

남   아, 왜! 너 좋은 시간을 보내겠구나.

여   너도 뮤지컬 좋아하지, 그렇지? 나랑 같이 갈 수 있니?

남   그러고 싶어.

|해설| 남자는 뮤지컬을 같이 보러 가자고 하는 여자의 제안을 승낙하
고 있다.

|어휘| yet 믱 아직   musical 몡 뮤지컬   win 동 얻다   be able
to-v ~할 수 있다

05 ②

M   Lisa's Supermarket is reopening on Main Street
this week. The grand reopening event will be on
Thursday, March 3 from 10:00 a.m. to 9:00 p.m. There
will be free ice cream for kids, and all fresh fruit and
vegetables will be 50% off. Please come and visit!

남   Lisa's Supermarket은 이번 주에 Main 가에 재개점합니다. 재
개점 행사는 3월 3일 목요일 오전 10시부터 저녁 9시까지 진행
됩니다. 아이들을 위한 무료 아이스크림이 있으며, 신선한 과일과
채소 모두 50% 할인될 겁니다. 방문하러 와주세요!

|어휘| reopen 동 다시 열다   free 형 공짜의, 무료의   fresh 형 신
선한   off 믱 할인되어

06 ③

M   Gina, would you like to go to the Paradise Zoo with
me?

W   I'd love to.

M   How about this Saturday?

W   I have a club meeting at two on Saturdays. It should
end at five.

M   That's okay. The zoo is only open at night, from seven
o'clock to 10:30 p.m.

W   That's perfect! Let's meet thirty minutes before the
zoo opens.

M   Okay.

남   Gina, 너 나랑 Paradise 동물원에 같이 갈래?

여   그러고 싶어.

남   이번 토요일 어때?

여   나 토요일마다 2시에 동아리 모임이 있어. 5시에 끝날 거야.

남   괜찮아. 동물원은 저녁 7시에서 10시 30분까지 밤에만 문을
열어.

여   딱 좋네! 동물원 개장하기 30분 전에 만나자.

남 그래.

|어휘| end [동] 끝나다

07 ②

M Beth, would you like to go to a flea market with me this afternoon?
W That sounds fun, but I can't. I have to tutor a student.
M All right, maybe next time. Isn't tutoring stressful, though?
W No, I really enjoy teaching. I want to be a math teacher someday.
M Oh, okay. Then tutoring is a good experience for you!

남 Beth, 오늘 오후에 나랑 벼룩시장에 갈래?
여 재미있을 것 같은데, 난 못 가겠다. 학생 개인 지도를 해야 해.
남 알았어, 다음에 가자. 하지만 가르치는 건 스트레스가 많지 않아?
여 아니, 나는 가르치는 게 정말 좋아. 언젠가 수학 선생님이 되고 싶어.
남 아, 그렇구나. 그럼 가르치는 것이 너에게 좋은 경험이네!

|어휘| flea market 벼룩시장 tutor [동] 가르치다, 개인 교습을 하다 stressful [형] 스트레스가 많은 though [부] 그렇지만, 하지만 math [명] 수학 someday [부] 언젠가 experience [명] 경험

08 ②

M Happy birthday, Jenny! This is for you.
W Wow! Thank you!
M It's my pleasure.
W I didn't think anyone remembered my birthday, so I was disappointed.
M I wanted to surprise you, so I didn't say anything until now.
W I was really surprised. I'm going to remember this day for a long time.

남 Jenny, 생일 축하해! 이건 널 위한 거야.
여 와! 고마워!
남 천만에.
여 난 아무도 내 생일을 기억 못 하는 줄 알고 실망했었어.
남 널 놀라게 해주고 싶어서, 지금까지 아무 말 안 했어.
여 정말 놀랐어. 난 오랫동안 이날을 기억할 거야.

|해설| 여자는 아무도 생일을 기억하지 못하는 줄 알았지만, 남자가 축하해줘서 기뻐하고 있다.

|어휘| It's my pleasure. 천만에. remember [동] 기억하다 disappointed [형] 실망한 surprise [동] 놀라게 하다

09 ④

W I'm so exhausted!
M Yeah, it was a long trip. I'm happy to be home!
W Me too. I want to rest, but I should unpack first.
M Before you do that, could you open the windows? It's a little hot in here.
W No problem. We need some fresh air.

여 나 너무 지쳤어!
남 그래, 긴 여행이었어. 집에 오니 좋다!
여 나도. 쉬고 싶지만, 먼저 짐을 풀어야겠다.
남 그거 하기 전에, 창문 좀 열어 줄래? 이 안이 약간 덥네.
여 알았어. 우린 신선한 공기가 좀 필요해.

|어휘| exhausted [형] 지친 rest [동] 쉬다 unpack [동] (짐을) 풀다

10 ①

W Jack, why is your room always so messy?
M I don't know. I am usually too tired or busy to clean it.
W Keeping your room tidy is very important. It makes you feel better.
M Really? I didn't know that.
W Try it. You'll feel less stressed.

여 Jack, 네 방은 왜 항상 그렇게 지저분하니?
남 모르겠어요. 보통 너무 피곤하거나 바빠서 청소할 수가 없어요.
여 방을 깨끗하게 하는 것은 정말 중요해. 네 기분을 나아지게 하거든.
남 정말요? 몰랐어요.
여 해보렴. 스트레스를 덜 받을 거야.

|어휘| messy [형] 지저분한 tired [형] 피곤한 tidy [형] 깨끗한, 정돈된 stressed [형] 스트레스를 받는

11 ③

W It's raining now, Sean. Don't forget your umbrella.
M Thanks, Stacy. I'll remember.
W I hope you don't have to wait at the bus stop for very long.
M I'm actually not taking the bus home tonight.
W Really? Why not?
M The new subway line opened last week, so I'm going to take the subway instead.

여 지금 비가 오고 있어, Sean. 우산 잊지 마.
남 고마워, Stacy. 기억할게.
여 네가 버스정류장에서 너무 오래 기다리지 않아도 되면 좋겠다.

남 사실 나는 오늘 밤에 집에 버스 타고 가지 않을 거야.
여 정말? 왜 안 타?
남 새 지하철 노선이 지난주에 개통되어서, 대신 지하철 탈 거야.

|어휘| subway line 지하철 노선 instead [부] 대신에

12 ②

M Good morning, Ms. Taylor. Do you like your room?
W I'm afraid not. I would like a different room.
M I'm sorry to hear that. Is it too small?
W No, it's not too small.
M What's wrong, then?
W It is very dark during the day. Can I switch to a brighter room?

남 좋은 아침입니다, Taylor 씨. 방은 마음에 드시나요?
여 아쉽게도 그렇지 않네요. 다른 방으로 하고 싶어요.
남 유감이네요. 방이 너무 작나요?
여 아니요, 그렇게 작지는 않아요.
남 그러면 뭐가 문제인가요?
여 낮에 너무 어두워요. 더 밝은 방으로 바꿀 수 있나요?

|어휘| dark [형] 어두운 day [명] 낮 switch to ~로 바꾸다 bright [형] 밝은

13 ①

W Do you have an appointment?
M No, I don't.
W Sorry, but you can't see the doctor if you didn't make an appointment.
M I know. But I just slipped on some ice and hurt my arm.
W I see. How bad is it?
M It's serious. I can't move it.
W In that case, I'll talk to the doctor. Wait for a moment, please.

여 예약하셨나요?
남 아뇨, 안 했습니다.
여 죄송하지만, 예약을 하지 않으셨다면 진료를 받으실 수 없습니다.
남 알고 있어요. 하지만 방금 빙판에 미끄러져서 팔을 다쳤어요.
여 그러셨군요. 얼마나 안 좋으신가요?
남 심각해요. 움직일 수가 없어요.
여 그렇다면 의사 선생님께 말씀드릴게요. 잠시만 기다려 주세요.

|어휘| have an appointment 예약[만날 약속]이 있다 make an appointment 예약[만날 약속]을 하다 slip [동] 미끄러지다 hurt [동] 다치게 하다 serious [형] 심각한

14 ⑤

M Have you seen my wallet?
W Your wallet? Didn't you just put it in your backpack?
M No, I didn't.
W Why don't you look under the bench?
M Well, there's nothing under the bench.
W Hmm... What about in the shopping cart?
M My wallet's not there either. Oh, wait. I think my wallet is in the locker.
W Oh yes. Here it is.

남 내 지갑 봤어요?
여 지갑이요? 방금 배낭에 넣지 않았어요?
남 아니, 안 넣었어요.
여 벤치 밑을 보지 그래요?
남 음, 벤치 밑에는 아무것도 없어요.
여 음… 쇼핑 카트 안에는요?
남 내 지갑이 거기에도 없어요. 아, 잠시만요. 내 지갑이 개인 물품 보관함 안에 있는 것 같아요.
여 아 있네요. 여기요.

|어휘| wallet [명] 지갑 locker [명] 개인 물품 보관함

15 ⑤

[Cell phone rings.]
W Hi, Mark.
M Hi, Shannon! Where are you now?
W I'm in the parking lot. I just got back from the grocery store.
M Good! I'll leave the front door open for you.
W Actually, could you come down and help me carry these bags? They're really heavy.
M Sure. I'll be there in a minute.

[휴대전화벨이 울린다.]
여 여보세요, Mark.
남 여보세요, Shannon! 지금 어디예요?
여 주차장에 있어요. 방금 식료품점에서 돌아왔어요.
남 좋아요! 당신을 위해서 현관문을 열어둘게요.
여 저, 내려와서 이 가방들 나르는 것 좀 도와줄래요? 정말 무겁네요.
남 그래요. 당장 갈게요.

|어휘| parking lot 주차장 grocery store 식료품점 carry [동] 나르다 heavy [형] 무거운 in a minute 당장, 즉각

16 ③

M Becky, I was just looking at your blog.

W Oh, really? What do you think?
M It's very well written. But the cartoons are the best part.
W Thanks! I worked hard on them.
M I can tell. They're unique.
W I want more people to see them.
M Why don't you make your own cartoon book?
W Maybe I will!

남 Becky, 나 방금 네 블로그를 보고 있었어.
여 아, 정말? 어때?
남 아주 잘 썼던데. 그런데 만화가 가장 훌륭한 부분이야.
여 고마워! 내가 그거 열심히 작업했어.
남 그런 것 같아. 만화가 독특해.
여 나는 더 많은 사람이 그걸 봤으면 좋겠어.
남 너만의 만화책을 만들어보는 게 어때?
여 아마 그래야겠다!

|어휘| unique [형] 독특한

17 ②

W Happy Monday!
M Hi, Julie. What did you do yesterday?
W I went to the dinosaur museum. But it turns out that it is closed on Sundays. So I couldn't enter.
M Oh, that's too bad. So did you just return home?
W I started to. But on my way home, I saw a big mall. So I went shopping instead.
M That's good.

여 행복한 월요일!
남 안녕, Julie. 어제 뭐 했니?
여 공룡 박물관에 갔었어. 하지만 일요일에는 문을 닫더라고. 그래서 들어갈 수 없었어.
남 아, 안됐다. 그래서 그냥 집으로 돌아갔니?
여 출발은 했어. 그런데 집으로 오는 길에, 큰 쇼핑몰이 보이는 거야. 그래서 대신 쇼핑을 하러 갔어.
남 좋았겠다.

|어휘| dinosaur [명] 공룡 museum [명] 박물관 turn out ~인 것으로 드러나다 enter [동] 들어가다 return [동] 돌아오다

18 ①

W Frank, I just read your article in the newspaper this morning. It was great!
M Thanks, Megan. I really enjoyed interviewing that Chinese novelist.
W Did you have to go to China?
M Yes, I was there for a month because I had to do some research.
W Oh, wow! How long did it take to write the article?
M About a week.

여 Frank, 오늘 아침에 막 신문에서 네 기사를 읽었어. 멋지더라!
남 고마워, Megan. 나는 그 중국 소설가를 인터뷰하는 게 정말 즐거웠어.
여 너 중국에 가야 했던 거야?
남 응, 조사를 좀 해야 해서 한 달 동안 거기 있었어.
여 아, 와! 그 기사를 쓰는 데는 얼마나 걸렸어?
남 일주일 정도.

|어휘| article [명] 기사 interview [동] 인터뷰하다 novelist [명] 소설가 do research 조사하다

19 ①

W What are you doing?
M I'm sending a package to my brother.
W Really? Don't you live with him?
M No, he's studying in the US.
W Wow! How long has he been there?
M For about two years.

② He lives in California.
③ He has been there twice.
④ He is almost 170 cm tall.
⑤ He went there to study English.

여 뭐 하고 있니?
남 남동생에게 소포 보내는 중이야.
여 정말? 너 남동생이랑 같이 살지 않아?
남 아니, 그 애는 미국에서 공부하고 있어.
여 와! 거기에 얼마나 있었는데?
남 2년 정도.

② 그 애는 캘리포니아에 살아.
③ 그 애는 그곳에 두 번 가 봤어.
④ 그 애는 키가 거의 170cm야.
⑤ 그 애는 그곳에 영어 공부를 하러 갔어.

|해설| 미국에 얼마나 있었는지 물었으므로, 체류 기간을 말하는 응답이 가장 적절하다.

|어휘| package [명] 소포

20 ③

W Excuse me, sir. How far is Central Park from here?
M It takes about forty minutes to get there on foot.
W Oh, wow. That's a long time.

M Do you have a bike? It only takes fifteen minutes by bicycle.
W No, I don't. Is there any other way I can get there?
M I recommend taking the subway.

① No, I don't want to go there.
② Central Park is very big.
④ Yes, people enjoy walking in the park.
⑤ You can pick up your bike next week.

여 실례합니다. 여기서 센트럴 파크가 얼마나 먼가요?
남 걸어서 거기 가는 데 40분쯤 걸려요.
여 아, 와. 긴 시간이네요.
남 자전거 있으세요? 자전거로 15분밖에 안 걸려요.
여 아니요, 없어요. 거기 갈 수 있는 다른 방법이 있나요?
남 지하철 타시는 것을 추천합니다.

① 아니요. 저는 거기 가고 싶지 않아요.
② 센트럴 파크는 아주 커요.
④ 네, 사람들은 공원에서 산책을 즐겨요.
⑤ 다음 주에 자전거를 가져가시면 됩니다.

|해설| 이용 가능한 교통수단을 물었으므로, 지하철 이용을 권하는 ③이 응답으로 가장 적절하다.

|어휘| on foot 걸어서 [문제] recommend [동] 추천하다

어휘·표현 다지기 p. 129

A

01 실망한	02 미끄러지다
03 밝은	04 가르치다, 개인 교습을 하다
05 ~보다 위에	06 어두운
07 주차장	08 겉(면)
09 기사	10 들어가다
11 독특한	12 조사하다
13 벼룩시장	14 식료품점
15 다시 열다	16 소설가

B

01 heavy	02 chance
03 messy	04 switch to
05 experience	06 exhausted
07 on foot	08 serious
09 stressed	10 be covered with

실전 모의고사 3회 pp. 130-131

01 ②	02 ③	03 ②	04 ①	05 ③
06 ①	07 ⑤	08 ②	09 ⑤	10 ①
11 ③	12 ②	13 ③	14 ③	15 ④
16 ④	17 ④	18 ④	19 ③	20 ⑤

01 ②

W You can find this in a bathroom. This has a long plastic handle and a brush at the end. You use this about three times a day to clean your teeth. You should buy a new one every few months. What is this?

여 여러분은 이것을 화장실에서 찾아볼 수 있습니다. 이것은 긴 플라스틱 손잡이가 있고 끝에 솔이 있습니다. 여러분은 치아를 깨끗이 하기 위해 하루에 세 번 정도 이것을 사용합니다. 여러분은 몇 달에 한 번씩 새로운 것을 사야 합니다. 이것은 무엇일까요?

|어휘| handle [명] 손잡이 brush [명] 붓, 솔

02 ③

W I need to pick out a tablecloth for tonight's dinner. Can you help me?
M Sure. I like the checkered one.
W I like that one too, but it's too small. How about the striped one?
M Okay. Should we get a round tablecloth or a square one?
W A round one.

여 나 오늘 저녁 식사를 위한 식탁보를 골라야 해. 나 도와줄 수 있니?
남 물론이지. 나는 체크무늬인 게 마음에 들어.
여 나도 그게 좋은데, 너무 작아. 줄무늬인 건 어때?
남 괜찮네. 우리 둥근 식탁보를 사야 하니, 아니면 네모난 것을 사야 하니?
여 둥근 것.

|어휘| pick out ~을 선택하다[고르다] tablecloth [명] 식탁보 checkered [형] 체크무늬의 striped [형] 줄무늬의 round [형] 둥근 square [형] 정사각형 모양의, 직각의

03 ②

M Good morning, Philadelphia! This is Jerry Miller with the weather report. It's cloudy today, and there is a high chance of rain tomorrow. The skies will be clear on Saturday, but there will be a lot of wind throughout the day. On Sunday, it will be warm and sunny.

남 좋은 아침입니다, 필라델피아 주민 여러분! 저는 일기 예보를 전해 드릴 Jerry Miller입니다. 오늘은 흐리고, 내일은 비가 내릴 가능성이 높겠습니다. 토요일에는 하늘이 맑겠지만, 종일 바람이 많이 불겠습니다. 일요일에는 따뜻하고 화창할 것입니다.

|어휘| clear [형] 맑은 throughout the day 종일

04 ①

W What are you looking for, Eric?

M My earphones. They were in my pocket. Maybe they fell out.

W Did you check your backpack? You usually keep them in there.

M I did, but they weren't in there. Will you check the living room for me?

W Sure. *[pause]* I can't find your earphones here.

M Then can I borrow yours today? I really need them now.

여 뭐 찾고 있니, Eric?

남 내 이어폰. 주머니에 있었거든. 아마 떨어졌나 봐.

여 책가방 확인했니? 너 보통 그 안에 두잖아.

남 확인했는데, 거기 없었어. 날 위해 거실 좀 확인해줄래?

여 그래. [잠시 후] 여기에서는 네 이어폰 못 찾겠어.

남 그럼 오늘 네 걸 빌릴 수 있을까? 지금 꼭 필요하거든.

|어휘| earphone [명] 이어폰 pocket [명] 주머니 borrow [동] 빌리다

05 ③

W Hi, everyone. This is my pet rabbit, Samantha. As you can see, her ears and nose are black, and the rest of her body is white. She is very friendly and playful. She likes it when I pet her soft fur. Her favorite food is carrots.

여 안녕하세요, 여러분. 이 동물은 반려 토끼, Samantha입니다. 보다시피, 귀와 코가 검고, 몸의 나머지는 하얗습니다. 매우 친근하고 장난기가 많습니다. 제가 부드러운 털을 쓰다듬으면 좋아합니다. 가장 좋아하는 음식은 당근입니다.

|어휘| pet [명] 반려동물 [동] 쓰다듬다 rest [명] 나머지 playful [형] 장난기 많은 soft [형] 부드러운 fur [명] 털

06 ①

M Caroline, will you go to a play with me tonight?

W Sure!

M It starts at seven thirty. Is that okay?

W Yes. But let's have dinner before the play.

M Sounds good. How about meeting an hour before it starts?

W Six thirty? I don't think that's enough time. How about meeting thirty minutes earlier?

M All right. See you then.

남 Caroline, 오늘 밤에 나랑 연극 보러 갈래?

여 그래!

남 7시 30분에 시작해. 괜찮아?

여 응. 그런데 연극 전에 저녁 먹자.

남 좋아. 연극 시작하기 1시간 전에 보는 것 어때?

여 6시 30분? 그건 충분한 시간은 아닌 것 같아. 30분 더 일찍 보는 건 어때?

남 그래. 그때 보자.

|어휘| play [명] 연극 enough [형] 충분한 earlier [부] 더 일찍

07 ⑤

M Hi, Christine. Do you want to study together after school today?

W I can't. Our school radio station is putting on a show at 6:00 p.m.

M Oh, okay. You're hosting the show, right?

W I am! I choose all the songs. I really love it.

M You should be a DJ and have your own show someday!

W That's my dream job!

남 안녕, Christine. 오늘 방과 후에 함께 공부할래?

여 난 못해. 학교 라디오 방송국에서 오후 6시에 프로그램을 상연하거든.

남 아, 그래. 네가 프로그램을 진행하지?

여 응! 내가 모든 노래를 골라. 난 정말 그 일이 좋아.

남 너 언젠가 DJ가 돼서 너만의 프로그램을 해야겠다!

여 그게 내 꿈의 직업이야!

|어휘| radio station 라디오 방송국 put on a show 프로그램을 상연하다 host [동] 진행하다 choose [동] 고르다

08 ②

W What was that noise?

M I didn't hear anything.

W There it is again! Don't you hear footsteps? I think something is following us.
M It's probably just the wind. Don't worry.
W What if it's a dangerous animal? I want to get out of here!
M All right. Let's go.

여 저 소리 뭐였어?
남 나는 아무것도 못 들었는데.
여 또 들려! 발소리 안 들려? 뭔가가 우리를 따라오는 것 같아.
남 아마 그냥 바람일 거야. 걱정하지 마.
여 위험한 동물이면 어떡해? 나 여기서 벗어나고 싶어!
남 알았어. 가자.

|해설| 여자는 정체 모를 소리를 듣고 무서워하고 있다.

|어휘| noise [명] 소리, 소음 footstep [명] 발소리 follow [동] 따라오다 what if ~? ~면 어쩌지? dangerous [형] 위험한 get out of ~에서 나오다

09 ⑤

M Do you need help with anything, Brittany? I can set the table.
W Oh, I'll do that after the curry is done.
M I can chop the onions, then.
W I've decided not to use onions this time. Could you peel some potatoes instead?
M Sure. How many do you need?
W Five should be enough.

남 뭐 좀 도와줄까, Brittany? 내가 상 차릴 수 있는데.
여 아, 그건 카레가 다 된 다음에 내가 할게.
남 그럼 내가 양파를 썰게.
여 이번에는 양파를 안 쓰기로 했어. 대신 감자 껍질 좀 벗겨줄 수 있어?
남 물론이지. 얼마나 많이 필요해?
여 5개면 충분해.

|어휘| set the table 상을 차리다 chop [동] 썰다 decide [동] 결정하다 peel [동] 껍질을 벗기다

10 ①

M What are you looking at, Joan? Are they club posters?
W Yes. I'm thinking about joining a school club.
M Would you like to join the book club with me?
W I don't have enough time to read books.
M What about the French club? I think it would be fun.
W Good idea. Let's join it!

남 뭐 보니, Joan? 동아리 포스터야?
여 응. 학교 동아리에 가입할까 생각 중이야.
남 나랑 독서 동아리에 가입할래?
여 난 책 읽을 시간이 충분하지 않아.
남 프랑스어 동아리는 어때? 그거 재미있을 것 같아.
여 좋은 생각이야. 거기 가입하자!

|어휘| join [동] 가입하다

11 ③

W Are you getting ready for school now, Mike?
M Yeah.
W Please don't ride your bike today. The roads are too slippery.
M Actually, my bike broke yesterday. I'll just walk.
W Are you sure? I can ask Mrs. Johnson to pick you up.
M No, it's okay. I don't mind walking.

여 Mike, 지금 학교 갈 준비하고 있니?
남 네.
여 오늘은 자전거 타고 가지 말아라. 길이 너무 미끄러워.
남 사실, 제 자전거가 어제 고장 났어요. 그냥 걸어갈 거예요.
여 정말이니? Johnson 씨에게 너를 태워달라고 부탁할 수 있는데.
남 아니요, 괜찮아요. 걷는 것 상관없어요.

|어휘| ride [동] 타다 road [명] 도로, 길 slippery [형] 미끄러운

12 ②

W Mr. Lee, can I talk to you for a minute?
M Sure. Do you have a question about the homework?
W No, I need to talk to you about the drama club.
M Okay.
W I want to skip rehearsals for a while. I need more time to study for my final exams.
M I understand. Studying is more important. I'll see you after the final exams.

여 이 선생님, 잠시 얘기할 수 있을까요?
남 물론이지. 숙제에 대한 질문이 있니?
여 아니요, 연극 동아리에 대해 드릴 말씀이 있어서요.
남 그래.
여 얼마간 예행연습을 빠지고 싶어요. 기말고사를 위해 공부할 시간이 더 필요해요.
남 이해한다. 공부하는 것이 더 중요하지. 기말고사가 끝나고 보자.

|해설| 여자는 기말고사 준비 때문에 당분간 연극 예행연습에 불참하겠다고 말하고 있다.

|어휘| for a minute 잠시 drama [명] 드라마, 연극 skip [동] (일을)

거르다, 빠지다 rehearsal [명] 예행연습, 리허설 for a while 잠시, 얼마 동안은 final exam 기말고사

13 ③

M May I help you?
W Yes, please. Is this sweater on sale?
M Yes. You can try it on if you'd like.
W Okay. *[pause]* It's great! I really love the picture of a slice of pizza on the pocket.
M It's one of our most popular items. And it's machine washable.
W How much is it?
M It's $10.

남 도와드릴까요?
여 네. 이 스웨터 할인 판매 중인가요?
남 네. 원하시면 입어보셔도 됩니다.
여 알겠습니다. [잠시 후] 멋지네요! 주머니에 있는 피자 조각 그림이 정말 마음에 들어요.
남 그건 저희의 최고 인기 상품 중 하나예요. 세탁기로 세탁할 수도 있죠.
여 얼마예요?
남 10달러예요.

|어휘| on sale 할인 판매 중인 try on ~을 입어보다 slice [명] 조각 machine washable 세탁기로 세탁 가능한

14 ③

W Excuse me. Where is the New World Hotel?
M Turn right at the hospital over there. Then go straight one block and turn left.
W Turn left?
M Yes. It will be on your right. It's next to the bank.
W Okay. Thanks for your help.

여 실례합니다. New World 호텔이 어디 있나요?
남 저쪽에 있는 병원에서 우회전하세요. 그러고 나서 한 블록 직진한 뒤 좌회전하세요.
여 좌회전이요?
남 네. 호텔은 오른편에 있을 거예요. 은행 옆이에요.
여 알겠습니다. 도와주셔서 감사합니다.

|어휘| go straight 직진하다

15 ④

W I'd like to check out, please.
M Okay. Did you enjoy your trip?
W I did! By the way, how can I get to the airport?
M You could take a bus, but you have a lot of luggage. A taxi would be better.
W Good idea. Could you call one for me?
M Sure.

여 퇴실하고 싶습니다.
남 네. 여행은 즐거우셨나요?
여 네! 그런데 공항에 어떻게 갈 수 있을까요?
남 버스를 타셔도 되지만, 짐이 많으시네요. 택시가 더 나으실 거예요.
여 좋은 생각이네요. 택시 한 대 불러 주시겠어요?
남 알겠습니다.

|해설| 여자의 말 'Could you call one for me?'에서 one은 택시를 가리키는 말이다.

|어휘| check out 퇴실하다 luggage [명] 짐

16 ④

M What are you doing tomorrow afternoon?
W I have a swimming lesson at 2:00 p.m.
M I think you should skip it. Why don't you come with me to visit Ms. Smith?
W Our old English teacher? Why?
M Tomorrow is Teachers' Day. Did you forget?
W I did! Thanks for reminding me.

남 내일 오후에 뭐 하니?
여 오후 2시에 수영 수업이 있어.
남 너 그거 빠져야 할 것 같은데. 나랑 Smith 선생님 뵈러 가지 않을래?
여 예전 우리 영어 선생님? 왜?
남 내일이 스승의 날이잖아. 잊었니?
여 깜빡했네! 상기시켜줘서 고마워.

|어휘| remind [동] 상기시키다

17 ④

M Are you okay? You look very tired.
W I am. I stayed up late last night.
M Why? Were you playing games on your phone?
W No, I was reading a mystery novel.
M So did you finish it?
W Yes. It was so interesting that I couldn't put it down.

남 괜찮아? 너 몹시 피곤해 보여.
여 피곤해. 어젯밤에 늦게까지 깨어 있었거든.

남 왜? 휴대전화로 게임하고 있었니?
여 아니, 추리소설을 읽고 있었어.
남 그래서 다 끝냈니?
여 응. 너무 재미있어서 책을 내려놓을 수가 없었어.

|어휘| stay up late 늦게까지 깨어 있다 mystery novel 추리 소설

18 ④

W Good afternoon. I would like to check in. My name is Hyejin Kim.
M Let me see... *[typing sound]* Here is your room key. Breakfast is served on the 10th floor from 6:00 a.m. to 10:00 a.m.
W Oh, great! I'm thinking of doing some sightseeing tomorrow. Do you have any suggestions?
M The Prado Museum is a must-see. I can arrange a guided tour for you.
W Thank you!

여 안녕하세요. 저 입실하고 싶은데요. 제 이름은 김혜진입니다.
남 한번 볼게요··· [자판 소리] 여기 손님 방 열쇠입니다. 조식은 오전 6시부터 10시까지 10층에서 제공됩니다.
여 아, 좋군요! 제가 내일 관광하려고 하는데요. 제안해주실 만한 것이 있나요?
남 프라도 미술관은 꼭 보셔야 할 겁니다. 손님을 위해서 가이드가 인솔하는 투어를 마련해 드릴 수 있어요.
여 감사합니다!

|어휘| check in 입실하다 serve [동] 제공하다 do sightseeing 관광하다 suggestion [명] 제안 must-see [명] 꼭 보아야 할 것 arrange [동] 마련하다 guided tour 가이드가 인솔하는 여행

19 ③

[Cell phone rings.]
W Hello?
M Hi, this is Bill Taylor. I'm Luke's teacher. Do you have a minute?
W Sure. Did something happen at school?
M No, I'm just concerned about Luke. He seems very quiet recently.
W Luke just got a new brother a few months ago. He thinks everyone likes his new brother more than him.
M You should give him more attention.

① I think he needs to wear glasses.
② Luke is very quiet.
④ Don't worry. He likes his new school.
⑤ The teachers' office is just around the corner.

[휴대전화벨이 울린다.]
여 여보세요?
남 안녕하세요, 저는 Bill Taylor입니다. Luke의 선생님이에요. 잠시 시간 좀 내주시겠어요?
여 그러죠. 학교에서 무슨 일이 있었나요?
남 아니요, 단지 Luke가 좀 걱정돼서요. Luke가 최근에 무척 조용한 것 같아요.
여 Luke가 몇 달 전에 남동생이 생겼거든요. 그 애는 모두 자신보다 새로 생긴 동생을 더 좋아한다고 생각해요.
남 그 애에게 관심을 더 가져주셔야겠어요.

① 그 애가 안경을 써야 할 것 같아요.
② Luke는 무척 조용해요.
④ 걱정하지 마세요. 그 애는 새로운 학교를 좋아해요.
⑤ 교무실은 모퉁이만 돌면 바로 있어요.

|어휘| happen [동] 일어나다, 발생하다 be concerned about ~을 걱정하다 recently [부] 최근에 [문제] attention [명] 관심, 주의 teachers' office 교무실

20 ⑤

[Cell phone rings.]
M Hi, Jin. I'm at the furniture store now.
W Hey, Dad. Did you pick out a desk for me?
M Not yet. What do you think of a wooden desk?
W Hmm... Does it have drawers?
M It does. But I think it's a little small.
W Can you bring home a brochure? Then we can look at it together.
M Of course! I'll ask the salesman to give me one.

① I already picked out your desk.
② It will fit in your room.
③ They will deliver the desk next week.
④ The furniture store is very close to my house.

[휴대전화벨이 울린다.]
남 안녕, Jin. 나 지금 가구점에 있어.
여 네, 아빠. 제 책상 고르셨어요?
남 아직. 나무로 된 책상 어떠니?
여 음··· 그거 서랍 있어요?
남 있지. 하지만 약간 작은 것 같구나.
여 책자를 집에 가져오실 수 있나요? 그러고 나서 같이 보면 되겠네요.
남 물론이지! 판매원에게 하나 달라고 할게.

① 나는 이미 네 책상을 골랐어.
② 그것이 네 방에 맞을 거야.
③ 다음 주에 책상이 배송될 거야.

④ 가구점은 우리 집에서 아주 가까워.

|어휘| furniture [명] 가구 wooden [형] 나무로 된 drawer [명] 서랍 brochure [명] (광고) 책자 [문제] fit [동] 맞다 deliver [동] 배달하다 close [형] 가까운 salesman [명] 판매원

어휘·표현 다지기 p. 139

A

01	체크무늬의	02	정사각형 모양의, 직각의
03	맑은	04	발소리
05	따라오다	06	나무로 된
07	최근에	08	썰다
09	줄무늬의	10	상을 차리다
11	짐	12	~면 어쩌지?
13	위험한	14	상기시키다
15	추리소설	16	미끄러운

B

01	handle	02	throughout the day
03	arrange	04	attention
05	be concerned about	06	stay up late
07	host	08	peel
09	pick out	10	skip

실전 모의고사 4회 pp. 140-141

01 ②	02 ④	03 ①	04 ③	05 ②
06 ①	07 ⑤	08 ④	09 ⑤	10 ③
11 ②	12 ②	13 ①	14 ⑤	15 ①
16 ⑤	17 ②	18 ①	19 ④	20 ③

01 ②

M I am a kind of animal. I don't have any fur or feathers. My skin is usually green or brown. I have a long tail and a long tongue. I like to climb walls and eat insects. What am I?

남 나는 동물의 일종입니다. 나는 털이나 깃털이 전혀 없습니다. 내 피부는 대개 초록색이거나 갈색입니다. 나는 긴 꼬리와 긴 혀가 있습니다. 나는 벽을 오르는 것과 곤충 먹는 것을 좋아합니다. 나는 무엇일까요?

|어휘| feather [명] 깃털 skin [명] 피부 tail [명] 꼬리 tongue [명] 혀 insect [명] 곤충

02 ④

W Look at this cake! I made it myself.
M It's very nice. You wrote "Love Forever" on the top.
W That's right. I used liquid chocolate. And I put a flower on the left side.
M It looks good. But why is there only one?
W I wanted to put a flower on the right side too. But there wasn't enough space.
M That's okay. It's still awesome!

여 이 케이크 좀 봐! 내가 직접 만들었어.
남 정말 멋지다. 위에 "Love Forever"라고 썼네.
여 맞아. 액체 초콜릿을 사용했어. 그리고 왼쪽에는 꽃을 하나 놨어.
남 보기 좋아. 그런데 왜 하나만 있어?
여 오른쪽에도 꽃을 하나 놓고 싶었어. 그런데 충분한 공간이 없었어.
남 괜찮아. 그래도 멋져!

|어휘| liquid [형] 액체 형태의 space [명] 공간 awesome [형] 멋진

03 ①

W Here's tomorrow's weather. There will be snow in Seoul. But it will be sunny in Daegu. The day will start out cloudy in Incheon, but it will be sunny in the afternoon. And in Busan, it will rain all day, so don't forget your umbrella.

여 내일의 날씨입니다. 서울에 눈이 오겠습니다. 하지만 대구는 화창하겠습니다. 인천은 구름이 낀 날씨로 하루를 시작하겠지만, 오후에는 화창하겠습니다. 그리고 부산은 온종일 비가 올 예정이니, 우산을 잊지 마십시오.

|어휘| all day 온종일

04 ③

M Is this your book?
W Oh! Actually, it's a library book. I forgot about it.
M When did you borrow it?
W About a month ago.
M You should take it back to the library today.

남 이거 네 책이니?
여 아! 사실, 그거 도서관 책이야. 그것에 대해 잊어버리고 있었네.
남 언제 빌렸는데?
여 한 달 전쯤.
남 너 오늘 그 책 도서관에 돌려줘야겠다.

|해설| 책을 도서관에 반납하는 것을 잊어버린 여자에게 남자가 충고하고 있다.

|어휘| actually 🖎 사실은 take ~ back ~을 돌려주다

05 ②

M Hello. My name is Patrick. I moved here from Seoul because my father changed jobs. In my free time, I like keeping a blog. When I grow up, I want to be a writer. And my favorite sport is soccer. I'm glad to meet everyone.

남 안녕하세요. 제 이름은 Patrick입니다. 아버지가 이직하셔서 서울에서 이곳으로 이사를 오게 됐어요. 시간이 날 때, 저는 블로그 하는 것을 좋아해요. 저는 자라서 작가가 되고 싶어요. 그리고 제가 가장 좋아하는 운동은 축구입니다. 모두 만나서 반갑습니다.

|어휘| free time 자유 시간 grow up 자라다

06 ①

[Cell phone rings.]

W Hello?

M Hi. I'm calling from the moving company.

W Oh. You're coming tomorrow at 10:00 a.m., aren't you?

M Well, it's supposed to rain in the afternoon. So I want to come one hour earlier.

W That's fine. How long will it take?

M We can move everything in two hours.

W Great! See you tomorrow!

[휴대전화벨이 울린다.]

여 여보세요?

남 안녕하세요. 이삿짐 운송 회사에서 전화드렸습니다.

여 아. 내일 오전 10시에 오시죠, 그렇죠?

남 음. 오후에 비가 온다고 하네요. 그래서 한 시간 더 일찍 갔으면 합니다.

여 괜찮아요. 얼마나 오래 걸릴까요?

남 2시간 만에 전부 옮길 수 있습니다.

여 좋아요! 내일 봴게요!

|어휘| move 🖎 이사하다, 옮기다 be supposed to-v ~하기로 되어 있다

07 ⑤

M I want to be an announcer someday. So I'm joining the school's broadcasting club.

W Oh, let's join together!

M Do you want to be an announcer, too?

W No. I want to be a journalist.

M Then you should become an editor at the school magazine, instead.

W Oh! That's a great idea.

남 나는 언젠가 아나운서가 되고 싶어. 그래서 학교 방송 동아리에 가입할 거야.

여 아, 같이 가입하자!

남 너도 아나운서가 되고 싶니?

여 아니. 나는 기자가 되고 싶어.

남 그러면 너는 대신에 교지의 편집자가 되어야겠다.

여 아! 그거 좋은 생각이다.

|어휘| announcer 🖎 아나운서 someday 🖎 언젠가 broadcasting 🖎 방송 journalist 🖎 기자 editor 🖎 편집자 school magazine 교지

08 ④

M I haven't been sleeping well these days. There's too much noise from upstairs.

W Why? Are there kids running around?

M No, it's a dog. It barks all night.

W Really? You should talk to your neighbors.

M I did that several times. But their dog still barks all the time!

남 요즘 잠을 잘 자지 못하고 있어. 위층에서 나는 소음이 너무 심해.

여 왜? 애들이 뛰어다니니?

남 아니, 개야. 밤새 짖거든.

여 정말? 이웃에게 이야기 좀 해야겠네.

남 여러 번 그렇게 했지. 하지만 개가 여전히 내내 짖어!

|어휘| noise 🖎 소음 upstairs 🖎 위층 bark 🖎 짖다 neighbor 🖎 이웃

09 ⑤

W Are you busy?

M No. I just finished doing my laundry. Do you need some help?

W Yes. I want to move these bookshelves. But they're too heavy.

M I can help you move them. But you should remove all the books first. It will make the shelves lighter.

W Okay. I'll do it right now.

여 바빠요?

남 아니요. 막 세탁하는 걸 마쳤어요. 도움이 필요한가요?

여 네. 이 책꽂이들을 옮기고 싶어요. 그런데 너무 무겁네요.

남 내가 옮기는 걸 도울 수 있어요. 하지만 우선 당신이 책을 모두 치워야겠네요. 그러면 책꽂이가 더 가벼워질 거예요.
여 알았어요. 지금 당장 할게요.

|해설| 남자가 여자에게 책꽂이에 있는 책을 다 꺼낼 것을 요청했다.

|어휘| do laundry 세탁을 하다 bookshelf [명] 책꽂이 remove [동] 치우다 light [형] 가벼운

10 ③

W I heard you did well on the midterm exams. Congratulations!
M Thank you. I studied hard during the vacation.
W How did you study?
M I took an online class. When I had a question, I emailed the teacher.
W I should try that for the next exam.

여 너 중간고사 잘 봤다고 들었어. 축하해!
남 고마워. 방학 동안 열심히 공부했어.
여 어떻게 공부했니?
남 온라인 강의를 들었어. 질문이 있을 때는, 선생님께 이메일을 보냈지.
여 다음 시험 때 그렇게 해봐야겠다.

|어휘| midterm exam 중간고사 Congratulations. 축하해요. vacation [명] 방학 email [동] 이메일을 보내다

11 ②

M It's almost time to go home. Can I walk you to the bus station?
W Actually, I'm not taking the bus today. Traffic is heavy because of an accident.
M Oh. I can give you a ride home if you'd like.
W I'll just ride a bike across the park to get home. I'd prefer to avoid the roads altogether.

남 집에 갈 시간이 거의 다 됐네. 버스 정류장까지 내가 걸어서 바래다줄까?
여 사실, 나 오늘 버스 안 탈 거야. 사고 때문에 교통이 혼잡하거든.
남 아. 네가 원한다면 집까지 태워줄 수 있어.
여 그냥 자전거 타고 공원을 가로질러 집에 갈 거야. 도로를 완전히 피하는 걸 택할래.

|어휘| traffic [명] 교통(량) accident [명] 사고 prefer [동] ~을 (더) 좋아하다[택하다] avoid [동] 피하다 altogether [부] 완전히, 아주

12 ②

[Telephone rings.]
W MG Computers. Can I help you?
M Hi. I bought one of your computers last week.
W I see. Is there a problem with it?
M It works very well. But it is making a strange sound.
W Please bring it to the nearest service center.
M Okay.

[전화벨이 울린다.]
여 MG Computers입니다. 도와드릴까요?
남 안녕하세요. 제가 지난주에 컴퓨터 한 대를 샀는데요.
여 네. 문제가 있나요?
남 아주 잘 작동합니다. 그런데 이상한 소리가 나요.
여 가장 가까운 서비스 센터로 가지고 와주세요.
남 알겠습니다.

|어휘| work [동] 작동하다 make a sound 소리를 내다 strange [형] 이상한

13 ①

M Hello. Can I help you?
W Yes. Do you have a restaurant?
M Actually, we have two. They're both on the 3rd floor.
W Do they deliver?
M Well, are you a guest here?
W Yes. I'm in room 702.
M In that case, you can order room service from your room's phone.

남 안녕하세요. 도와드릴까요?
여 네. 식당이 있나요?
남 사실 두 곳이 있어요. 둘 다 3층에 있습니다.
여 배달해주시나요?
남 음, 여기 투숙객이신가요?
여 네. 702호예요.
남 그러면 방에 있는 전화로 룸서비스를 주문하시면 됩니다.

|어휘| both [대] 둘 다 floor [명] 층 guest [명] 투숙객, 손님 room service 룸서비스(호텔에서 투숙객이 주문한 음식을 방으로 가져다주는 서비스)

14 ⑤

M Oh, I lost my cell phone! Can you help me find it?
W Sure. Did you look around the jungle gym?
M Yes, but there was nothing there.
W Let me check by the see-saw for you.

M Did you find it?

W No. Why don't you go up the slide and check there? I saw that you were riding it.

M Okay. *[pause]* My cell phone isn't here either.

W Oh, look! It's under the slide!

M You're right! Thanks.

남 아, 내 휴대전화를 잃어버렸어! 찾는 것 좀 도와줄래?

여 물론이지. 정글짐 주변을 봤니?

남 응, 하지만 거기엔 아무것도 없었어.

여 내가 시소 옆을 확인해 볼게.

남 찾았어?

여 아니. 미끄럼틀 위에 올라가서 확인해 보는 게 어때? 네가 그거 타고 있는 걸 봤거든.

남 알았어. [잠시 후] 내 휴대전화는 여기에도 없어.

여 오, 봐! 미끄럼틀 아래에 있어!

남 그러네! 고마워.

|어휘| lose [동] 잃어버리다 jungle gym 정글짐 slide [명] 미끄럼틀

15 ①

[Cell phone rings.]

W Hello?

M Hi, it's Frank. Do you want to watch the sunrise together at the beach tomorrow?

W Oh, that sounds fun.

M Great! Set your alarm clock so we don't miss it.

W Sure. What time does the sun rise?

M At 6:35 a.m.

W That's so early. Can you call me at 5:00 a.m.? I might oversleep.

M Okay. I will.

[휴대전화벨이 울린다.]

여 여보세요?

남 안녕, 나 Frank야. 내일 해변에서 해돋이 함께 볼래?

여 아, 그거 재미있겠다.

남 좋아! 놓치지 않게 알람시계 맞춰 놔.

여 그래. 해가 몇 시에 뜨지?

남 아침 6시 35분에.

여 너무 이르다. 나한테 5시에 전화해 줄 수 있니? 내가 늦잠 잘 수도 있어서.

남 알았어. 그럴게.

|해설| 여자는 늦잠 잘 것을 걱정해 남자에게 전화해 달라고 부탁했다.

|어휘| sunrise [명] 해돋이 set an alarm clock 알람시계를 맞추다 miss [동] 놓치다 oversleep [동] 늦잠 자다

16 ⑤

W You look bored, Mark. You should have brought a book to read.

M I like to read books, but they are too heavy to carry.

W Then why don't you try reading e-books? They are convenient.

M Sounds like a great idea!

W Yeah! You can just download them onto your smartphone.

M Thank you for letting me know.

여 너 지루해 보인다, Mark. 읽을 책을 가져오지 그랬어.

남 난 책 읽는 것을 좋아하긴 하는데, 그건 들고 다니기에 너무 무거워.

여 그럼 전자책을 읽어 보는 건 어때? 그건 편리하잖아.

남 좋은 생각 같다!

여 맞아! 네 스마트폰에 내려받기만 하면 돼.

남 알려줘서 고마워.

|어휘| bored [형] 지루한 carry [동] 가지고 다니다, 휴대하다 convenient [형] 편리한 onto [전] ~ 쪽으로

17 ②

M Hi, Stella. What did you do yesterday?

W I went to the zoo. How about you?

M I visited my uncle's house.

W What did you do there?

M I played chess with my cousin.

W Oh, are you good at it?

M No. I couldn't win a single game. It was fun, though.

남 안녕, Stella. 어제 뭐 했니?

여 동물원에 갔었어. 너는?

남 난 삼촌 집에 갔었어.

여 거기서 뭐 했니?

남 사촌과 체스를 했어.

여 오, 너 그거 잘하니?

남 아니. 한 게임도 못 이겼어. 그렇지만 재미있었어.

|어휘| chess [명] 체스 be good at ~을 잘하다 single [형] 단 하나의 though [부] 그렇지만

18 ①

W Hi, Charlie. What's up?

M I'm not in your class, but I'd like to write for the school newspaper.

W Great! You don't have to be one of my students to work for the newspaper.

M Really? I'm glad to hear that.

W We're meeting tomorrow at 4:00 p.m. in the school theater. Come join us!

여 안녕, Charlie. 무슨 일이니?

남 제가 선생님 수업을 듣진 않지만, 학교 신문에 글을 쓰고 싶어서요.

여 좋아! 신문 작업을 위해 내 수업을 듣는 학생일 필요는 없단다.

남 정말요? 잘됐네요.

여 우린 학교 극장에서 내일 오후 4시에 만날 거야. 와서 함께 하렴!

|어휘| theater 몡 극장

19 ④

M What are you doing, Mom?

W Do you remember when that car hit our fence the other day?

M Yes, of course I do.

W Well, I'm going to try to fix the fence.

M Can I help you?

W Sure. Hand me the hammer and those nails.

① No. A repairman will fix the fence.

② Don't worry, honey. It wasn't your fault.

③ I'm sorry, but I don't have time right now.

⑤ Okay, I will pick you up after I'm finished.

남 엄마, 뭐 하고 계세요?

여 일전에 저 자동차가 우리 집 울타리를 쳤던 것 기억하니?

남 네, 물론 기억하죠.

여 음, 내가 울타리를 고쳐보려고 해.

남 도와드릴까요?

여 그래. 망치와 저 못 좀 건네주렴.

① 아니. 정비사가 울타리를 고칠 거야.

② 걱정 말렴, 얘야. 네 잘못이 아니었어.

③ 미안하지만 난 지금 당장은 시간이 없어.

⑤ 좋아, 끝나면 내가 너를 데리러 갈게.

|어휘| hit 동 치다 fence 몡 울타리 fix 동 고치다 [문제] repairman 몡 정비사 fault 몡 잘못 hammer 몡 망치 nail 몡 못

20 ③

W Minsu, wake up! You fell asleep again.

M Oh, I'm sorry.

W We need to finish this homework by tonight.

M I know. But I'm really exhausted today.

W Why are you so tired? Did you study all night for an exam?

M No. Actually, I got back from my trip at 1:00 a.m.

W Wow! No wonder you can't stay awake!

① You should leave now.

② That's strange. Do you know why?

④ That's okay. I finished my homework earlier today.

⑤ Sorry, I didn't realize you had other plans already.

여 민수야, 일어나! 너 또 잠들었어.

남 아, 미안해.

여 우리 오늘 밤까지 이 숙제를 끝내야 하잖아.

남 알아. 근데 오늘 너무 지친다.

여 왜 그렇게 피곤하니? 시험 때문에 밤새워 공부했니?

남 아니. 실은, 여행에서 새벽 1시에 돌아왔거든.

여 와! 네가 깨어 있지 못할 만도 하네.

① 너 지금 출발해야 해.

② 그거 이상하네. 너 왜 그런지 아니?

④ 괜찮아. 나는 오늘 예상보다 일찍 숙제를 끝마쳤어.

⑤ 미안해, 네가 이미 다른 계획이 있는지 몰랐어.

|어휘| fall asleep 잠들다 exhausted 형 지친 trip 몡 여행 [문제] no wonder ~은 전혀 놀랄 일이 아니다 stay awake 자지 않고 깨어 있다 realize 동 깨닫다

어휘·표현 다지기
p. 149

A

01 피부	02 잠들다
03 소음	04 짖다
05 잘못	06 방송
07 액체 형태의	08 혀
09 편집자	10 공간
11 깃털	12 기자
13 중간고사	14 교통(량)
15 피하다	16 책꽂이

B

01 all day	02 realize
03 convenient	04 single
05 theater	06 oversleep
07 remove	08 stay awake
09 be supposed to-v	10 set an alarm clock

실전 모의고사 5회 pp.150-151

01 ③	02 ③	03 ③	04 ①	05 ⑤
06 ④	07 ②	08 ⑤	09 ③	10 ①
11 ①	12 ⑤	13 ②	14 ③	15 ②
16 ④	17 ④	18 ③	19 ③	20 ④

01 ③

M You can find this on roads. This usually has three colored lights: red, yellow, and green. Each color has a different meaning. The red light means "stop," the yellow light means "be careful" and the green light means "go." What is this?

남 여러분은 이것을 도로에서 찾을 수 있습니다. 이것은 대개 빨간색, 노란색, 그리고 초록색의 세 가지 색의 빛을 가지고 있습니다. 각각의 색은 다른 의미를 가집니다. 빨간색 빛은 '멈추라'를 의미하고, 노란색 빛은 '주의하라'를 의미하고, 초록색 빛은 '가라'를 의미합니다. 이것은 무엇일까요?

|어휘| light [명] 빛 different [형] 다른 meaning [명] 의미 careful [형] 주의하는

02 ③

W Hey John, let's get a new cushion for my puppy.
M That sounds like a great idea. There are a lot of cushions here.
W Which one do you like best?
M How about this one? It's square and has a checkered pattern.
W Well, I prefer the round one with paw prints on it.
M Okay. Let's buy that one.

여 저기, John, 우리 강아지를 위해 새 방석을 삽시다.
남 좋은 생각인 것 같아요. 여기에 방석이 많네요.
여 당신은 어떤 것이 제일 좋아요?
남 이것은 어때요? 네모 모양이고, 체크무늬가 있어요.
여 음, 나는 발 무늬가 있는 둥근 게 더 좋아요.
남 좋아요. 그걸로 삽시다.

|어휘| cushion [명] 쿠션, 방석 pattern [명] 패턴, 무늬 round [형] 둥근 paw [명] (동물의 발톱이 달린) 발 print [명] 무늬

03 ③

W Good morning. Here is Atlanta's weather forecast. On Monday, we expect cloudy skies throughout the day. On Tuesday, it will rain. If you planned to go on a picnic, you'd better postpone it until Wednesday. From Wednesday until Friday, it will be sunny.

여 좋은 아침입니다. 애틀랜타의 일기 예보를 전해드립니다. 월요일에는 온종일 흐린 하늘을 예상합니다. 화요일에는 비가 내릴 예정입니다. 만약 나들이를 계획하고 계셨다면, 수요일까지 미루시는 게 낫겠습니다. 수요일부터 금요일까지는 맑겠습니다.

|어휘| weather forecast 일기 예보 expect [동] 예상하다 throughout [전] 내내 plan [동] 계획하다 had better ~하는 편이 낫다 postpone [동] 미루다

04 ①

M Hi, Laura!
W Good morning, Bob. Tomorrow is your last day in New York, right?
M Yes, it is. My flight leaves at 8:00 a.m. tomorrow.
W I can give you a ride to the airport if you want.
M That would be great. Thanks for being so helpful.

남 안녕, Laura!
여 안녕, Bob. 내일이 뉴욕에서의 마지막 날이네, 맞지?
남 그래, 맞아. 내 항공편은 내일 아침 8시에 출발해.
여 네가 원한다면 공항까지 태워다 줄 수 있어.
남 그러면 좋겠다. 정말 기꺼이 도움을 줘서 고마워.

|어휘| flight [명] 항공기, 항공편 helpful [형] 기꺼이 돕는

05 ⑤

M Good morning, students. As you know, your new homeroom teacher will arrive tomorrow. Her name is Mrs. Baker. She will teach science. She is very intelligent and friendly. She has been teaching for fifteen years. I think you will all learn a lot from her.

남 안녕하세요, 학생 여러분. 알다시피, 내일 새로운 담임 선생님이 오십니다. 성함은 Baker 선생님이십니다. 선생님은 과학을 가르치실 것입니다. 매우 똑똑하고 다정하시죠. 15년 동안 가르치는 일을 해오셨습니다. 여러분 모두 선생님께 많이 배울 수 있을 것이라고 생각합니다.

|어휘| homeroom teacher 담임 교사 intelligent [형] 총명한, 똑똑한

06 ④

M Sarah, can you still meet me tonight?
W We have plans for tonight?

M Yes. You suggested that we have dinner together at 6:30.
W Oh, I forgot. I'm sorry. How about tomorrow instead?
M All right. So, are you okay with 6:30?
W How about 30 minutes later? I leave work at 6:00, but there will be a lot of traffic.
M Sure.

남 Sarah, 너 오늘 밤에 나 만나는 거 여전히 가능한 거지?
여 우리가 오늘 밤에 계획이 있다고?
남 응. 6시 30분에 같이 저녁 먹자고 네가 제안했잖아.
여 아, 잊어버렸어. 미안해. 대신 내일은 어때?
남 괜찮아. 그럼, 6시 30분은 괜찮은 거야?
여 30분 더 늦게는 어때? 내가 6시에 퇴근하는데, 차가 아주 많을 거야.
남 그러자.

|해설| 여자가 차량 정체 때문에 약속을 30분 늦추자고 했으므로 두 사람이 만날 시각은 7시이다.

|어휘| plan [명] 계획 suggest [동] 제안하다 traffic [명] 교통(량)

07 ②

W Where are you going, Tom?
M Hi, Jane. I'm on my way to my singing lessons.
W I didn't know you liked singing. Do you want to be a singer?
M Not really. My dream is to be a singing teacher.
W Oh, wow. Maybe you could teach me how to sing sometime!

여 어디 가니, Tom?
남 안녕, Jane. 노래 수업에 가는 길이야.
여 네가 노래 부르는 걸 좋아하는지 몰랐어. 가수가 되고 싶은 거야?
남 그렇진 않아. 내 꿈은 노래 강사가 되는 거야.
여 아, 와. 언젠가 네가 나한테 노래 부르는 것을 가르쳐줄 수 있겠다!

|어휘| sometime [부] 언젠가

08 ⑤

M Your phone is vibrating, Ashley.
W Oh, it's a text message from my mom.
M What did she say?
W She said that she's proud of me for getting a job.
M That's very sweet of her.
W I know! She also wrote that she's lucky to have a daughter like me.

남 네 휴대전화 진동 울린다, Ashley.
여 아, 엄마한테 온 문자야.
남 뭐라고 말씀하셨어?
여 내가 직장을 구해서 자랑스럽다고 하셨어.
남 엄마 참 다정하시다.
여 맞아! 엄마는 나 같은 딸을 둔 것이 행운이라고도 적으셨어.

|어휘| vibrate [동] 진동하다 text message 문자 (메시지) be proud of ~을 자랑스러워하다 sweet [형] 다정한 lucky [형] 운이 좋은

09 ③

W Thank you for making time for this interview, Mr. Lawrence.
M It's my pleasure.
W Can you tell me about your new movie?
M Sure. I play the main character. He loses his memory in an accident.
W Wow, that's interesting. It's based on a novel, isn't it?
M Yes, it is.
W Sorry, but do you mind if I get a drink of water?
M That's fine. Go ahead.

여 이 인터뷰에 시간 내주셔서 감사합니다, Lawrence 씨.
남 천만에요.
여 새 영화에 대해 말씀해 주시겠습니까?
남 그러죠. 저는 주인공을 맡았습니다. 그는 사고로 기억을 잃어요.
여 와, 흥미롭네요. 소설을 바탕으로 한 영화죠, 그렇죠?
남 그렇습니다.
여 죄송하지만, 물 한 잔 마셔도 괜찮을까요?
남 괜찮습니다. 그러세요.

|해설| 여자가 물을 마셔도 되냐고 물으며 인터뷰를 잠시 중단했다.

|어휘| make time 시간을 내다 interview [명] 인터뷰 main character 주인공 lose [동] 잃다 memory [명] 기억 be based on ~에 기반을 두다 novel [명] 소설

10 ①

M You look cold, Tiffany!
W I am. I bought a new winter coat, but it doesn't keep me very warm.
M Have you tried wearing long underwear?
W No, I haven't.
M You should! It really helps.
W Oh, does it?
M Yes. It keeps you warm by trapping your body heat. So you can also save some money on heating costs.

남 너 추워 보인다, Tiffany!

여 맞아. 새 겨울 코트를 샀는데, 그리 따뜻하지 않아.
남 긴 내의 입어 봤어?
여 아니.
남 꼭 입어 봐! 그게 진짜 도움이 돼.
여 아, 그래?
남 응. 그게 체열을 빠져나가지 않게 가둬서 널 따뜻하게 해줄 거야. 그래서 난방비도 좀 절약할 수 있어.

|어휘| underwear [명] 내의, 속옷 trap [동] 가두다 body heat 체열 save [동] 절약하다 heating cost 난방비

11 ①

M Why are you leaving so early, Natalie?
W Mom can't give me a ride to school today.
M Oh, that's right. Are you going to take the subway?
W No, I'll take the bus. It takes too long by subway. I would have to transfer three times.
M I see.

남 왜 이렇게 일찍 가니, Natalie?
여 오늘 엄마가 저를 학교에 태워 주실 수 없어서요.
남 아, 그렇구나. 지하철 탈 거니?
여 아니요, 버스 탈 거예요. 지하철로는 너무 오래 걸려요. 세 번이나 갈아타야 하거든요.
남 알겠다.

|어휘| give ~ a ride ~을 태워 주다 transfer [동] 환승하다

12 ⑤

M Did you have a nice trip to Seoul last weekend, Christine?
W No, it was terrible!
M What happened? Didn't you like your hotel?
W My hotel was terrific! But I caught a cold on the first day of my visit.
M Oh, no! What did you do after you got sick?
W I just played games on my smartphone all day.

남 지난 주말에 서울 여행 즐거웠니, Christine?
여 아니, 끔찍했어!
남 무슨 일 있었어? 호텔이 마음에 안 들었니?
여 호텔은 정말 좋았어! 하지만 여행 첫날 감기에 걸려버렸어.
남 아, 저런! 아픈 뒤로는 뭐 했어?
여 그냥 온종일 스마트폰으로 게임했어.

|해설| 여자는 여행 첫날 감기에 걸려 여행을 즐기지 못했다.

|어휘| terrible [형] 끔찍한 terrific [형] 매우 멋진 catch a cold 감기에 걸리다

13 ②

M Good morning. What can I do for you today?
W I need some small photos for my resume.
M Okay. It will be $20 for ten photos.
W That's fine. Do you have a black jacket? I want to wear one in the photo.
M Sure. There are several options to choose from. I'll show you.
W Thanks!

남 안녕하세요. 오늘 무엇을 도와드릴까요?
여 이력서에 쓸 작은 사진이 필요해요.
남 네. 사진 10장에 20달러입니다.
여 좋습니다. 검은색 재킷이 있나요? 사진에서 입고 있으면 해요.
남 물론이죠. 손님이 고르실 수 있는 몇 가지 선택권이 있습니다. 보여드릴게요.
여 감사합니다!

|어휘| resume [명] 이력서 several [형] 몇몇의 option [명] 선택(할 수 있는 것), 선택권 choose [동] 선택하다

14 ③

M Megan, do you know how to get to the flower shop?
W Oh, it's easy to find. Go straight one block and then turn left on Iris Street.
M Turn left?
W Yes. Then go straight for two blocks. It will be on your right.
M Got it. Thanks for your help!

남 Megan, 꽃 가게에 어떻게 가는지 알아?
여 아, 거기 찾기 쉬워. 한 블록 직진한 다음 Iris 가에서 좌회전해.
남 좌회전?
여 응. 그런 다음 두 블록 직진해. 너의 오른쪽에 있을 거야.
남 알았어. 도와줘서 고마워!

|어휘| on one's right 오른쪽에

15 ②

W Greg, does your dog like taking baths?
M Yes, she loves it. Why are you asking?
W My father brought a dog yesterday. I tried to wash him, but I couldn't.
M Why? Did he keep moving?
W Yes! He also barked a lot. Could you help me give him a bath?
M Sure, no problem.

여	Greg, 너희 집 개는 목욕하는 거 좋아하니?
남	응, 좋아해. 왜 물어보는 거야?
여	아버지가 어제 개를 데려오셨거든. 목욕시키려고 했는데, 못 했어.
남	왜? 개가 계속 움직여서?
여	응! 많이 짖기도 했고. 목욕시키는 것 좀 도와줄 수 있어?
남	그래, 물론이지.

|해설| 여자는 자신의 개를 목욕시키는 일이 어렵다며 남자에게 도움을 요청하고 있다.

|어휘| take a bath 목욕하다   give ~ a bath ~을 목욕시키다

16 ④

M	Tiffany, do you think that I've gained weight recently?
W	Yes, I think so. Your clothes look tight on you.
M	I know. I should start exercising, but I don't have time to go to the gym.
W	Then why don't you get off the bus a stop early and walk home every day?
M	I'll try that!

남	Tiffany, 최근에 나 체중이 늘어난 것 같아?
여	응, 그런 것 같아. 너한테 옷이 꽉 조여 보여.
남	그러게. 운동을 시작해야 하는데, 헬스장에 갈 시간이 없네.
여	그럼 매일 버스에서 한 정거장 일찍 내려서 집에 걸어가는 건 어때?
남	그렇게 해봐야겠다!

|어휘| gain weight 체중이 늘다   tight 휑 꽉 조이는   gym 몡 헬스장, 체육관   get off ~에서 내리다   stop 몡 정거장

17 ④

M	What book would you like to read next for our book club?
W	I want to read a book about history or science.
M	But we have already read those kinds of books. How about a fun and easy one?
W	What do you have in mind?
M	How about a children's novel? I heard *The Giver* won several children's book awards.
W	That sounds great.

남	우리 독서 모임에서 다음에 무슨 책을 읽었으면 좋겠어?
여	역사나 과학에 대한 책을 읽고 싶어.
남	하지만 그런 종류의 책들은 이미 읽었잖아. 재밌고 쉬운 건 어때?
여	뭐 생각해 둔 거 있어?
남	아동용 소설은 어때? 〈The Giver〉가 여러 아동문학상을 수상했대.

여	괜찮겠다.

|해설| 남자가 제안한 아동용 소설에 여자는 괜찮겠다며 긍정적인 반응을 보였다.

|어휘| book club 독서 모임   kind 몡 종류   have in mind ~을 염두에 두다   award 몡 상

18 ③

M	Good morning. Where would you like to go?
W	Central Park, please. How long will it take?
M	With this traffic, it will take about forty minutes.
W	And how much will it be?
M	About $50. But it could be more.
W	All right. That's fine.

남	안녕하세요. 어디로 가실 건가요?
여	센트럴 파크요. 얼마나 걸릴까요?
남	이런 교통량이면, 40분 정도 걸릴 거예요.
여	그리고 비용은 얼마나 될까요?
남	50달러 정도요. 하지만 더 될 수도 있어요.
여	네. 괜찮습니다.

|해설| 목적지를 묻고 목적지까지의 예상 소요 시간과 비용을 말하는 것으로 보아, 남자는 택시 운전사임을 알 수 있다.

|어휘| take 통 (시간·비용 등이) 걸리다

19 ③

W	Is there a room available for tonight?
M	What kind of room would you like?
W	A single room, please. Is breakfast included?
M	All of our rooms come with breakfast.
W	Okay. Can you tell me what the rate is?
M	The rate is $120 a night.

① No, it's not available.
② Yes, that would be fine.
④ The checkout time is 12:00 p.m.
⑤ It is served from 8:00 a.m. to 11:00 a.m.

여	오늘 밤에 이용할 수 있는 방이 있습니까?
남	어떤 종류의 방을 원하세요?
여	1인실이요. 아침식사가 포함되나요?
남	네. 모든 방에 아침식사가 딸려 있습니다.
여	알겠습니다. 요금을 알려주시겠어요?
남	요금은 1박에 120달러입니다.

① 아니요. 이용이 불가합니다.
② 네, 괜찮을 것 같네요.

④ 퇴실 시간은 오후 12시입니다.
⑤ 오전 8시부터 11시까지 제공됩니다.

|어휘| available [형] 이용 가능한 single room 1인실 include [동] 포함하다 come with ~이 딸려 있다 rate [명] 요금 [문제] checkout [명] 퇴실 serve [동] 제공하다

20 ④

W What are you doing, Sean?
M I'm writing down my New Year's resolutions.
W Oh, what are they?
M I want to drink less soda and exercise more often.
W Sounds wonderful!
M How about you? Do you have any New Year's resolutions?
W I want to spend more time with my family. Everyone is busy with school and work, so it's hard to do things together.
M I'm sure that would make them really happy.

① How many brothers do you have?
② I'm looking forward to seeing them.
③ Sorry. I don't have time to do something together today.
⑤ What do you and your friends like to do together?

여 뭐 하고 있어, Sean?
남 내 새해 결심을 적고 있어.
여 아, 뭔데?
남 탄산음료를 더 적게 마시고 더 자주 운동하고 싶어.
여 멋지다!
남 너는 어때? 새해 결심 있니?
여 나는 가족들과 더 많은 시간을 보내고 싶어. 모두 학교와 직장 때문에 바빠서, 함께 뭔가를 하기 힘들거든.
남 그렇게 하는 것이 가족들을 정말 행복하게 해줄 거라고 확신해.

① 너는 남자형제가 몇 명 있어?
② 그들을 보는 게 기대돼.
③ 미안해. 오늘 같이 뭔가 할 시간이 없어.
⑤ 너와 네 친구들은 함께 뭐 하는 걸 좋아해?

|어휘| resolution [명] 결심 soda [명] 탄산음료 spend [동] 보내다 [문제] look forward to v-ing ~하는 것을 기대하다

어휘·표현 다지기 p. 159

A

01	포함하다	02	기억
03	이력서	04	가두다
05	탄산음료	06	제안하다
07	상	08	미루다
09	체중이 늘다	10	담임 교사
11	언젠가	12	목욕하다
13	총명한, 똑똑한	14	문자 (메시지)
15	의미	16	~을 자랑스러워하다

B

01	heating cost	02	tight
03	be based on	04	resolution
05	helpful	06	transfer
07	rate	08	body heat
09	vibrate	10	have in mind

실전 모의고사 6회 pp. 160-161

01 ④	02 ②	03 ③	04 ①	05 ⑤
06 ⑤	07 ②	08 ②	09 ④	10 ③
11 ④	12 ②	13 ①	14 ⑤	15 ②
16 ③	17 ④	18 ④	19 ⑤	20 ⑤

01 ④

W You hang your coat or hat on this. Usually, you can find this near a door. This is a tall pole. Hooks stick out of this. This is usually made of metal, wood, or plastic. What is this?

여 여러분은 이 위에 외투나 모자를 겁니다. 보통 문 근처에서 이것을 찾을 수 있습니다. 이것은 긴 막대입니다. 여기에 고리가 툭 튀어나와 있습니다. 이것은 보통 금속, 나무, 또는 플라스틱으로 만들어집니다. 이것은 무엇일까요?

|어휘| hang [동] 걸다, 매달다 pole [명] 막대기, 장대 hook [명] 고리 stick out 툭 튀어나오다 be made of ~로 만들어지다 metal [명] 금속

02 ②

M Do you like my flower pot? I made it in art class.
W It's great! I like the ladybug on the flower.
M Thanks. I wanted to draw a bumblebee instead, but it was too hard.
W Are you going to plant something in it?
M No. I'm going to give it to my friend.

남 내 화분 마음에 드니? 내가 미술 수업 시간에 만들었어.
여 멋져! 나는 꽃 위의 무당벌레가 마음에 들어.
남 고마워. 대신 꿀벌을 그리고 싶었는데, 너무 어려웠어.
여 그 안에 뭔가 심을 거니?
남 아니. 내 친구에게 줄 거야.

|어휘| flower pot 화분 ladybug [명] 무당벌레 bumblebee [명] 꿀벌 instead [부] 대신에 plant [동] 심다

03 ③

M Good morning! This is Anthony Brown with the weather. It will snow all day today, so be careful on the roads! Tomorrow, it will be very foggy but the temperature will rise. The day after tomorrow, there is a 30% chance of rain.

남 좋은 아침입니다! 저는 날씨를 전해드리는 Anthony Brown입니다. 오늘은 종일 눈이 올 것으로 예상되니, 도로에서 주의하십시오! 내일은 안개가 매우 많이 끼겠으나 기온은 오르겠습니다. 모레에는 비가 내릴 확률이 30%입니다.

|어휘| temperature [명] 기온 rise [동] 오르다 chance [명] 가능성

04 ①

M Hi, Beth. Are you going on vacation this weekend?
W Yes, I am. I'm so excited!
M Who is going to take care of your dog?
W I'm going to ask my best friend to do it. Why?
M Oh. Could I take care of him instead? I really love your dog.
W Sure! Thanks a lot.

남 안녕, Beth. 이번 주말에 휴가 가니?
여 응, 그래. 나 너무 신나!
남 네 개는 누가 돌볼 예정이야?
여 내 가장 친한 친구에게 돌봐달라고 부탁하려고. 왜?
남 아. 내가 대신 돌봐줘도 될까? 나 너희 개 정말 좋아하거든.
여 물론이지! 정말 고마워.

|해설| 남자의 마지막 말 'Could I ~?'는 상대에게 허락을 구하는 표현이다.

|어휘| go on vacation 휴가를 가다 excited [형] 신이 난 take care of ~을 돌보다

05 ⑤

W We're introducing a new style of ice skates today. They are available in white, black, and green. Only the softest leather is used to make these skates. They are perfect for beginner figure skaters. At the low price of $199, you should buy a pair today!

여 오늘 저희는 새로운 스타일의 스케이트화를 소개하려고 합니다. 흰색, 검은색, 초록색으로 구매하실 수 있습니다. 이 스케이트화를 만들기 위해 가장 부드러운 가죽만이 사용되었습니다. 이 스케이트화는 피겨스케이트를 타는 초보자에게 안성맞춤입니다. 199달러라는 낮은 가격으로, 오늘 (스케이트화) 한 켤레 구매하시기 바랍니다!

|어휘| introduce [동] 소개하다 leather [명] 가죽 beginner [명] 초보자 low [형] 낮은 pair [명] 한 쌍[켤레]

06 ⑤

W Hey! Can you still meet me at the library after school today?
M Definitely. We should study for the history test.
W Great. Let's meet at 4:00 p.m.
M I can't. I have soccer practice at 3:30 p.m. Can we meet at 5:30 p.m.?
W No problem. I'll see you in front of the library.
M All right. See you then.

여 얘! 너 오늘 방과 후에 도서관에서 나 만날 수 있는 것 맞지?
남 물론이지. 우리 역사 시험공부 해야 해.
여 좋아. 오후 4시에 만나자.
남 안 돼. 나 3시 30분에 축구 연습 있어. 5시 30분에 볼 수 있니?
여 좋아. 도서관 앞에서 보자.
남 알겠어. 그때 보자.

|어휘| definitely [부] 그렇고말고 in front of ~의 앞에서

07 ②

M Molly, I liked your speech on your trip to Italy.
W Thanks! I think the topic is really interesting.
M You must enjoy traveling.
W I do. I want to travel around the world someday.
M You should become a pilot!
W No, I don't want to fly planes. I want to help take care of the passengers by serving them food and drinks.

남 Molly, 너의 이탈리아 여행에 대한 강연 좋았어.
여 고마워! 이 주제가 정말 흥미로운 것 같아.
남 너 틀림없이 여행하는 것을 즐길 것 같아.
여 맞아. 언젠가는 세계를 여행하고 싶어.
남 너 비행기 조종사가 되어야겠다!
여 아니야, 난 비행기를 조종하고 싶지 않아. 나는 승객들에게 음식과

음료를 제공하면서 그들을 살피는 일을 돕고 싶어.

|해설| 여자는 마지막 말에서 승객을 돕는 일이 좋다고 했다.

|어휘| speech 명 강연, 연설   topic 명 주제   someday 부 언젠가   pilot 명 비행기 조종사   passenger 명 승객

08 ②

W Hi, Tony. Did you have a good day at school?
M I did! I have some news!
W What is it?
M I got a perfect score on my Spanish test!
W That's wonderful! I knew you could do it.
M Thanks!

여 안녕. Tony. 학교에서 좋은 하루 보냈니?
남 네! 저 말씀드릴 게 있어요!
여 뭔데?
남 저 스페인어 시험에서 만점 받았어요!
여 멋지구나! 나는 네가 해낼 줄 알았어.
남 감사해요!

|어휘| perfect score 만점   Spanish 명 스페인어   [문제] shy 형 수줍음을 많이 타는   indifferent 형 무관심한   jealous 형 질투하는   nervous 형 초조한

09 ④

M Are you okay, Diane? You look tired.
W No, I'm sick. I have a runny nose and a sore throat.
M I'm sorry to hear that. Did you take some medicine?
W I took some this morning, but it didn't help.
M Why don't you go to the doctor?
W Yeah… I should make an appointment now.

남 너 괜찮니, Diane? 피곤해 보여.
여 안 괜찮아, 나 아파. 콧물이 나고 목도 아파.
남 안됐구나. 약 좀 먹었니?
여 오늘 아침에 먹었는데, 도움이 되지 않네.
남 병원에 가보지 그래?
여 그래… 지금 예약해야겠다.

|어휘| have a runny nose 콧물이 나다   have a sore throat 목이 아프다   medicine 명 약   help 동 도움이 되다   make an appointment 예약하다

10 ③

W Oh my gosh! Your bedroom is a mess. You promised me that you would clean it.

M I know. Sorry, Mom. I'll clean it right now.
W Can you start by picking up your clothes? They're all over the floor.
M Okay. I'll make my bed and sweep the floor after that.
W Great.

여 세상에! 네 침실이 엉망이구나. 청소하겠다고 나와 약속했잖니.
남 맞아요. 죄송해요, 엄마. 지금 당장 치울게요.
여 옷부터 주울 수 있겠니? 바닥에 온통 널려 있구나.
남 네, 그거 한 뒤에 잠자리도 정리하고 바닥도 쓸게요.
여 좋아.

|어휘| mess 명 엉망인 상태   promise 동 약속하다   pick up ~을 집다[들어올리다]   floor 명 바닥   make one's bed 잠자리를 정돈하다   sweep 동 (방 등을 빗자루로) 쓸다

11 ④

M Kelly, is that your science project? It looks big and heavy.
W Yes, it is. It's due today.
M Can you take it on the bus by yourself?
W Actually, I was wondering if you could give me a ride.
M My car broke down yesterday. Let's use your mom's car.
W Okay.

남 Kelly, 그거 네 과학 과제니? 크고 무거워 보인다.
여 네, 맞아요. 오늘까지 하기로 되어 있는 거예요.
남 너 혼자 그걸 버스에 들고 탈 수 있겠니?
여 사실, 아빠가 저를 좀 태워주실 수 있는지 궁금했어요.
남 내 차가 어제 고장 났단다. 너희 엄마 차를 쓰자.
여 알겠어요.

|해설| 남자는 마지막 말에서 여자의 엄마 차를 이용하자고 했다.

|어휘| due 형 ~하기로 예정된[되어 있는]   by oneself 혼자   break down 고장 나다

12 ②

W What are you doing tonight, Cory?
M I'm taking a salsa class. It starts at 7:00 p.m.
W That's great! Are you taking it for exercise?
M No. My girlfriend wants me to take the class with her.
W Wow, I'm sure that you'll have a great time!

여 오늘 밤에 뭐 하니, Cory?
남 나 살사춤 수업 들어. 오후 7시에 시작해.
여 멋지다! 운동을 위해 듣는 거야?

남 아니. 내 여자친구가 나랑 수업을 같이 듣고 싶어 해.
여 와, 너희 좋은 시간 보낼 것 같다!

|어휘| salsa [명] 살사(춤) exercise [명] 운동

13 ①

W Hello, sir. How may I help you?
M Can I open a checking account, please?
W Okay. Is there anything else I can do for you?
M I also need a new debit card.
W Sure. Please fill out these forms first.
M Okay. How long will it take to get the card?
W It will take three or four days.

여 안녕하세요, 고객님. 무엇을 도와드릴까요?
남 예금 계좌를 개설할 수 있을까요?
여 네. 제가 도와드릴 것이 더 있나요?
남 새 현금 카드도 필요합니다.
여 네. 이 양식을 먼저 작성해주세요.
남 알겠습니다. 카드를 받는 데 얼마나 걸릴까요?
여 삼사일 정도 걸릴 예정입니다.

|어휘| checking account 예금 계좌 debit card 직불[현금] 카드 fill out (서식 등을) 작성하다 form [명] 양식

14 ⑤

M Mom, do you know where the remote control is?
W It's always by the plant or in front of the TV, you know.
M But it's not in either of those places.
W Why don't you look in the drawer, then?
M There's nothing in the drawer.
W Hmm… Did you look on the sofa?
M Oh, I found it! It's on the rug. It must have fallen off the sofa.

남 엄마, 리모컨이 어디 있는지 아세요?
여 알다시피, 항상 식물 옆이나 TV 앞에 있단다.
남 하지만 그 두 곳 중 어느 곳에도 없어요.
여 그럼 서랍 안을 들여다보지 그래?
남 서랍 안에 아무것도 없어요.
여 음… 소파 위를 봤니?
남 아, 찾았어요! 깔개 위에 있어요. 소파에서 떨어졌나 봐요.

|어휘| remote control 리모컨 drawer [명] 서랍 rug [명] 깔개 fall off 떨어지다

15 ②

M Hi, Mrs. O'Brien.
W Hello, Max. Do you need something?
M Can I change my seat? I need to sit closer to the board.
W Oh, I'm sorry. I forgot that you can't see far away very well. Can you remind me again tomorrow? I'll find a new seat for you then.
M Okay. Thank you.

남 안녕하세요, O'Brien 선생님.
여 안녕, Max. 필요한 것 있니?
남 제 자리 좀 바꿀 수 있을까요? 칠판에 더 가까이 앉아야 해서요.
여 아, 미안해. 네가 먼 곳을 그다지 잘 보지 못한다는 걸 깜빡했네. 내일 다시 나에게 상기시켜줄 수 있니? 그때 너를 위한 새 자리를 찾아볼게.
남 알겠습니다. 감사합니다.

|해설| 남자는 먼 곳을 잘 볼 수 없기 때문에 여자에게 자리를 바꿔 달라고 부탁하고 있다.

|어휘| seat [명] 자리, 좌석 board [명] 칠판 remind [동] 상기시키다

16 ③

W Have you made any friends at your new school yet, Jake?
M Not yet. I'm too shy.
W Making new friends is always difficult.
M My old friends and I used to play soccer. I miss them.
W Why don't you join the school soccer team? You can meet new people that way.
M Sounds great!

여 Jake, 새로운 학교에서 친구들 좀 사귀었니?
남 아직. 난 너무 부끄럼을 많이 타.
여 새로운 친구들을 사귀는 것은 늘 어렵지.
남 내 옛 친구들하고 난 축구를 하곤 했었어. 그 친구들이 그리워.
여 학교 축구부에 가입하는 건 어때? 그런 식으로 새로운 사람들을 만날 수 있을 거야.
남 그거 괜찮네!

|어휘| miss [동] 그리워하다 join [동] 가입하다

17 ④

W Hi, Jason. Why didn't you come to Emma's party last Sunday?
M I really wanted to go. But I just couldn't make it.
W Ah, now I remember. You said you had a basketball

game, didn't you?

M Well, actually, that was last Friday.

W Then what did you do?

M I participated in a dance audition.

W Oh, that's so cool!

여 안녕, Jason. 왜 지난 일요일에 Emma의 파티에 오지 않았니?

남 정말 가고 싶었어. 하지만 갈 수가 없었어.

여 아, 이제야 기억나네. 농구 경기가 있었다고 했지, 그렇지 않니?

남 음, 사실 그건 지난 금요일이었어.

여 그럼 뭘 했어?

남 댄스 오디션에 참가했어.

여 오, 정말 멋지다!

|어휘| make it (모임 등에) 가다 remember [동] 기억나다 participate in ~에 참가하다 audition [명] 오디션

18 ④

W Hello. How may I help you?

M I made an appointment for my dog, Paris. She needs a checkup.

W Please come into my office. Does she have any problems?

M She scratches a lot. I think she has dry skin.

W Let me see. *[pause]* She has fleas. You need to give her a bath with this shampoo.

M Okay. Thank you.

여 안녕하세요. 무엇을 도와드릴까요?

남 제 개 Paris를 위해서 예약했어요. 건강진단을 받아야 해서요.

여 제 진료실로 들어오시죠. 어떤 문제가 있나요?

남 개가 많이 긁어요. 피부가 건조한 것 같아요.

여 제가 한번 볼게요. [잠시 후] 벼룩이 있네요. 이 샴푸로 Paris를 목욕시켜주세요.

남 네. 감사합니다.

|해설| 남자가 자신의 개의 건강 상태를 확인하기 위해 동물병원에 방문한 상황이다.

|어휘| checkup [명] 건강진단 office [명] 사무실, 진료실 scratch [동] 긁다 dry [형] 건조한 flea [명] 벼룩

19 ⑤

M Haley, where is your umbrella?

W Oh, no! I guess I lost it.

M Where did you have it last?

W I had it with me while I was waiting for the bus at the bus station.

M Oh, you probably left it there. You should go back and look for it.

W It's okay. I'll buy another one.

① That's not mine.
② It stopped raining.
③ What does it look like?
④ I looked everywhere for it.

남 Haley, 네 우산 어디 있니?

여 아, 안 돼! 저 그거 잃어버린 것 같아요.

남 마지막으로 그걸 가지고 있던 게 어디였는데?

여 버스 정류장에서 버스를 기다리는 동안에는 가지고 있었어요.

남 아, 아마 거기에 두고 온 것 같다. 돌아가서 찾아보렴.

여 괜찮아요. 다른 걸 살 거예요.

① 그거 제 것 아니에요.
② 비가 멈췄어요.
③ 그것은 어떻게 생겼어요?
④ 모든 곳을 다 찾아봤어요.

|어휘| probably [부] 아마도 leave [동] 두고 오다

20 ⑤

M I'm going to order a pizza for dinner. What would you like on it?

W Sausage and pepperoni, please. Those are my favorite toppings.

M But I'm a vegetarian. Could you pick something else?

W Okay. What about tomatoes and spinach?

M Sure. Would you like some soda too?

W No, thanks. It has too much sugar in it.

① I can pick up the pizza.
② Either one would be fine.
③ I can pay for it. It's my treat!
④ There is no soda in the fridge.

남 저녁으로 피자를 한 판 주문할 거야. 위에 뭘 올리면 좋겠어?

여 소시지랑 페퍼로니로 해줘. 그게 내가 가장 좋아하는 토핑이야.

남 하지만 나는 채식주의자야. 다른 것을 골라줄 수 있을까?

여 그래. 토마토와 시금치 어때?

남 좋아. 탄산음료도 좀 먹을래?

여 아니, 괜찮아. 그건 설탕이 너무 많이 들어 있어.

① 내가 피자 사 올게.
② 둘 중 어떤 것이든 괜찮아.
③ 내가 계산할 수 있어. 내가 낼게!
④ 냉장고에 탄산음료가 없어.

|해설| 'Would you like ~?'는 상대에게 무언가를 권하는 표현이다.

|어휘| topping [명] 토핑, 고명 vegetarian [명] 채식주의자 pick [동] 고르다 spinach [명] 시금치 [문제] fridge [명] 냉장고

어휘·표현 다지기

p. 169

A

01	강연, 연설	02	(방 등을 빗자루로) 쓸다
03	약	04	약속하다
05	만점	06	가죽
07	막대기, 장대	08	화분
09	무관심한	10	긁다
11	채식주의자	12	승객
13	언젠가	14	무당벌레
15	혼자	16	콧물이 나다

B

01	stick out	02	participate in
03	mess	04	definitely
05	remote control	06	make one's bed
07	have a sore throat	08	break down
09	checkup	10	due

시험 직전 모의고사 1회

pp. 170-171

01 ⑤	02 ④	03 ⑤	04 ③	05 ⑤
06 ①	07 ②	08 ②	09 ④	10 ③
11 ③	12 ②	13 ⑤	14 ④	15 ③
16 ②	17 ③	18 ②	19 ③	20 ③

01 ⑤

W You can find this in the kitchen. This has a lid. Usually, there is a handle on the top of this. You put this on the stove to boil water. When the water boils, this whistles. What is this?

여 여러분은 이것을 부엌에서 발견할 수 있습니다. 이것은 뚜껑을 가지고 있습니다. 보통 이것의 맨 위에는 손잡이가 있습니다. 여러분은 물을 끓이기 위해 레인지 위에 이것을 놓습니다. 물이 끓으면, 이것은 쌕쌕하는 소리를 냅니다. 이것은 무엇일까요?

|어휘| lid [명] 뚜껑 handle [명] 손잡이 stove [명] (요리용) 레인지 boil [동] 끓이다, 끓다 whistle [동] (주전자가) 삑삑[쌕쌕] 하는 소리를 내다

02 ④

W Thanks for coming to my party, Tyler.
M It's my pleasure. This card is for you.
W Wow, did you make it yourself? I like the three hearts!
M Yes. I also wrote "Happy B-Day" under the hearts.
W It looks wonderful!
M Thanks, Amy. I'm glad you like it.

여 내 파티에 와줘서 고마워, Tyler.
남 내가 기쁘지. 이 카드는 너를 위한 거야.
여 와, 네가 직접 카드를 만든 거야? 하트 세 개가 마음에 든다!
남 응. 하트 밑에 "생일 축하해"라고 쓰기도 했어.
여 근사해 보인다!
남 고마워, Amy. 네가 좋다고 하니 나도 기뻐.

|어휘| wonderful [형] 아주 멋진 glad [형] 기쁜

03 ⑤

M Good morning! This is Jerry Waters, the weatherman for Daily News. It's snowing now in Seoul, but it will stop this afternoon. There are severe winds in Beijing this morning, and there is a high chance of rain tomorrow.

남 좋은 아침입니다! 저는 Daily News의 일기 예보관 Jerry Waters입니다. 지금 서울은 눈이 내리고 있지만, 오후에는 그칠 것입니다. 오늘 아침 베이징에는 심한 바람이 있으며, 내일은 비가 내릴 가능성이 높습니다.

|어휘| weatherman [명] 일기 예보관 severe [형] 심한

04 ③

M Mom, I don't want to go to school today.
W Why? Are you feeling unwell?
M I have a science test today, but I forgot to study.
W No wonder you're so worried. You still need to go to school, though.
M What if I fail the test?
W It will be okay. Just try your best.

남 엄마, 저 오늘 학교 가기 싫어요.
여 왜? 아프니?
남 오늘 과학 시험이 있는데, 깜박하고 공부를 안 했어요.
여 네가 많이 걱정하는 게 당연하네. 그래도 학교는 가야지.
남 시험에서 낙제하면 어쩌죠?
여 괜찮을 거야. 그저 최선을 다하렴.

|해설| 여자는 과학 시험을 앞두고 걱정하는 남자를 격려하고 있다.

|어휘| unwell [형] 아픈 no wonder ~하는 것이 당연하다 still [부] 그럼에도 불구하고 fail [동] (시험에) 떨어지다, 낙제하다 try one's best 최선을 다하다

05 ⑤

W Hello, everyone. My name is Mrs. Baker, and I am your new art teacher. I'm from Seattle, Washington. On the weekends, I enjoy spending time with my husband and daughter. We usually ride bikes together and go horseback riding. I'm looking forward to teaching you all this year!

여 안녕하세요, 여러분. 제 이름은 Baker이고, 여러분의 새로운 미술 선생님입니다. 저는 워싱턴주 시애틀에서 왔어요. 주말마다 저는 남편과 딸과 함께 시간을 보내는 것을 즐깁니다. 우리는 보통 함께 자전거를 타기도 하고 승마를 하러 가기도 하죠. 올해 여러분 모두를 가르치는 것을 고대하고 있습니다!

|어휘| ride [동] 타다 horseback riding 승마 look forward to v-ing ~하는 것을 고대하다

06 ①

W Hi, Mike. Can you still go to the ballet with me on Friday?

M Definitely! When does it start?

W It starts at eight o'clock. Would you like to have dinner first?

M Okay. What do you want to have?

W How about sushi?

M Sounds good. Let's meet at six thirty.

W The traffic will be bad then. Let's meet 20 minutes earlier than that.

M Okay. See you then.

여 안녕, Mike. 너 금요일에 나랑 발레 보러 가는 것 맞지?

남 그렇고말고! 공연이 언제 시작하지?

여 8시에 시작해. 먼저 저녁 먹을래?

남 그래. 뭐 먹고 싶니?

여 초밥 어때?

남 좋아. 6시 30분에 만나자.

여 그때는 교통이 안 좋을 거야. 그것보다 20분 더 일찍 만나자.

남 알겠어. 그때 보자.

|해설| 여자는 6시 30분보다 20분 더 일찍 만나자고 했다.

|어휘| definitely [부] 그렇고말고

07 ②

M Sophie, I saw the photograph you took. It looks terrific!

W I'm glad you like it.

M You are very talented. You're good at both drawing and taking pictures.

W Thank you. Drawing is one of my hobbies, and I want to be a photographer.

M I see. I hope to go to one of your exhibitions someday.

남 Sophie, 네가 찍은 사진 봤어. 아주 좋더라!

여 네가 좋다고 하니 기뻐.

남 너 정말 재능 있어. 넌 그림도 잘 그리고 사진도 잘 찍는구나.

여 고마워. 그림 그리는 것은 내 취미 중 하나이고, 난 사진작가가 되고 싶어.

남 그렇구나. 언젠가 네 전시회에 갈 수 있게 되기를 바랄게.

|어휘| terrific [형] 아주 좋은 talented [형] 재능이 있는 draw [동] 그림을 그리다 hobby [명] 취미 exhibition [명] 전시회 someday [부] 언젠가

08 ②

W Hey, Brian. It's time to wake up!

M Can I stay in bed a little longer? I don't feel well.

W What's the matter? Are you sick?

M I think I caught a cold. I walked home in the rain last night.

W What a pity! Let's take your temperature.

여 얘, Brian. 일어날 시간이야!

남 저 조금만 더 누워 있어도 돼요? 몸이 안 좋아요.

여 무슨 일이니? 아프니?

남 저 감기에 걸린 것 같아요. 어젯밤에 비를 맞으면서 집에 걸어왔거든요.

여 저런, 안됐구나! 체온 좀 재보자.

|해설| 여자의 마지막 말 'What a pity!'는 상황이나 상대에 대한 안타까움을 나타내는 표현이다.

|어휘| wake up 일어나다, 깨다 catch a cold 감기에 걸리다 in the rain 빗속에, 비를 맞으며 pity [명] 유감 take one's temperature 체온을 재다

09 ④

M Hi, Becky. How was the new superhero movie?

W It was fantastic! I loved the costumes and special effects.

M That's great. I'm planning to watch it tonight.

W Have you bought a ticket?
M Not yet.
W I think you should get one as soon as you can. They will sell out quickly.
M Oh, you're right. Thanks for letting me know. I'll buy a ticket right now.

남 안녕, Becky. 새 슈퍼히어로 영화 어땠어?
여 환상적이었어! 의상이랑 특수효과가 정말 좋았어.
남 멋지다. 나는 오늘 밤에 그걸 볼 계획이야.
여 표는 샀니?
남 아직.
여 가능한 한 빨리 표를 사는 게 좋을 거야. 빨리 매진될 거거든.
남 아, 맞아. 알려줘서 고마워. 지금 바로 표를 사야겠다.

|어휘| fantastic [형] 환상적인 costume [명] 의상 special effect 특수효과 as soon as one can 가능한 한 빨리 sell out 매진되다

10 ③

W Nathan, do you have your mask?
M Oh, thanks. I almost forgot. The air is really bad today.
W Yes. The air pollution has been terrible lately. The air is even bad inside our apartment.
M Why don't we buy some plants? I heard that they help to produce fresh air.
W Sounds like a great idea. Let's drop by a flower shop on our way to the supermarket.

여 Nathan, 마스크는 챙겼어?
남 아, 고마워. 하마터면 잊어버릴 뻔했네. 오늘 공기가 정말 안 좋다.
여 그래. 요즘 대기 오염이 심해. 심지어 우리 아파트 안도 공기가 좋지 않아.
남 우리 식물을 좀 사는 게 어때? 식물이 신선한 공기를 만드는 데 도움이 된다고 들었어.
여 그거 괜찮은 생각이다. 우리 슈퍼마켓 가는 길에 꽃 가게에 들르자.

|어휘| air [명] 공기 pollution [명] 오염 terrible [형] 심한 lately [부] 요즈음, 최근에 inside [전] ~ 안에 plant [명] 식물 produce [동] 생산하다 drop by ~에 들르다 on one's way to ~로 가는 길에

11 ③

M Why are you packing, Hani?
W I'm going to Yeosu to visit my uncle this Friday.
M That's pretty far from Seoul. How are you getting there?
W I usually take the bus. But the traffic is going to be bad because it's the holiday season.
M Yeah. How about taking the train? It will be faster.
W That's a good idea. I think I should.

남 왜 짐을 싸고 있니, 하니야?
여 이번 주 금요일에 삼촌을 찾아뵈러 여수에 갈 예정이야.
남 거기는 서울에서 꽤 멀잖아. 거기에 어떻게 갈 거야?
여 보통은 버스를 타. 하지만 휴가철이라서 교통이 안 좋을 것 같아.
남 맞아. 기차를 타는 건 어때? 그게 더 빠를 거야.
여 좋은 생각이다. 그래야겠어.

|어휘| pack [동] (짐을) 싸다, 꾸리다 pretty [부] 어느 정도, 꽤 far [형] 먼 holiday [명] 휴가

12 ②

W Why didn't you come to baseball practice yesterday, Sean? Were you on vacation?
M No, I wasn't. My grandfather was sick, so I needed to visit him in the hospital.
W I'm sorry to hear that. Is he feeling better?
M Yes, he is much better now.

여 어제 야구 연습 왜 안 왔니, Sean? 휴가 중이었어?
남 아니. 할아버지께서 편찮으셔서, 병문안을 가야 했어.
여 유감이야. 할아버지께서는 괜찮아지셨니?
남 응, 지금은 훨씬 나아지셨어.

|어휘| practice [명] 연습 vacation [명] 휴가

13 ⑤

M It's really nice to be here.
W I agree. Those flamingos are beautiful.
M They really are. Now let's go and see the penguins and crocodiles.
W Okay. But can we grab some snacks first?
M Sure. There is a stand that sells some drinks and cookies over there.
W Great!

남 여기 오니 정말 좋다.
여 나도. 저 플라밍고들 아름답다.
남 정말 그러네. 이제 펭귄과 악어를 보러 가자.
여 좋아. 하지만 먼저 간식을 먹어도 될까?
남 물론이지. 저쪽에 음료와 쿠키를 파는 가판대가 있어.
여 좋아!

|어휘| flamingo [명] 플라밍고 crocodile [명] 악어 grab some snacks 간식을 먹다 stand [명] 가판대

14 ④

M Excuse me. How do I get to the bakery?
W Walk straight for about 20 meters. Then turn left on Brooklyn Street.
M Okay.
W Walk for a few meters until you see the flower shop on your left. The bakery is next to it.
M Thank you!

남 실례합니다. 제과점에 어떻게 가야 하나요?
여 20미터 정도 쭉 걸어가세요. 그러고 나서 Brooklyn 가에서 좌회전하세요.
남 알겠습니다.
여 왼편에 꽃 가게가 보일 때까지 몇 미터 걸어가세요. 제과점은 그 옆에 있습니다.
남 감사합니다!

|어휘| straight ㊝ 똑바로 next to ~의 옆에

15 ③

M Good morning, Ellie. Why are you in such a rush?
W My alarm clock broke, so I got up late. Jake and I are taking the bus to the beach today.
M That's a long ride. Will you have time to eat first?
W No. Can you make some sandwiches for us to bring?
M No problem. Just a minute.

남 좋은 아침이야, Ellie. 왜 그렇게 서두르는 거니?
여 알람시계가 고장 나서, 늦게 일어났어요. Jake랑 저는 버스 타고 해변에 갈 예정이거든요.
남 멀리 가는구나. 먼저 밥 먹을 시간이 있겠니?
여 아니요. 저희가 가져갈 샌드위치 좀 만들어주실 수 있어요?
남 물론이지. 잠깐만 기다리렴.

|어휘| in a rush 서둘러 break ㊍ 고장 나다

16 ②

W How long have you been watching TV, Chris?
M I'm not sure. Maybe two hours? I really like this show.
W It's a beautiful day today. Why don't you go outside and play basketball with your friends?
M That's a good idea. I'll call Mark. Maybe he has finished his homework.
W Have fun!

여 TV를 얼마나 오랫동안 보고 있는 거니, Chris?
남 잘 모르겠어요. 아마 2시간 정도요? 저 이 프로그램을 정말 좋아해요.
여 오늘 날이 좋은데. 밖에 나가서 친구들과 농구를 하지 그러니?
남 그거 좋겠네요. Mark에게 전화할래요. 그 애는 아마 숙제를 끝냈을 거예요.
여 재미있게 보내렴!

|어휘| outside ㊝ 밖에, 밖으로 maybe ㊝ 아마도 have fun 재미있게 보내다

17 ③

M What are you doing, Lisa?
W I'm trying to choose an ice cream cake for Mrs. Johnson's birthday.
M She will probably want to share it with her family. But those cakes look too small.
W You're right. Then what about cookies? She often enjoys sweets with coffee.
M That sounds terrific!

남 너 뭐 하니, Lisa?
여 Johnson 씨 생일을 위해 아이스크림 케이크를 고르려는 중이야.
남 그분은 아마 그걸 가족과 나눠 먹고 싶어 하실 거야. 하지만 저 케이크들은 너무 작아 보이네.
여 네 말이 맞아. 그러면 쿠키는 어떨까? 그분은 종종 커피와 함께 단 것을 즐겨 드시거든.
남 아주 좋은 생각이야!

|어휘| probably ㊝ 아마 share ㊍ 나누다 sweet ㊎ 단것

18 ②

M Hi, Tina. I would like to get a haircut today.
W Okay. What kind of hairstyle would you like?
M I want the same style as my brother.
W Are you sure? His hair is very short.
M I'm sure. I just joined the swim team, so I need to have short hair.
W Oh, okay.

남 안녕하세요, Tina 씨. 오늘은 머리를 자르려고요.
여 알겠습니다. 어떤 머리 스타일이 좋으세요?
남 형이랑 같은 스타일로 하고 싶어요.
여 정말요? 형 머리는 정말 짧잖아요.
남 정말이에요. 제가 막 수영부에 가입해서, 머리카락이 짧아야 해요.
여 아, 알겠습니다.

|어휘| get a haircut 이발하다 join ㊍ 가입하다

19 ③

W You look stressed, Kevin. What's wrong?
M I have a big project due soon, but my teammates aren't helping me.
W Oh, no.
M I don't know what to do.
W Did you talk to your teacher about it?
M No, I didn't.
W Then you should let your teacher know what's going on. She can talk to your teammates.
M Okay, thanks for your advice.

① Let me help you.
② When is your project due?
④ There are five people on my team.
⑤ I don't know what's going on here.

여 Kevin, 너 스트레스받는 것 같아 보여. 무슨 일이니?
남 곧 마감인 큰 프로젝트가 있는데, 팀원들이 날 도와주지 않아.
여 아, 저런.
남 내가 어떻게 해야 할지 모르겠어.
여 그것에 대해 선생님께 말씀드렸니?
남 아니, 안 했어.
여 그럼 무슨 일이 일어나고 있는지 선생님께 알려야 해. 선생님께서 네 팀원들에게 말씀하실 거야.
남 알겠어, 조언 고마워.

① 내가 도와줄게.
② 프로젝트가 언제 마감이니?
④ 우리 팀은 5명이야.
⑤ 여기서 무슨 일이 벌어지고 있는지 모르겠어.

|어휘| stressed [형] 스트레스를 받는 due [형] 마감인, 만기가 된 teammate [명] 팀원 **[문제]** advice [명] 조언

20 ③

W Billy, can I talk to you for a minute?
M Sure, Mrs. Scott.
W I've noticed that your grades have been getting worse recently.
M I'm sorry. I have orchestra practice after school every day, so I don't have much time to study.
W I understand. But when do you usually have practice?
M From 6:00 p.m. to 8:00 p.m.

① I'm afraid I can't.
② It will not take long.
④ I took violin lessons for five years.
⑤ I don't like playing music that much.

여 Billy, 잠깐 얘기 좀 할 수 있을까?
남 물론이죠, Scott 선생님.
여 최근에 네 성적이 점점 안 좋아지고 있다는 걸 알게 됐어.
남 죄송해요. 제가 매일 방과 후에 오케스트라 연습이 있어서, 공부할 시간이 많지 않아요.
여 이해한다. 그런데 보통 언제 연습이 있니?
남 오후 6시에서 8시까지요.

① 죄송하지만 안될 것 같아요.
② 오래 걸리지 않을 거예요.
④ 저는 5년 동안 바이올린 교습을 받았어요.
⑤ 저는 곡을 연주하는 것을 그렇게 좋아하진 않아요.

|해설| 여자는 오케스트라 연습 시간이 언제인지 묻고 있다.

|어휘| notice [동] 알아채다 grade [명] 성적 recently [부] 최근에

시험 직전 모의고사 2회

pp. 172-173

01 ③	02 ②	03 ⑤	04 ②	05 ④
06 ②	07 ④	08 ①	09 ①	10 ③
11 ③	12 ②	13 ①	14 ⑤	15 ②
16 ③	17 ①	18 ④	19 ①	20 ④

01 ③

W You can find this in the kitchen. This keeps your food from going bad. This is shaped like a rectangle. You can put magnets on this. When you open this, you will see several drawers and shelves. It is cold inside this. What is this?

여 여러분은 부엌에서 이것을 발견할 수 있습니다. 이것은 음식이 상하는 것을 막습니다. 이것은 직사각형 모양입니다. 여러분은 이것에 자석을 붙일 수 있습니다. 이것을 열면, 몇 개의 서랍과 선반이 보일 것입니다. 이것의 내부는 차갑습니다. 이것은 무엇일까요?

|어휘| go bad 썩다, 상하다 shaped like ~와 같은 모양을 한 rectangle [명] 직사각형 magnet [명] 자석 several [형] 몇몇의 drawer [명] 서랍 shelf [명] 선반

02 ②

M Sara, what are you looking for?
W Hi, Dad. I can't find my scarf.
M What does it look like?
W It has stars and moons on it.

M　Hmm… Are there strings on the ends?

W　No, that's Mom's scarf. My scarf doesn't have any.

M　Okay. I'll help you look for it.

남　Sara, 뭘 찾고 있니?

여　아, 아빠. 저 목도리를 못 찾겠어요.

남　어떻게 생겼는데?

여　별이랑 달이 그려져 있어요.

남　음… 끝에 가는 끈들이 있니?

여　아니요. 그건 엄마 목도리예요. 제 목도리는 아무것도 안 달려있어요.

남　알았다. 내가 찾는 것을 도와줄게.

|어휘| look for ~을 찾다　scarf 몡 목도리, 스카프　string 몡 (가는) 끈, 줄

03　⑤

M　Good morning, this is David Johnson with today's weather. The sky is clear now. However, the temperature will drop, and it will snow after 12:00 p.m. You should wear a warm jacket if you go outside.

남　좋은 아침입니다. 저는 오늘 날씨를 전해드릴 David Johnson입니다. 현재 하늘은 맑은 상태입니다. 하지만 기온이 떨어지고, 오후 12시 이후에는 눈이 내리겠습니다. 외출하신다면 따뜻한 외투를 입으셔야겠습니다.

|어휘| temperature 몡 기온, 온도　drop 동 떨어지다

04　②

W　Hi, Sam! Do you have any plans this weekend?

M　Why do you ask?

W　I was hoping that you could come to my piano concert.

M　I didn't know you played the piano! When is it?

W　It's at 2:00 p.m. on Saturday.

M　I want to go, but I can't. I have to work.

여　안녕, Sam! 너 이번 주말에 무슨 계획 있니?

남　왜 물어보는 거야?

여　네가 내 피아노 연주회에 올 수 있으면 했지.

남　네가 피아노를 치는 줄 몰랐네! 연주회가 언젠데?

여　토요일 오후 2시에 해.

남　가고 싶지만, 못 가겠다. 나 일해야 하거든.

|해설| 남자는 연주회에 오라는 여자의 제안에 응하고 싶지만, 그럴 수 없는 상황이다.

|어휘| concert 몡 연주회

05　④

W　Hello, I'm Emma. My family and I just moved here from San Francisco, California. I am 14 years old. I have a twin brother and a younger sister. Their names are Luke and Maggie. My favorite foods are pasta and strawberry ice cream. Nice to meet you!

여　안녕, 나는 Emma라고 해. 우리 가족과 나는 캘리포니아주 샌프란시스코에서 막 이곳으로 이사 왔어. 나는 14살이야. 쌍둥이 남자 형제와 여동생이 있어. 이름은 Luke랑 Maggie야. 내가 가장 좋아하는 음식은 파스타랑 딸기 아이스크림이고. 만나서 반가워!

|어휘| move 동 이사하다　twin 혱 쌍둥이의　favorite 혱 가장 좋아하는　strawberry 몡 딸기

06　②

M　Hi, Emily! Are you doing anything after school tomorrow?

W　No, I don't have any plans.

M　Would you like to see the movie *Blue Planet* with me tomorrow night then?

W　Sure! What time?

M　The movie starts at 8:30 p.m.

W　That's too late for me. Can we go to the 6:00 p.m. showing instead?

M　Sure. I'll see you in front of the theater 30 minutes before it starts.

W　Okay. See you then.

남　안녕, Emily! 내일 방과 후에 뭔가 하니?

여　아니, 아무 계획도 없어.

남　그럼 내일 밤에 나랑 〈Blue Planet〉 영화 보러 갈래?

여　그래! 몇 시?

남　영화는 저녁 8시 30분에 시작해.

여　나한테는 너무 늦네. 대신 6시 영화를 보러 갈 수 있을까?

남　물론이지. 영화 시작하기 30분 전에 극장 앞에서 보자.

여　좋아. 그때 보자.

|해설| 두 사람이 만나기로 한 시각은 영화 시작 시각인 6시보다 30분 전인 5시 30분이다.

|어휘| showing 몡 (영화) 상영　in front of ~의 앞에서

07　④

W　Hi, Andrew! Congratulations on winning first prize at the talent show.

M　Thanks. I practiced a lot.

W　I really enjoyed listening to you sing "Dance With Me

Tonight."
M I'm so glad you enjoyed it.
W You should be a singer!
M I actually want to be an actor. I like playing lots of different characters.

여 안녕, Andrew! 장기자랑에서 일등 한 것 축하해.
남 고마워. 연습 많이 했어.
여 네가 'Dance With Me Tonight'을 부르는 것 정말 잘 들었어.
남 네가 좋았다니 나도 기분이 아주 좋네.
여 너는 가수가 되어야겠다!
남 사실 나는 배우가 되고 싶어. 나는 여러 다양한 역할을 연기하는 것을 좋아하거든.

|어휘| congratulations on ~에 대한 축하 win first prize 일등을 하다 talent show 장기자랑 practice [동] 연습하다 a lot 많이 actually [부] 사실 actor [명] 배우 character [명] 등장인물, 배역

08 ①

M Why are you so late? I've been waiting for an hour!
W I'm sorry. I got off the bus at the wrong stop.
M Why didn't you call me?
W I left my cell phone at home. I didn't think I would need it.
M I really hate waiting. Please don't be late again!

남 너 왜 이렇게 늦었어? 한 시간 동안 기다렸잖아!
여 미안해. 버스에서 엉뚱한 정류장에 내렸어.
남 왜 나한테 전화 안 했어?
여 집에 휴대전화를 놓고 왔어. 그게 필요할 거라는 생각을 못했어.
남 나 기다리는 거 정말 싫어해. 다시는 늦지 말아줘!

|어휘| get off (버스 등에서) 내리다 wrong [형] 잘못된, 엉뚱한 stop [명] 정류장

09 ①

[Cell phone rings.]
W Hello, Chris. Where are you?
M I just left the office.
W I'm at the restaurant, but there aren't any empty tables.
M That's disappointing. Why don't we go to the Mexican restaurant near City Hall?
W Sounds good. I will call them now. I hope there is a table for us.
M Thanks. I will get there as soon as I can.

[휴대전화벨이 울린다.]
여 안녕, Chris. 어디야?
남 나 방금 퇴근했어.
여 난 음식점에 있는데, 빈 테이블이 하나도 없네.
남 실망스럽네. 우리 시청 근처에 있는 멕시코 음식점에 가지 않을래?
여 좋아. 지금 음식점에 전화해볼게. 우리 자리가 있으면 좋겠다.
남 고마워. 가능한 한 빨리 거기로 갈게.

|어휘| leave the office 퇴근을 하다 empty [형] 빈 disappointing [형] 실망스러운

10 ③

M Why are you driving so slowly?
W I'm driving 30 km per hour. Don't you see the school over there? We're in a school zone.
M Oh, I didn't realize that.
W We should drive slowly because children might cross the street.
M You're right. Everyone should drive carefully around schools.

남 왜 그렇게 천천히 운전하니?
여 시속 30km로 운전하는 중이야. 저기 학교 보이지 않니? 우리 지금 어린이 보호구역에 있잖아.
남 아, 그걸 깨닫지 못했네.
여 아이들이 길을 건널지도 모르니까 천천히 운전해야 해.
남 네 말이 맞아. 모두 학교 주위에서 주의해서 운전해야 해.

|어휘| per [전] ~마다 school zone 어린이 보호구역 realize [동] 깨닫다 cross [동] (가로질러) 건너다 carefully [부] 주의하여

11 ③

W Why is your hair all wet, Mike?
M I walked to work this morning.
W But it's freezing and snowing outside.
M I know. I forgot to check the weather before I left.
W I heard that it's going to snow all day. Let me drive you home after work.
M That would be great!

여 머리카락이 왜 온통 젖은 거니, Mike?
남 오늘 아침에 걸어서 출근했거든.
여 하지만 밖은 너무나 춥고 눈이 내리고 있잖아.
남 알아. 출발하기 전에 날씨 확인하는 걸 깜박했어.
여 종일 눈이 온다고 들었어. 퇴근 후에 내가 차로 집에 데려다줄게.
남 그러면 좋지!

|어휘| wet [형] 젖은 freezing [형] 너무나 추운

12 ②

W Hi, Josh. What are you using that blue fabric for?
M I'm going to make a cape.
W Really? Is it for a costume party?
M No, it's for the school play. The king is going to wear it.
W Oh, wow! Let me know if you need any help.

여 안녕, Josh. 그 파란색 천은 뭐에 쓰려고?
남 망토를 만들 거야.
여 정말? 가장무도회에서 쓰려는 거니?
남 아니, 교내 연극용이야. 왕이 그것을 입을 예정이야.
여 아, 와! 도움이 필요하면 내게 알려줘.

|어휘| fabric [명] 직물, 천 cape [명] 망토 play [명] 연극

13 ①

W Hello. I'd like to check in.
M Okay. Do you need to check any baggage?
W Yes. I have one bag.
M Put it on the scale, please. *[pause]* I'm sorry, but your suitcase is over the weight limit.
W Oh, no! How much does it weigh?
M Eighty pounds. You need to pay the overweight baggage fee. It's $200.
W I understand.

여 안녕하세요. 탑승 절차를 밟고 싶습니다.
남 네. 부치실 짐이 있나요?
여 네. 가방 하나 있어요.
남 저울 위에 올려주세요. [잠시 후] 죄송하지만, 손님의 여행 가방이 중량 제한을 초과했네요.
여 아, 이런! 무게가 얼마나 나가는 거죠?
남 80파운드입니다. 중량 초과 수하물 수수료를 내셔야겠네요. 200달러입니다.
여 알겠습니다.

|해설| check any baggage, weight limit, baggage fee 등의 표현으로 미루어 보아 두 사람이 공항에서 대화하고 있음을 알 수 있다.

|어휘| check in 탑승[투숙] 절차를 밟다 baggage [명] 수하물, 짐 scale [명] 저울 suitcase [명] 여행 가방 weight limit 중량 제한 weigh [동] 무게가 ~이다 overweight [형] 중량 초과의 baggage fee 수하물 수수료

14 ⑤

M Anna, did you eat my candy?
W No, I didn't.
M Well, I put it on the table in the morning, but it's not there. Where is it?
W I don't know. Did you look under the table?
M Yes, but it's not there.
W How about on the sink?
M No, it isn't there either.
W Oh, look! It's in the cupboard. Mom might have put it in there.

남 Anna, 네가 내 사탕 먹었니?
여 아니, 안 먹었어.
남 글쎄, 내가 아침에 테이블 위에 올려놨는데, 거기에 없어. 그게 어디에 있지?
여 나는 몰라. 테이블 아래 봤니?
남 응, 그런데 거기 없어.
여 싱크대 위는?
남 아니, 거기에도 없어.
여 오, 봐! 찬장 안에 있어. 엄마가 거기에 넣어 두셨는지도 몰라.

|어휘| sink [명] 싱크대 cupboard [명] 찬장

15 ②

W Dad, are you busy now? I need your help.
M I was getting ready to cut the grass. What do you need, Stacy?
W Could you check my history homework? I have to give a presentation on it tomorrow.
M Can I help you this evening instead? I'd be happy to help you then.
W Okay.

여 아빠, 지금 바쁘세요? 아빠 도움이 필요해요.
남 잔디를 깎으려고 준비하고 있었어. 무슨 도움이 필요하니, Stacy?
여 제 역사 숙제 좀 봐주실 수 있어요? 내일 그것에 관해서 발표해야 하거든요.
남 대신 오늘 저녁에 도와줘도 될까? 그때 도와주는 게 좋을 것 같은데.
여 알겠어요.

|어휘| grass [명] 잔디 presentation [명] 발표, 프레젠테이션

16 ③

M Tina, you look so pale.

W My daughter's teacher just called me.
M Is there any problem with your daughter?
W She fell down the stairs and broke her arm.
M Oh, no. That's terrible!
W She's in the hospital now. I want to see her, but I need to finish my work.
M I can finish it for you. Why don't you leave now?
W Really? Thanks!

남 Tina, 안색이 너무 창백해 보여요.
여 저희 딸 선생님께서 방금 전화하셨어요.
남 딸에게 무슨 문제라도 있나요?
여 그 애가 계단에서 넘어져서 팔이 부러졌대요.
남 오, 이런. 큰일이네요!
여 지금 병원에 있대요. 딸을 보고 싶은데, 일을 끝내야 해요.
남 제가 대신 마무리할게요. 지금 출발하지 그러세요?
여 정말요? 고마워요!

|해설| 남자는 여자의 딸이 병원에 있다는 말에 딸에게 가보라고 말하고 있다.

|어휘| pale [형] 창백한 fall down 넘어지다 stairs [명] 계단

17 ①

W Hi, Paul. What are you going to do this weekend?
M I don't have any plans yet. What about you?
W I'm thinking of going to Namsan.
M What are you going to do there?
W I'm going to take pictures of the cherry blossoms. Would you like to join me?
M I'd love to!

여 안녕, Paul. 이번 주말에 뭐 할 거야?
남 아직 아무 계획 없어. 너는?
여 남산에 갈까 생각 중이야.
남 거기서 뭐 할 건데?
여 벚꽃 사진을 찍을 거야. 너도 같이 갈래?
남 좋아!

|어휘| cherry blossom 벚꽃

18 ④

W Good morning, Mr. Jones. Please come in.
M Hello, Mrs. Smith. I brought a few wallpaper samples for you.
W Oh, thank you. I like this blue one with the diamonds.
M That pattern will make the living room look smaller. I recommend this white one.
W Well, isn't it too simple?
M The bright color will match perfectly with your new leather sofa.

여 안녕하세요, Jones 씨. 들어오세요.
남 안녕하세요, Smith 씨. 고객님을 위해서 벽지 샘플을 조금 가져왔어요.
여 아, 감사합니다. 저는 다이아몬드 무늬가 있는 이 파란색 벽지가 마음에 드네요.
남 그 무늬는 거실을 더 작아 보이게 할 거예요. 저는 이 흰색 벽지를 추천합니다.
여 음, 그건 너무 단순하지 않나요?
남 밝은 색상이 고객님의 새 가죽 소파와 완벽하게 어울릴 거예요.

|어휘| wallpaper [명] 벽지 pattern [명] 무늬 recommend [동] 추천하다 simple [형] 단순한 bright [형] 밝은 match [동] 어울리다 leather [명] 가죽

19 ①

M Welcome to our store. Did you know we're having an end-of-season sale?
W Oh, that's great! I didn't know, but I really need to get a new sweater.
M Then it's your lucky day! All our winter clothes are 50 percent off.
W Are these snow boots also on sale?
M No, I'm afraid not. Shoes aren't included in the sale.
W What a shame!

② That's a good idea.
③ I'm glad to hear that.
④ Thank you for coming.
⑤ They're uncomfortable.

남 저희 매장에 오신 것을 환영합니다. 저희가 시즌 말 할인 판매를 하고 있는 것 아셨나요?
여 아, 잘됐네요! 모르고 있었지만, 제가 정말 새 스웨터를 사야 하거든요.
남 그렇다면 운이 좋은 날이네요! 저희 겨울옷이 전부 50% 할인 판매 중이에요.
여 이 겨울 부츠도 할인 판매 중인가요?
남 아니요, 그건 아니에요. 신발은 할인 판매에 포함되지 않습니다.
여 아쉬운 일이네요!

② 좋은 생각이에요.
③ 그 말을 들으니 기쁘네요.
④ 와주셔서 감사합니다.
⑤ 그건 불편해요.

|어휘| boots [명] 부츠, 장화 on sale 할인 판매 중인 include

ⓢ 포함하다 [문제] shame ⓝ 아쉬운 일 uncomfortable ⓐ 불편한

20 ④

M What have you been doing in your room all day, Michelle?

W I'm reading a science fiction novel. I really like it so far.

M That sounds interesting. What is it about?

W It's about two scientists. They found a way to travel back in time.

M Wow! Can I borrow it sometime?

W <u>Actually, it is a library book.</u>

① That's correct.

② It's too expensive.

③ I prefer watching movies.

⑤ Reading books is my favorite hobby.

남 종일 방에서 뭐 하고 있니, Michelle?

여 공상 과학 소설을 읽는 중이야. 지금까지는 정말 마음에 들어.

남 재미있겠다. 뭐에 관한 거야?

여 두 과학자에 관한 거야. 그들은 시간을 거슬러 여행하는 방법을 발견했어.

남 와! 언젠가 나 그 책을 빌려도 될까?

여 <u>사실 이건 도서관 책이야.</u>

① 그건 옳아.

② 그건 너무 비싸.

③ 나는 영화 보는 게 더 좋아.

⑤ 독서는 내가 매우 좋아하는 취미야.

|해설| 언젠가 책을 빌려줄 수 있겠냐고 물었으므로, 책을 빌려줄 수 있는지 여부에 관한 ④가 가장 적절하다.

|어휘| science fiction 공상 과학 소설 so far 지금까지 borrow ⓢ 빌리다 sometime ⓟ 언젠가 [문제] correct ⓐ 옳은 expensive ⓐ 비싼 prefer ⓢ 더 좋아하다

기초부터 실전까지 중학 듣기 완성

1316
LISTENING LEVEL 1

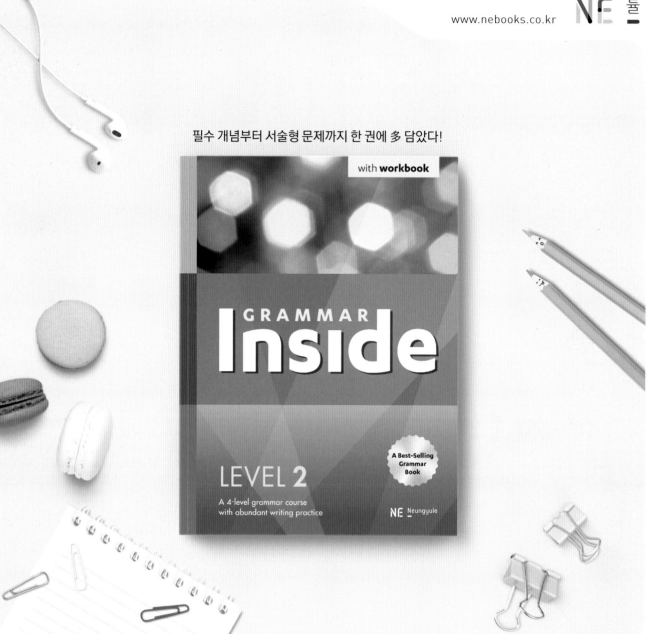